The
Garland Library
of
War and Peace

The
Garland Library
of
War and Peace

Under the General Editorship of

Blanche Wiesen Cook, *John Jay College, C.U.N.Y.*

Sandi E. Cooper, *Richmond College, C.U.N.Y.*

Charles Chatfield, *Wittenberg University*

Militarism

by

Guglielmo Ferrero

with a new introduction
for the Garland Edition by
Sandi E. Cooper

Garland Publishing, Inc., New York & London
1972

The new introduction for this
Garland Library Edition is Copyright © 1972, by
Garland Publishing Inc.
24 West 45 St., New York, N.Y. 10036

All Rights Reserved

Library of Congress Cataloging in Publication Data

Ferrero, Guglielmo, 1871-1942.
    Militarism.

    (The Garland library of war and peace)
    Reprint of the 1902 ed., which is a translation,
with additions, of Il militarismo.
    1. Militarism. 2. Peace. 3. War. 4. Caesarism.
I. Series.
JX1952.F5 1972   355.02'13   76-147469
ISBN 0-8240-0260-1

Printed in the United States of America

Introduction

Guglielmo Ferrero (1871-1942), journalist, historian, sociologist and political analyst, enjoyed an international reputation which has survived his death. His observations and commentaries on the politics and societies of ancient Rome, Napoleonic Europe and the twentieth century West remain among the most acute and intelligent contemporary discussions of those subjects. The seventy-one years of his life spanned developments that made the world of his childhood unrecognizable in the world of his old age. Ferrero's own interests mirrored the great agonies and deep traumas of a civilization where change was too rapid, too sudden, and therefore, too destructive to be assimilated.

It was appropriate that he spent the last twelve years of his life, and in fact died, in exile from his beloved Tuscan countryside. No man of Ferrero's temperament, inclinations, love of justice and freedom could have survived as a vegetable in the climate of Mussolini's Italy. To the end of his life, Ferrero retained his deep faith in the great liberal traditions of the West, in particular, the respect for human dignity and the rights of others. He deplored force and violence in the everyday operations of political life. When the tumultuous forces of the post-World War I

5

INTRODUCTION

ear appeared in the early 1920's, Ferrero was among the first to cry out and to immerse himself in the struggle against neo-barbarism.

He came from an Italian family of Piemontese origin which enjoyed the comforts of middle-class status. Although born near Naples, he was raised in Tuscany after his father, an engineer, was transferred north. As a child, Ferrero was interested in a variety of academic subjects ranging from mathematics to law. He finally received degrees in letters and in jurisprudence from the universities of Bologna and Turin. Perhaps the most important formative experiences of his youth was his exposure to the dynamic intellectual circle which had gathered in Turin in the last years of the nineteenth century. There, the well-known professors and soon to be famous students and disciples created an intellectual life that transcended classroom contacts and even stretched out to include labor and socialist leaders.[1] In the Turinese cenacolo, *Ferrero met the famous criminologist, Cesare Lombroso who was very taken by the young man's intelligence. Lombroso invited Ferrero to collaborate on a new work which appeared in 1893 as* La donna delinquente, la prostituta e la donna normale. *This study of normal and abnormal behavior*

[1] *A valuable description of the intellectual climate at Turin is available in Paolo Spriano,* Socialismo e classe operaia a Torino dal 1892 al 1913, *particularly chapter III, "Il Socialismo dei Professori" (Turin: G. Einaudi, 1958). In addition, the subject is discussed for a slightly later period in English by John M. Cammett,* Antonio Gramsci and the Origins of Italian Communism *(Stanford University Press, 1967), ch. 2.*

6

INTRODUCTION

in women received considerable publicity and aroused a lively debate. Ferrero's name was projected to a nation-wide public. Eight years later, in 1901, he was married to Gina Lombroso, daughter of his senior mentor and collaborator.

In the 1890's, however, Ferrero had not clearly defined his interests and his "career" commitment. He was fascinated by the history of jurisprudence and wanted to write on the evolution of justice. Instead of beginning in the usual place, archives, he chose to take an extended trip through Europe to get to know men and their environment. From his travels, he produced L'Europa giovane (1897) which was a grand statement of faith in the future. In the 1890's also, he was associated with the Milanese paper. Il Secolo and he developed a reputation as a journalist of considerable acumen.

In the aftermath of the Italian defeat at Adowa, Ferrero returned home. Italy was brought to the verge of civil war and dictatorship by this "humiliation" to her national honor. The defeat touched off profound waves of discontent in every area of Italian life culminating in strikes, martial law, public demonstrations, suspension of civil liberties. A great debate rent Italian life, raging on all social levels, over the "meaning" of Italy, its role as a power given its limited wealth and enormous domestic miseries. The Peace Society of Milan (Società della Pace di Milano) invited Ferrero to deliver a series of lectures on militarism. The lectures were a resounding success or

INTRODUCTION

a great disaster depending on one's point of view in the national crisis of conscience. In 1898, they appeared in book form entitled Il Militarismo *and in 1902, were translated into English in the revised and expanded version reprinted here. In his preface, Ferrero stated that he wrote this book "in order to contribute my quota to the grand work of pacifying civilized nations." According to a friend of the Ferrero family, the book infuriated the ruling classes and was a work which the nationalists never forgot nor forgave.*[2]

Ferrero's reputation as a historian stemmed originally from his five-volume study of the greatness and decline of Rome, 1902-1907. Following its appearance, invitations to lecture abroad poured in which took the author to Paris, South America and the United States.[3] *The work enjoyed a wide circulation for reasons which did not endear Ferrero to professional, academics and scholars and did not get him a university chair, since it did not follow the conventions of traditional scholarship. This history of Rome was an immensely readable, richly descriptive*

[2] *Jacques Pirenne, "In memoria di Gugliemo Ferrero"* Nuova Revista Storica *XXXII (Naples, January, 1948). p. 6.*

[3] *President Theodore Roosevelt supposedly extended the invitation to Ferrero to come to the United States after reading Ferrero's work and being impressed by his analogy between ancient Roman and Tammany Hall politics. According to the* New York Times *obituary of Ferrero, this American visit "made" Ferrero's international reputation. In this country, he was awarded an honorary degree by New York University in 1908. See "Ferrero is Dead: Italian Historian" in* The New York Times, *Wednesday, August 5, 1942, p. 19.*

INTRODUCTION

*work that explained the past through numerous
analogies to contemporary political phenomena. For
Ferrero, history and politics were reciprocal sides of a
coin; they informed each other. He studied a past
epoch for what he could learn about the present and
from what he knew of the present. He understood the
present very considerably through what the past had
left. This mutual infusion of time past and present
can lead to the cheapest form of propaganda or to
highly intelligent discussion of complex phenomena.
In Ferrero's hand, the latter occurred. In the late
1930's, when he turned to study the Napoleonic
period, the contemporary political ramifications of
his work were very clear.*

*Following 1918, Ferrero emerged as one of the
most acute observers of the developing turmoils in
Italian and European political life. He warned immediately of the dangers to the liberal state and the
democratic view of life. In 1919, commenting on the
dangers inherent in d'Annunzio's adventure in Fiume,
Ferrero pointed to the role of men in high places
encouraging law-breaking.[4] The restless violence
characteristic of post-war politics led him to an
understanding of the dangers which the developing
Red-White dialectic would bring to the liberal state
that remained paralyzed in face of challenges from
left and right. Ferrero foresaw the coming hysteria,
the anti-Bolshevik disease, of the twentieth century.
No admirer of the Russian Revolution himself,*

[4]Da Fiume a Roma, *published later in Milan: Athena, 1945.*

9

INTRODUCTION

Ferrero nonetheless feared equally the quality of politics based on anti-revolutionary hysteria. When the advent of Mussolini justified his apprehensions about the inability of liberal democracy to meet the challenges of lawlessness, Ferrero joined the small group of liberal intellectuals and politicians that protested. A coalition formed by the liberal newspaper editor, Giovanni Amendola, drew up the famous Manifesto of the Anti-Fascist Intellectuals which he signed. It appeared in May, 1925.[5]

Of course, it was too late. Neither liberal nor socialist had either the golden tongue nor the persuasive power to rid Italy of the black-shirted gangs and restore parliamentary government, free speech, free press, and real security of person. Ferrero retired to his country place. Finally in 1930, the Fascists inexplicably permitted him to leave. He accepted an invitation to teach at the University of Geneva in the Institute for Advanced Studies in International Affairs. At sixty years, Ferrero began his career as a university professor.

The most important writings of his last years dealt with the aftermath of the French Revolution.

---

[5]*Printed in Paolo Alatri,* L'antifascismo italiano *(Rome: Editori Riuniti, 1961), pp. 405-412. Signatories included Benedetto Croce, Guido de Ruggiero, Luigi Salvatorelli, Luigi Einaudi among others. The entire roster is a compendium of the leading personages of Italian cultural and intellectual life.*

INTRODUCTION

L'Aventure: Bonaparte en Italie[6] *provided fresh insight on the Italian compaigns of 1796-1797 which had made Napoleon's reputation. Ferrero's study concentrated, however, on the long range ramifications for Italy and not on the personal "achievement" of the conqueror. The book proclaimed the highly transitory nature of Napoleonic power which the author detested as despotic. Readers could hardly escape the inferences for would-be Napoleons of the 1930's. In a second volume concerned with this epoch, Ferrero's total hatred for Napoleon led him to glorify Talleyrand and the period of 1814-1815.[7] The Congress of Vienna, preceded by the military defeat of the despot, is assessed as a period where justice and human rights were recovered. Again, Ferrero's study of history was informed by the present as well as by his steady devotion to principles of justice. The age of the Congress of Vienna was the time when decency was reasserted. It would come again.*

Professional historians and critics have found his work too weighted in favor of Talleyrand, of course, and perhaps too moralistic. For the aging Ferrero, it was his contribution as an intellectual to the resistance against despotism and barbarism in the twentieth century. His final work was Pouvoir

[6]*Paris: Plon, 1936. In English, available as* The Gamble: Bonaparte in Italy, 1796-1797 *(New York: Walker, 1961). The Italian translation did not appear until after World War II.*

[7]*In English, entitled* The Reconstruction of Europe *(New York, 1941). The book depended heavily on Talleyrand's Memoirs which Ferrero generally did not criticize.*

INTRODUCTION

*(Power), a general analysis of legitimacy and illegiti-
macy in the exercise of authority. Many consider it
his finest book. It was finished shortly before his
death.*

    *Clearly Ferrero's studies of the past were not
insulations aginst present realities. As a committed
intellectual, he could not violate his conscience by
ignoring the degradation of human values which were
manifested in the 1920's and 1930's. As an Italian, he
had a familiarity with this new phenomenon which
only World War II brought to others. The differences
between the young Ferrero who wrote* L'Europa
giovane *and* Il Militarismo *in the 1890's and the
mature Ferrero of the inter-war years reflects the
catastrophe of the twentieth century unleashed by
World War I—not merely the aging of a young man. In
the early works, Ferrero could rightly trace the
evolution of civilizing and humanizing trends over
vast stretches of time without doubting that these
directions would continue and mature in the
twentieth century. He could treat the phenomena of
war and violence with balance and detachment in the
1890's. The scientific, positivist approach to normal-
ity and abnormality used in the study of women
co-authored with Lombroso could justifiably pervade
the pages of* Il Militarismo.

    *There, war was treated essentially as an economic,
not an ideological phenomenon. Ferrero identified its
function in ancient societies as essentially the accumulation of capital spearheaded by a small*

INTRODUCTION

aggressive élite which wanted to escape the grinding poverty of its underdeveloped, agricultural or nomadic economies. In contrast, modern civilization, based on work and consumption, developed less violent means to amass capital and create wealth. In the late nineteenth century, Ferrero observed that the relationship between richer, advanced and industrialized nations (the United States, England, Germany) and poorer ones (Italy, Spain, Russia) was similar to the relationship between mother countries and colonies, excepting the political ties, of course. The poorer states were dependent on the richer ones. The best oranges from poor Mediterranean regions fed the workers in foreign northern cities. Poorer nations exported commodities which commanded far less than they spent on imports. Wealth was magnetized to already richer nations. Thus, poorer nations flirted with disaster if they undertook to sustain elaborate military establishments and engage in power plays. Militarism was an unqualified disaster for them. The richer states already had learned this, Ferrero thought. They rarely gambled their wealth in risky warrior adventures. It was appropriate for a British publisher to bring Il Militarismo forth in English as the Boer War was beginning to rock domestic tranquility in that nation.

Ferrero's analysis of war and militarism must be understood in terms of the optimism generated by nearly four decades of peace among the great powers of Europe. He saw war as a gradually disappearing

13

INTRODUCTION

*phenomenon, growing useless and harmful to matur-
ing civilization. Ferrero was not a pacifist in any sense
of the term, despite the dedication to Italy's leading
peace worker, E.T. Moneta, at the beginning of the
book. In his discussion of the Spanish-American war,
for instance, Ferrero supported the idea that states
which are justly governed "should interpose and
introduce . . . a theoretically and practically superior
government" in areas which are controlled
despotically. Such "liberal imperialism" was necessary and useful, in Ferrero's estimation, to further the
"advance towards justice" which was characteristic of
civilization. (pp. 49-50)*

*Ferrero's discussion of war in the ancient world
demonstrated that he was far from being an absolute
pacifist. He recognized the important role war had
played in the development of civilization, even though
the achievement and preservation of civilization meant
abandoning war eventually. If states and peoples still
found war useful, observed Ferrero, it was because
that was their only way of curbing the forces of mod-
ernization. It is no wonder that the ruling classes of
Italy in the wake of Adowa found Ferrero's book far
from their liking.*[8]

Sandi E. Cooper
Division of Social Sciences
Richmond College — C.U.N.Y.

[8] *The author of this introduction wishes to thank John M. Cammett,
John Jay College—C.U.N.Y., for his help.*

14

MILITARISM

MILITARISM

BY

GUGLIELMO FERRERO

LONDON
WARD, LOCK & CO., LIMITED
NEW YORK AND MELBOURNE
1902

TO

ERNESTO TEODORO MONETA

FOUNDER AND PRESIDENT OF THE

FIRST ITALIAN PEACE SOCIETY

WITH RESPECT AND GRATITUDE

PREFACE

THIS translation of my book, "Il Militarism," published in Italy a year ago, is really almost a new work, because the greater part of the Italian text has been entirely recast, and profoundly modified, and whole chapters have been added. The events that have occurred since its publication, continued meditation on the great problems of which it treats, some of the objections raised by critics during the animated discussions that broke out in Italy on its appearance, have induced me to try to improve my work by making these changes.

I have written the book in order to contribute my quota to the grand work of pacifying civilized nations, entered upon by so many enlightened spirits, and I agree with them in holding that a general European war, especially a war between England and France, would be a world calamity, and would produce incalculable evils without recompense.

I venture to hope that my book may prove a useful contribution to the noble crusade of peace. In this spirit I have written it, and in this spirit I now offer it to my English readers.

GUGLIELMO FERRERO.

TURIN (ITALY), *January* 31, 1899.

PUBLISHER'S NOTE TO THE ENGLISH TRANSLATION.

THIS being a translation from a Standard Italian work, it has been thought best to leave the text exactly as in the original, without attempting either to bring it up to the present date, or to correct the occasional inaccuracies which are generally to be found in works written from the foreign point of view.

October, 1902.

CONTENTS

PEACE AND WAR AT THE END OF THE NINETEENTH CENTURY

CHAPTER I

PEACE AND WAR AT THE END OF THE NINETEENTH CENTURY

I

FREQUENTLY, when I have remarked in conversation, "War is losing much of its pristine importance in modern civilized life: whether it be that no longer such great odds depend on it, or because the moral conscience of man is perfecting itself," I have been answered: "This is an illusion that always arises on the eve of a great war. We are on the eve of a terrible one which will transform Europe into a huge battlefield. Man is born brutal, he is by nature a wolf: how could you change him into a lamb? Civilization only renders the instruments of war more terrible in the hands of man. So long as there shall be men on the earth there will be wars, and the advance of morality can do nothing against the inexorable law of force which dominates the world."

We will not dwell on the fact that for the past twenty years this same thing has been repeated—that we are on the eve of an universal war. If there is a fragment of truth in this argument, it is that the alarming ferocity innate in man has not been one iota diminished by the civilization of the nineteenth century. Without doubt customs have changed for the better since it rarely happens now that an ordinary individual kills or injures his fellow; indeed, it has become a rare thing for a man to come to a violent death. Two or three centuries ago, on the contrary, assaults and murders were common occurrences, little more than everyday incidents in high life no less than among the people; and we can be certain that had we lived in the seventeenth century, many of us by this time would already have hacked the body of some fellow with sword or dagger, or in some manner have stained our hands with human blood. But the modification of customs does not imply any diminution in the innate ferocity of man. As dynamite can be stored in warehouses left dormant for years, transported from spot to spot without danger, and yet retain its orignal power, if ignited, to uproot mountains, so it is with human ferocity. It lies dormant in the civilized man of our century, but beware if a spark comes to kindle its terrible destructive force.

It is not, therefore, rash to suppose that a diabolical entanglement of violent passions and errors urges men to war, since for so many centuries, in so many terrific combats, man has exhibited so much ferocity and such a blind thirst for destruction. But even admitting that this be true: what does it prove? The spirit of man is replete with bad passions and exaggerated ideas, civilization is only a progressive repression of these bad passions, and a progressive rectification of these errors. The problem of existence for every individual is the same: it can be summed up in these terms : to seek pleasure, to avoid pain. Now the problem of existence is the same for a society as it is for the individuals who form it. The whole existence of society is an effort—whether profitable or futile—towards the acquirement of happiness,

which is the same as saying towards justice and truth,
every increase in the general happiness of a nation being
accompanied by some progress in justice and knowledge.
The whole history of man is but the history of the
attempts made to find a more complete solution of this
problem ; what we call the advances of civilization are simply
the successive and laborious approaches to a more and more
perfect and durable solution of this great problem : " *to be
happy*"—not each of us for himself, but altogether, in the
community of social life. Thus we see that civilization consists
principally in an increase of universal happiness which is only
to be reached through moral and intellectual progress, by
means of which so many evils born of passion and error are
mitigated and by degrees destroyed. Why should not war be
amongst these evils ? Certainly any one who considers war as
a form of struggle which is the negation of justice—for in war
the morally superior and morally inferior have equal chances
of victory—could not understand how the progress of justice
could fail to diminish or abolish it, for long periods at least,
from civilization. No evil, indeed, is capable of amelioration,
unless it has in it some element of good—however slight this
element may be. But if it were possible to prove that war,
in its final results, does not absolutely deny justice, that the
ultimate victory belongs to the communities which have the
greater share of right and truth on their side, it would then be
evident that war is rather one of the many vehicles of truth
and justice than a negation thereof; that it tends rather to
increase than to diminish the sum of justice in the world, and
is therefore at times a factor of civilization and moral progress.
But for this same reason it is evident that war instead of being
eternal, tends at some time to disappear, when civilization
will have increased—owing to multiple factors, war amongst

others—so as no longer to tolerate the infinite evil which is
in war.   If all this were true, war would almost be subject to
a law of self-annihilation.

II

But is this true ?

As a rule war is considered simply as a manifestation of
brute force—an encounter between two armies, in which that
which is best armed and guided by the ablest general
conquers ; a true assertion, but an insufficient one—one, however, with which most people content themselves, apparently
satisfied with the idea that the success of the issue depends
on the ability of the general, the quality of the armament, the
sum a nation can spend in arms, on the valour of the soldiers,
the superficial and frothy patriotic education provided in schools
and barracks.   Instead of this, war is an encounter between
two States, and it is supported with less suffering and greater
probability of victory by the State which is governed with
greater justice, and in which the relations between men and
social classes lead to a greater degree of loyalty.   To some
countries war is a light-hearted matter, so to say ; to others
a sad one.   It is a light or a sad undertaking to a country
according as its government is good or bad, according to
the degree of justice in its social system.   Amongst civilized
and Christian nations to-day, the more unjustly a people is
governed—that is to say, the more it is dominated by petty
and selfish oligarchies, and the more despotic and violent
is its administration—so in proportion is war a ruinous and
dangerous undertaking for it.   On the other hand, a people
governed more justly, that is, by a more liberal, economical
and honest government, is less in danger of the moral and

economical oppression of one caste over another, whether
this be exercised by means of or outside of political power,
and it is in a position to contemplate far more serenely
the dangers and hardships entailed by war. In other words,
the State which proves strongest in war is that in which
morals and life at ordinary times are the furthest removed
from the cruelty, egoism, and violence which during war
become the normal conditions of life and action.

III

A proof of the truth of this affirmation is to be found in
the last struggle between civilized and Christian nations—
the Spanish-American War.

Can we consider the United States of North America as
a model of a society founded on justice ? It would certainly
be imprudent to answer with an unqualified Yes, because
this society is too unequal a conglomeration of good and evil,
of vice and virtue. How can one give an unreserved opinion
on a nation which possesses the most perfect penitentiary
institutions in the world for the shelter and education of
criminals, and which at the same time tolerates the arbitrary
punishment of crime by infuriated mobs ?—A nation which
protects the rights of inventive genius so rigorously and
wisely by the law of patents, a society which has thus reached
a most perfect comprehension of this last and subtlest ideal
of property, whose immaterial essence so many nations still
fail to conceive, but which countenances also the public
organization of those associations of malefactors which are
allowed to impose the most monstrous levies on the populations of entire cities by means of intrigue and fraud ?—A
nation where the laws punish duels as homicide, and where

year after year the massacre of tens of thousands of men by railway accidents, due to the criminal negligence of rapacious companies, is tolerated ?—A nation whose Government retains so much of the wolf nature inherent in the worst European Governments, which allows the most colossal squandering of public moneys, which practises those many administrative artifices by which the true sense, theoretically so clear, of *meum* and *teum* is obscured, such as that most ingenious of all, protectionism ?

But the gravity of a social evil should always be measured in proportion to the force of resistance of the society which it afflicts.   If there are many iniquities in American society, if abominable and unavenged oppression of the strong over the weak is not lacking, and if many means are known for corrupting justice and robbery, and deceiving one's fellows ; if certain of these evils appear to have grown there to a formidable degree unknown in our countries ; nevertheless, in American society is to be found a recompense far greater— that of living amidst far happier natural, social, and historical conditions.

The most essential social bond, which exists as a definite standard of the degree of justice and therefore of civilization, which a community has reached, is the remuneration of labour. A country may possess one institution or another—the family, education, penal or civil justice—better regulated than in other states ; but the excellence of these institutions proves nothing for the moral superiority of that nation, if its system of re-muneration of labour is more iniquitous than in other states where these social institutions are ruder and more imperfect. In the United States, owing to the abundance of land, the relative but not excessive scarcity of capital and men, human work obtains magnificent remuneration ; and obtains it, at least in certain parts of the Union, in the midst of a marvellous and almost perfectly organized civilization. The fabulous prodigality with which the earth pours from her full bosom, after an accumulation of thousands of centuries, the first abundance of her treasures; the possession of the elaborate culture of our civilization free from so many atavisms, prejudices, and dead traditions which encumber the foundations of our society; the extreme freedom and ease of the individual, not handicapped as we are in changing occupations, habits, social caste, received ideals, and social axioms by a social tradition, become almost sacred; the innumerable opportunities in the midst of such constant material and intellectual change for the association of individual talents and energies; the prodigious rapidity with which these combinations can be formed and dissolved; the frequent return of opportunities brought about by the rapidly revolving wheel of fortune; the instability of all things—of good but no less of bad; the purely temporary nature of all conditions; the almost complete want of any definite solutions;—of necessity imply that there is no defeat without reconquest, no decay without rebirth. These conditions prevailing in America, render it easy to any ordinarily intelligent and energetic man to obtain for his work remuneration which errs rather on the side of being beyond than beneath his deserts; never so low as to force him to live without other satisfaction than that of not dying of hunger; without rendering possible, however, those fabulous remunerations to be obtained in new countries, still in their infancy and almost uninhabited—demoralizing remunerations on account of their liberality, which are only possible where civilization is not yet fully organized. It is a matter of small importance, then, if American industrial protectionism, for the

B

benefit of a few, renders many things unreasonably expensive ;
if the money collected by taxes is often spent badly and
frequently misappropriated ; if oligarchies of capitalists impose
levies on the population by means of monopolies. Many
may obtain enormous profits from these iniquities, but without
reducing the condition of others to such a point as only to
allow of their not dying of hunger. Vast industrialism
disciplines but does not degrade a nation. Indeed, the fact
that American capital is employed by preference in the
creation of aristocratic industries, like the mechanical ones,
which demand a great deal of instruction and a certain
intellectual superiority in the worker, and that the good
instinct of the whole people makes them give their preference
in the market to articles of the highest quality, both in material
and workmanship, has resulted in producing a working class
composed, not merely of rude weavers and spinners, of ignorant
labourers employed in the simplest trades, who exercise nothing
but brute force—as happens in many European countries. We
find here, on the contrary, what I might be allowed to call an
aristocracy of labour, well educated, and used to an almost
luxurious standard of life, a class of workers, in consequence,
who cannot be too much imposed on by intrigues of capital
without risk of lowering the quality of the work demanded of
them. Brutal and degrading works devolve upon negroes,
Chinese, and Italian emigrants. It is true that the workers
of the United States are, like others, subject to periods of
enforced idleness, proportionate to the immense and rapid
advance of their industrial speculations, and consequently
more intense than similar European crises ; but the crisis and
misery are of short duration, for the workers who are superfluous in one trade rapidly turn to another which lacks
hands.

The lot of the middle class, amidst considerable adversity, is equally good.

Thanks to the almost complete lack of intellectual protectionism—that is, of academical degrees which ensure the monopoly of certain professions—thanks, in consequence, to the lack of a government *curriculum* of unprofitable and obligatory studies, America is exempt from an intellectual proletariat and from the *declassés*, the chronic disease of the middle classes in Europe. Let him who can do a thing well step forward and do it, no one will question *where* he learnt it : such is the degree required of an American engineer, barrister, clerk, or employé. And as the opportunities to do well are innumerable, every one can develop the talents with which Nature has endowed him, changing his occupation according to circumstances and opportunity. Whereas for a young man belonging to the middle class in continental Europe, the choice of a profession is a solemn deed, entailing practically the consecration of his whole future to one object from that hour deemed immutable, and against which his will from thenceforward will have but little force. For the American this choice is always transitory and variable in accordance with circumstances ; he is never a victim of the tyranny of a choice made once for all for his whole life, often whilst still immature ; and he rarely finds himself in either of those two situations so ruinous to the middle classes in Europe, more especially in the Latin countries : the absolute uncertainty of success, and the utter despair of ever recovering from a sudden ruin. Where all professions are handsomely remunerated so as to allow to all a luxurious life, an American is always ready to see the particular stream at which he has been drinking dried up, and be prepared to pack up his belongings and set off in search of another.

In recompense, he need never feel himself condemned
to the long-life misery of being tied down to a profession,
chosen badly but irrevocably, or to the wretched pursuit
of a dying industry ruined by competition or economic
evolution. The strong spiritual energies of this class, constantly fostered by surrounding circumstances, occasionally
give rise to violent tempests, it is true, and bring the scum to
the surface, but they never rot in a state of pestilential inertia
from which exhale the vapours of dark pessimism and the
fevers of vain revolutionary ideas. The sight of the soul
remains always clear and unveiled, though it often be capable
of penetrating none but material objects ; the will remains
young and active, because constantly exercised by the simple
and healthy gymnastics of action.

And thus it is that work, the great trial that God, according to the Bible, imposed on the human race, the servile yoke
which man has borne for so many ages, and to escape which
classes and nations have spilt so much blood, changes its
nature, and instead of degrading man, ennobles him. A new
passion, common to all the Anglo-Saxon races, has become
the mainspring of the morality of a civilization, new also,
itself—the ardent passion for work, the ambition to reach by
its means an excellence hitherto unknown. Nothing is more
difficult to man than moderation. Instead of seeking happiness in the wise exercise of his forces, and in the healthy
indulgence of divers pleasures which demand a certain effort
of will and self-control, he seeks it in the frantic pursuit of
one particular pleasure, which, though frequently unhealthy
and dangerous, gives inebriating joy for a minute, and dis-
penses with the necessity of tedious self-control. Thus hard
but not too exhausting work, alternated with sufficient repose,
would procure for man the most durable and pleasurable

mode of life ; but he, on the contrary, is rather inclined to yield to the seductions of the enfeebling pleasures of repose prolonged beyond the period necessary for the recuperation of his forces—that is, of absolute laziness—or of the sublime and fatal voluptuousness to be obtained through the abuse of his intellectual forces, in an attempt to multiply his efforts and successes in the struggle for life. The excess of labour can procure a voluptuous spiritual exaltation in which man feels as though his energies were doubled, in which fatigue appears delight, so easy and pleasant does work become to him : a delight which few can resist by taking necessary repose, for the exaltation of overwork cannot last indefinitely, and nearly always terminates in painful physical and mental disease. Thus whilst moderate labour may be healthily pleasurable, absolute idleness or the abuse of work are morbid passions ; and we find that in certain communities—Turkey, for instance —absolute idleness is regarded as the supreme pleasure of existence, and is led by those who are considered perfect and happy—the highest classes—and in other countries, such as England and the United States, the greatest joy of life is found in hard work, in the utmost exercise of the human faculties within the bounds of possibility.

In the American the passion for work is combined with the pride in doing his best, the ambition not to allow himself to be overcome by any difficulties, and to reach an unsurpassed grade of excellence. All men work with a view to some reward ; but some are satisfied with pay, others, besides at money reward, seek to satisfy their own *amour-propre*, and to obtain the admiration of others. It is the same with the work of nations, and indeed, from the reward generally sought after, the quality of the work may be judged. Although Americans are commonly accused of cupidity, their work ranks among the most disinterested, because they aim not only at accumulating money, but also, they display an insatiable thirst for perfection, which tends to idealize their work ; and into nearly all they do they put extra labour, not with the object of gaining more money, but of improving the quality of the work. The decisive proof of the superiority of American work was given by industrial protectionism which, in continental Europe, has lowered the standard of goods, because the manufacturers, content with the easy profits obtained by protectionism, consider themselves exempt from the trouble of perfecting their own goods. American industries, on the contrary—the mechanical ones more particularly—have reached a marvellous degree of perfection, notwithstanding protectionism, because the manufacturers were stimulated, not merely by a desire to gain money, but also by the ambition of displaying a degree of excellence in their productions till then unknown to the world. American goods, moreover, have notoriously the reputation of costliness and high finish.

No doubt this passion for work and this ambition for excellence, so deep-rooted in the American and English mind, may be due to the fact that work is not too hard and its remuneration good. The Americans are made of the same clay as other white men, and great hardship in work and very poor recompense for it would have created in them, as in other civilized peoples, insupportable weariness of labour and indifference to its quality. But as luckily for them this is not so, the passion for work and its excellence became the ruling force of their nation, and the moral basis of their society, for to these two sentiments are attributable the greatest qualities and the worst defects of the American—amongst their defects, the weakness of family ties, the inordinate admiration of success, and the lack of scruples in the struggle ; amongst their good qualities, their force of will, their courage, their strong spirit of social solidarity and justice, the capacity to act on other than directly personal motives and interests.

What power does not this sentiment give to American and English society ? The greatness of a nation depends on a high standard of moral solidarity, and this is high only where each respects in others the rights he himself claims, and admits for himself the same duties which he would impose upon others under similar circumstances ; it arises from the recognition of the fact that if men differ from one another in talent, culture, and wealth, they are nevertheless morally equal, and that no one of them is morally bound to serve his fellow without receiving just and equivalent remuneration. Where this sentiment of the moral equality of men is most deeply felt, every one resents the injustice done to others, and in thought and action aims at social justice. But the conditions most favourable to the development of this sentiment are those under which no one depends for his livelihood on the capricious benevolence of others, but like the American and Englishmen, only on his own capacities to serve in some way his fellows, receiving their services in exchange, and these not measured arbitrarily by some power outside himself, but governed by his own judgment. This liberty develops in him the sense of moral dignity, which is the backbone of the human character and of the sentiment of moral equality. When, on the contrary, men depend for their livelihood on the caprice of others, the patron claims for himself other rights than he recognizes in his protégé. When the protégé admits this, there is born the sentiment known as servility— the protégé acquiescing in the fact that the patron on whom he

depends has the licence to commit iniquities and to be overbearing. These things may annoy him when he is the direct
victim, but do not offend his torpid sense of justice when
inflicted on others, and indeed in the long run he often
grows indifferent. But the man who is alive to the sense of
his moral equality with others does not bow to injustice, for
this sentiment becomes such a stimulus to his energies that
it generates in him an insatiable desire to perfect his own
conditions and those of others, and to free them from the
ever-diminishing degree of injustice which, to his refined
conscience, appear more intolerable the meaner they are—
a desire which he satisfies in diverse ways, and which
maintains in a free society a continuous and lively circulation of ideas, and an interest in moral and social reform.
Indifference to injustice, on the contrary, renders man
apathetic and lazy, leading to aimlessness in life and
inertness of intellect, as we shall better demonstrate in speaking of Spain, in societies organized, not in accordance with
principles of liberty, but of protection.

But in the American the sentiment of social solidarity is
strengthened by the proud ambition never to give way to
obstacles, and to aim always at the highest perfection in all
things. This introduces a new altruistic stimulus to life,
rendering man capable of acting from other than selfish
motives. If this stimulus, born of pride, cannot be considered
especially noble, it is nevertheless a precious one if we
consider the gross egoism of man. It is always a great thing
to raise man from his native selfishness, if only by means of
pride ; and still greater if his ambition to conquer is stimulated, not with a view to obtaining the good opinion of
others, but of satisfying his own. Thus it is with the
American who has in him, in his pride to succeed well in all

he undertakes, the chief incentive to raise himself from the pettiness of private interest, and to labour not only for himself but also for a perfection in which he will find none but ideal satisfaction.

In short, what has made American society appear to Europeans in the light of an enchanted world, is that it combines two qualities which seemed each naturally to exclude the other by absolute contrariety : the refinement of culture and morals only possible to a long-established civilization, and the freedom of the individual from those oppressive historical, political, moral, and intellectual tyrannies which the State accumulates and imposes on all our anciently civilized countries. Hence arises the marvellous range of moral energies in the individual, which, in the United States, vents itself in an unmeasured ambition to do great things, and to which the benignity of surrounding Nature gives such full satisfaction. Who has not heard say that in America the dimensions of everything were designed by men with double or triple sight? An aristocracy of wealth served by an infinite mass of inanimate slaves, animated by a soul of steam or electricity, which spare their masters the trouble even of slight exertion : this is the ideal of life to the American, to satisfy which his ingenuity conceives and constructs every year a prodigious number of machines to perform the greatest and the meanest of services—to convey electricity across continents, to squash flies, and to clean shoes. Everything there is on a gigantic scale : the newspapers print sufficient paper every day to envelop the world ; their houses rival the tower of Babel ; their great offices have the dimensions of cities ; donations to public schools can be reckoned by tens of millions of dollars, and the fortunes of the very rich by thousands. This is the modern form taken by that instinct of greatness which in the past gave rise to the mightiest aristocratic creations of history, then directed towards art and now to mechanical industry; that same instinct which led the Romans to create the Colosseum and the Baths, the Venetians to create the Grand Canal, the Florentines Santa Maria del Fiore, and which now leads the Americans to create a world where real things have taken the proportions we behold. These grandiose aristocracies—so prodigal of beauty, wealth, and grandeur—pass away, because the benignity of the natural and social conditions amidst which they grow are rapidly exhausted; and so also the day will come when the population of the United States will have multiplied a hundred-fold, and the earth will be a little tired, and then the Americans also will have to be more economical. Then our descendants, when recollecting the fabulous prodigality of the past, will receive an impression analogous to that which we receive when looking back on the princely grandeur of Venice; they will find in them both two different forms of the same sentiment, the ambition for greatness, which at times takes hold of social communities and entire nations, and whose first incentive in the Americans was fundamental justice and the splendid liberality of the remuneration given to human work.

Thus social iniquities in America are as cyclones that rise, go their way, annihilating men and their work along the course of their terrible progress, and then dissolve into nothing. In a word, iniquity is one of the violent and intermittent forms of evil, like fire, and tempests and earthquakes amongst physical phenomena, and acute and mortal diseases amongst the phenomena of organic life. The most terrible of all, I hear some one exclaim. Indeed no: the most terrible in appearance, perhaps, but the most innocent in reality. The violent forms of evil wrench some fruit from the tree of life, break a few branches, denude it of some beautiful leaves, and this is the extent of the evil of which they are capable. The really terrible forms of evil are slow and continuous : not those which annihilate, but those which insidiously corrupt life ; those which attack the root, and diffuse themselves upwards from it, poisoning the purest lymph in the live trunk. The terrible in life and nature is not the violent outburst of evil in passing devastations, but the slow and continuous spread of malignant essences, which continuously distil in the secret recesses of being, and spread by means of the most subtle natural influences through the veins of creation. The fury of a storm destroys pastures, cattle, houses : many people die in consequence of it, much property is destroyed ; but calm returns shortly, and only a vague recollection of the tempest remains. But in the countries which nature has for centuries inoculated with the germs of fever, where man finds himself attacked by an enemy always present and invisible ; where he breathes the fever the earth exhales at sunrise and sundown, and drinks fever dissolved in water and in the juice of fruits ; where whole populations die slowly, without having received any external shock ;—the poison, secreted and absorbed for centuries by the earth, destroys their constitutions by slow degrees.

IV

This is the reason why Spain is so much less happy than the United States. Iniquity does not burst forth there in transitory furies, but it exhales from the earth and slowly poisons like a miasma. An old society leaning on pillars of injustice, which has grown darker from century to century,

bolstered up by the dust of innumerable iniquities, from
this earth poisoned slowly, molecule by molecule, exhales a
malaria whence all the classes which build up Spanish society
must perish, unable to find the conditions necessary for
healthy development.

The main characteristic of Spanish society is that it is
formed, not on principles of liberty, but of protection, for the
greater number, more especially of the easy and educated
class, who form the morality and culture of a country, and
depend for existence not on their own labour, but on the
caprice of others. It is this which renders unjust the
remuneration of labour. Men find little opportunity to do
anything in Spain, because a few, protected by the State,
have usurped unjust reward, greater than is due to their
merit, thereby diminishing the recompense available to others
to a degree that renders work repugnant. Spain is apparently
ruled by a parliament ; but this *regime* covers a hidden caste
despotism, because the most essential condition to liberty—as
demonstrated by a great Italian writer on political science,
Gaetano Mosca [1]—the plurality of political forces in the government of a society, is totally lacking. In other words, all the
classes or social groups who, owing to wealth or culture, are
in a position to direct or misdirect public affairs in Spain,
form part of or are interested in the Government, and by
means of it they grasp or seek to grasp an undue reward for
their services. The nobility, which consists almost entirely
of proprietors of arable land, is in need of Government
protection, by means of taxation, against the competition
of American grain. The great financiers accumulate wealth
principally by speculating in public finances. The great in-
dustrialists and merchants grow rich illicitly by the monopolies

---

[1] In his book " Elementi di Scienza politica " (Turin, 1896)

and protection conceded by the Government. The middle class largely depends on public appointments and politics, for parliament is composed of lawyers, journalists, and jobbers, who live by defending the great financiers and speculators. The prelates, endowed with State farms, can but be obsequious to it.

Thus there does not exist, as in England, a middle class independent of the Government, capable of controlling and opposing it ; but only the ignorant and miserable masses who are forced to contribute very largely through taxes to the maintenance and enrichment of the governing oligarchy. They must, moreover, play their part in the comedy of universal suffrage by voting, that is to say, for the candidate whom the *coteries* in power have already selected. And for this it is necessary to keep them in ignorance.

In such a society the ideal object in life is naturally to shirk any severe labour and responsibility. For some the seductions of idleness are too strong, for others the difficulties of work too great, so that, while some do little or nothing, the rest are forced to overwork in order to do their share. Hence they grow to regard happiness as consisting, not in the liberality of remuneration and the satisfaction of work well done, but in making the smallest effort possible. They take no pleasure or pride in their work, and have no other aim than to obtain, with the least possible trouble, some sort of money remuneration. The ignorant and bigoted rich have no regard for agriculture ; they live far away from their estates ; the only interest they take in them is to draw their rents, which they mercilessly extort from the peasants, in order to spend the money in urban luxuries and dissipations, protected by iniquitous governmental taxations. And how should the rude peasants who are forced to lead such hard

and laborious lives, for the pleasures of others, take more
interest in the land than their masters?   Not even the small
landed proprietors—except in a few districts, such as Anda-
lusia—possess the true love of agriculture, or cultivate the
ground with zeal and passion.   They are only the unconscious
heirs of ancient practices and traditions which they have inherited from their fathers, and will bequeath to their sons.
Their ignorance is of the densest, and they have no incentive to improve themselves.   They are satisfied if, by means of
small frauds, usuries, and persistent usurpations, they succeed
in augmenting their property by a few acres.   The Spanish
peasant does not trouble to better his system of cultivation.
Ignorant, superstitious, conservative, of the severest morals,
his whole spiritual existence consists in the most elementary
egoism.   The artisan classes are equally ignorant, with the
exception of the few turbulent workers in the great Catalonian factories.   They are poor, bigoted, illiterate, lazy, and
consider work merely as a service to the Government and
wealthy classes.   They have little moral sense, and no
character, and are a true hot-bed of the crime and mendicity
which infest Spain.   Nor are the industrial and commercial
upper middle classes relatively superior.   With the exception
of those engaged in certain industrial pursuits traditional to
the country, they show neither originality, enterprise, love of
perfection, or any passion for study or culture.   The Catalonian
manufacturers aim only at accumulating large profits, and for
this reason Spanish industry ranks among the humblest and
roughest, despite the fact that it had once secured itself a
rich colonial market, on most advantageous terms, with high
productive tariffs in favour of the commerce and industry of
the mother-land.

    The moral malady that afflicts the middle classes is more

complicated and painful. If the middle class prospers in
America, because it knows how to preserve the equilibrium
between character and riches, exercising thought and will in
the healthy gymnastics of action, in Spain, on the contrary, the atavistic prejudices against industrial labour, the
degeneration of several very noble trades through the carelessness of the men who followed them, the difficulty of commerce
and industry proper to impoverished countries that lack
capital, prevent the middle-class youth from entering on this
healthy life, and leave him only the resource of liberal
professions and Government appointments. A youth belonging to the lower *bourgeoisie* is thus set to study, at the cost of
serious family sacrifice ; he enters the military schools, which
he leaves as an officer at the age of 16 or 17, after having
learnt very little. He is thus fully equipped to form part
of the most ignorant class of officers in the world. Or he goes
to the University to swell the ranks of those poor and idle
students—too numerous in all Latin nations, but poorer and
lazier in Spain than elsewhere. These University studies
are still simpler, more careless and incomplete, than in France
or Italy. The youths waste their time in dissipation, till
they find themselves at the end of their University education
as ignorant as when they started, and as incapable of rendering
any useful or becoming service to their fellows. It only
remains for them to gain, by means of baseness and servility,
the favour of some great family or political leader, and to
obtain through his influence some liberal profession, State
appointment, or political opening. Only a few cunning or
lucky men, however, succeed in reaching fame, fortune, or
honour through politics or appointments in a poor country,
where the circulation of wealth is as slow as a torpid and
muddy stream. To others there only remain the most

poorly paid employments, and the decently clothed squalor of the petty *bourgeoisie* that tries to live like the easy classes without possessing the means to do so. In recompense for this, however, they obtain life appointments when once they enter the ranks of the permanent functionaries ; nor do they need, in order to obtain this, to give proof of their aptitude to do a given work. A little influence suffices, and the work is then light and free from responsibility to him who does not care to work too hard. Thus he is able to satisfy to the full the ideal of every Spanish middle-class youth : to be an official at Madrid, to work little ; to be able well dressed to take part in the *prado* promenade in the *corridas* and theatre ; to be received amongst the minor guests in some great family ; to go to bed late, get up late in the morning, go to business late, and leave it early without having done much work. Only the more fortunate and intelligent and the least scrupulous, run any chance of shining in Madrid society ; of attaining to well-paid posts where they can sell their influence at a high price ; of becoming celebrated orators to whose lectures flock the ladies of Madrid, or the leaders of political factions. The remainder are condemned to a poor and obscure life, with only one advantage : that of being exempt from the need of serious work or study. The Spanish administration, which is composed of similar functionaries, is, in consequence, the most ignorant in Europe, and its politics the richest in talk and the poorest in deeds and ideas.

For all these reasons—so contrary to what we observe in American society—according to the psychological process demonstrated, the defect of Spanish society is the lack of energy, the indifference of the upper classes, which oscillates between extravagant pride and base servility, for the sentiment of justice, personal dignity and moral equality is feeble in all classes. The whole of society always finds itself in the position of protector or protected, every one being in turn the *protége* of some one and the protector of somebody else ; and hence arises the universal indifference to the injustice of those in power, and to the consequent social ills—the harshness of the relations between rich and poor, the apathy and fatalism of the multitudes who do not heed the troubles of others, and scarcely note their own. Thus it is in the natural order of things that Jesuitism should have more weight in Spain than elsewhere ; and that Catholicism—this Proteus, which in America and Belgium is becoming liberal, tolerant, and active—should remain here the religion of vanity, ignorance, and sloth, *fêtes*, ceremonies, and processions ; the luxury of the great prelates; bountiful charity to vagabonds ; flattery to the vanity and idleness of women ; absolution for sins born of laziness and egoism, such as libertinage, envy, avarice, vanity, and calumny ; pitiless rigour against the virtues due to labour and generosity, such as pride, compassion for social evils; the desire for culture and breadth of ideas ; moral formalism and bigotism which deform the soul, arrogance towards the State, and the ambition to be beyond its bounds. This is a true picture of Spanish Catholicism : a formidable instrument for shattering the moral energies of man, for reducing character to something limp and devoid of backbone. And thus the work of the Church tends to complete the moral enervation of Spanish society, founded on the unjust remuneration of labour. Hence all hedge themselves round with petty individual and family selfishness, and remain deaf to the demands of modern civilization, that incites men to great and hardy deeds, rewarding then with liberal recompense.

C

V

Now, the United States does not yet possess a standing army. Till recent years they had a few old ships rather than a fleet, and even now their fleet is but of some few years' standing. Besides this, they have the established reputation of being the least heroic and chivalrous, the most bourgeois and mercantile country in the world. The Spaniards, on the contrary, possess an army and fleet whose traditions are ancient; they possess militia and naval equipages raised by conscription, generals and admirals by profession, and an ancient reputation for national valour.

Might we not reasonably have concluded that of these two nations the Americans would have regarded the possibility of imminent war with terror, and the Spaniards, on the contrary, with confidence? But this was not the case: the American people calmly faced the prospect of war with Spain. To them it was a truly cheerful war. During three years a portion of the American people watched with interest the Cuban insurrection; they openly provided the insurgents with gold, iron, and dynamite; they publicly proclaimed that Weyler was a murderer who merited the gallows. Who amongst them gave a thought to the war that might arise from these popular and diplomatic interferences in the great duel? Doubtless, in this common courage, in this species of public petulance, there was a considerable portion of the light-mindedness and unconsciousness of a people who did not consider all that war might imply, and who allowed themselves to be led away by their feelings. But, however rash was the attitude of the people towards the probability of war, in any case it was, in the eyes of Europe, one of the principal forces of the American Government in dealing with the Cuban question. With practical foresight it was able to combine the collective courage of the country, preparing their forces for the inevitable conflict, and declaring war as soon as these forces were sufficient to assure them victory. After this they showed no hesitation. The declaration of war was made with calm resolution ; and if it was not generally considered an ordinary act of the national policy, neither was it looked upon as particularly alarming, nor as the universal calamity, the light in which so many people in the more ignorant European countries regard war, that *matribus detestata*. Beyond a slight burst of patriotic exultation, public feeling in America received no shock at the news of the coming war, and industry in no way interrupted its indomitable regularity throughout the continent.

On the other hand, the war against the insurgent island, no less than that with America, was a fearful calamity for the Spanish people. The army in Cuba was composed, for the most part, of wretched peasants sent there by force, while the flower of the educated classes, thanks to the convenient law of substitution, remained at home to cheer the departing soldiers, and to receive on their return these wretched shadows of the florid youths who had landed on the beautiful but accursed island. The ardent patriotism of the Spanish upper classes, more particularly during the Spanish-American War, proved itself to be, above all else, a literary and oratorical sentiment. The feud between the petty parliamentary cliques never ceased ; indeed, they rather grew more venomous. Few of the great families subsidized the war, and there was presented the spectacle of a European country collecting money, by means of theatre and *corridas* benefits, to carry on war with one of the richest nations in the world. Very few upper-class youths took part in the war as common soldiers. Workers and peasants were sent to fight in the ranks of the non-graduated soldiers—the masses, in short, who were the unwilling instruments of this bloody deed so repugnant to them, not so much on account of their breadth of ideas, as owing to their ingenuous and rude egoism. They were mere blind instruments whose courage was only maintained by the fear of punishment. So true is this, that as the war by degrees grew fiercer in Cuba, the Spanish Government was compelled to intensify the reign of terror with which it habitually coerces Spain ; to multiply the states of siege ; to increase the power of the police ; to imprison pellmell, and under the most diverse pretexts, all those who were suspected of too liberal dispositions, for fear that the revolutionary parties might succeed in rousing to rebellion the masses exasperated by the enormous tribute of blood, money, and suffering demanded of them by the Spanish Government. The final consequence of the Spanish-American War was that the whole of Spain was placed under martial law, a proof that the Government counted little on the concurrence of the people in face of this struggle with the enemy. Indeed, the truth is that a large portion of the population, not concerned in politics, showed great indifference to the outcome of the war. It is well known that the inhabitants of Madrid would not allow the *corridas* to be postponed owing to the news of the battles of Cavité and Santiago ; and whilst far away their brothers were being massacred they continued their dissipations.

VI

Thus we see war conducted cheerfully on one hand, sadly on the other ; and this not merely due to the difference between easy and difficult warfare. The mercantile American Government, composed entirely of bourgeoisie, presided over by a former tradesman, knew how to prepare for conflict, to measure the forces necessary, and to deal the blow with certainty at the proper moment. That their adversaries were very poor and the American very rich detracts in no wise from their merit, since eight years ago they were still weaker, and possessed no naval force. Moreover, it does not suffice for a nation to own riches ; it must know how to spend money well, and to prepare itself properly and seriously for war. The Spanish Government, on the contrary, which still has military character and tradition, and which, in spite of the country's poverty, spent during the last three years several milliard dollars on the attempted suppression of the Cuban insurrection, was unable to quell the uprising. It then engaged in combat with the United States when totally unprepared. Hence America was able to destroy two Spanish fleets, with small loss of men on her side, and to conquer Cuba, defended by 200,000 soldiers, by landing there little over 20,000 men, after a somewhat haphazard assault on Santiago.

This unreadiness was, indeed, at the bottom of all the Spanish misfortunes. The Cuban rebels, as to whose number various writers differ, were, at the outside, calculated at some 40,000 ; only a certain number were armed with guns, whilst the majority possessed only common knives. They had little ammunition or money, and what they had reached them from America, across the line of the maritime blockade. Consequently they never attacked the enemy resolutely, but merely wore it out with little skirmishes. Against these poorly armed bands the Spaniards sent in various relays 200,000 men, the greatest army that ever crossed the Atlantic, an army led by generals educated in European schools, with the open sea behind it, and a Government which could obtain loans of millions of pounds from European bankers. How was it, then, that after three years the insurrection was still so little subdued that bands of rebels marauded in safety only a few miles from Havana? Unfortunately for Spain, her army consisted merely of armed and uniformed soldiers—if, indeed, they all possessed arms and uniforms—but the other apparatus necessary nowadays to an army were lacking: waggons, beasts of burden, provisions, ambulances. The result was that the soldiers could not leave the towns to defend the country for more than two or three days at a stretch, without the risk of dying of hunger or remaining without ammunition, so that all the reinforcements sent to Cuba were in the way rather than being of service. They were distributed in the towns and fortresses throughout the island, but they remained there idle, whilst the insurgents became masters of the country. For this reason the Spanish Government at last resorted to the cruel tactics of General Weyler, of reducing the rebels by famine, by devastating the country, thus compelling them to collect in the towns, to die there of hunger, leaving the land uncultivated around them. Then, when General Shafter laid siege to Santiago, it was several times announced that a body of militia commanded by General Pandos was to come from Havana to the assistance of the besieged at Santiago; and, indeed, it appears strange that while 200,000 soldiers were on the island, Santiago should have been left to be conquered by the small American army. But the fact was that the Spaniards, through lack of all the apparatus necessary to an army with long country marches before it, had no means of overland communication between the various Cuban towns, but could only communicate by sea, so that from the moment that the Americans were masters of the coast, the great naval towns were quite cut off from aid. If the Spanish Government had equipped an army of 40,000 men for Cuba, provided with all the necessaries for a modern army, so that, divided in columns, they could leave the towns and fortresses and hold the country for miles together ; if this army had attacked the rebels, the insurrection would have been quelled in a few months, with small loss of blood and at infinitely smaller expense.

But why was not Spain capable of organizing such an army, whilst the United States, so far poorer in military tradition, were able to create a fleet in a few years capable of all that was required of it ? The cause of this must be sought for in the character of the two Governments and the two nations, in the moral strength of the one and the moral weakness of the other. The Spanish Government is a slave of *routine*, little capable of reforming its institutions, even in face of grave and imminent danger ; because it is led by a selfish oligarchy, outside of which, as we have shown, there exists only a miserable and oppressed multitude who are its victims, and not an intelligent and educated bourgeoisie capable of opposing it ; because its administration is narrow, and chosen, not in the interests of the good government of its country, but with a view to finding employment for the *protégés* of politicians, and of providing in some manner for the maintenance of the middle classes. This results in a lack of any proper control over public opinion, which can only be exercised by educated and intelligent people ; and in public offices not being given to those who deserve them, but to toadies to those in power ; and finally, in the Government not acting for the public good, but in the hopes of pleasing this or that portion of the reigning oligarchy. Under such circumstances the ministers lose the faculty of making any serious reform, and the Spanish ministry showed itself quite ·incapable of warfare. A year's serious labour would have been necessary to organize a proper Cuban army. But with a set of officials whose appointment was due rather to the intrigue of politicians than to their own merits—directed by old men, jealous of one another, who had raised themselves by intrigue, and were only anxious not to allow themselves to be outdone by the intrigues of rivals, not unfrequently corrupt and bowed down under the weight of prejudices—what ministry could pass any serious or important measures of reform ? A sense of the futility of making any attempt disarmed the most resolute, and every one trusted blindly to chance. Besides this, it appears that several shipping companies and other large firms made a lucrative thing out of the transport of soldiers to Cuba, so that it was to their interests that great numbers should be sent there, as it was also to the interests of the officers, for thus they went in larger numbers to Cuba, where there was little fighting to be done and much to be gained. These companies, having great weight with the Government, urged it to multiply the transports of soldiers, ruining thereby the public treasury, and making greater confusion in Cuba, but enriching themselves —a monstrous iniquity deserving of heavy punishment, but which was committed with impunity in Spain in the midst of universal indifference, because justice lay dormant, and because those who, through wealth or education, were in a position to direct the moral conscience of the country, and to prevent such scandals, were all attached to the Government, and therefore interested in encouraging, or compelled to tolerate in silence, these abominable crimes against their native land.

In the United States, on the contrary, the Government is
not the sole representative of all that is strong in talent,
culture, or wealth in American society. Public functionaries,
and those concerned in politics, represent only a portion of
the educated classes, and they have no decided superiority
over the rest. The officials, moreover, do not consider their
posts as a mere sinecure, enabling them to live permanently
on the Treasury, without anxiety for the morrow. They
are for the most part men who carry on their business like
any other business, who go on with it as long as it is to
their interest, and give it up when they think they could
do better elsewhere. Thus the Government knows that it is
subject to the criticism of the country ; that it has to deal
with energetic opposition ; and that, if the nation is willing to
put up with many shortcomings in the administration because
they cause it no great inconvenience and would take too
much time to set to rights, it does not concede to the Government absolute impunity. Wherefore a Government which
should engage in a war without having made sufficient pre-
paration would meet with condign punishment in universal
disapproval. Besides this, that pride to succeed in every
undertaking, which a free and adventurous life develops in
every American, also assists the statesmen. It pledges their
amour propre, and makes them deliberate ; while their Spanish
confrères, used only to looking after their own interests and
those of their friends, remain indifferent to the results of
their politics so long as they do not themselves have to pay
for it, knowing full well that no one will demand of them
too exact an account of their failures. Lastly, the instability
of American official appointments renders it possible for the
Government, when it wishes an administration to do some
given work, such as organizing a fleet or preparing for war,

to seek and find the men capable of doing it well—men who are also stimulated by the ambition common to Americans to show off their own worth. Hence it was possible for the American Government to provide a fleet at brief notice and at a small cost; and impossible for Spain, at the expense of thousands, to get together an army.

The Spanish-American War was of such brief duration that the United States only needed their fleet and their small army : both of them composed of professional soldiers not raised by conscription. The volunteers—that is, the nation itself in arms—had not time to enter on action, except in very small bodies. Is it to be believed that if the Americans had had to rely entirely on their volunteer army, they would have been beaten by the Spanish regiments raised by conscription and educated in barracks ? Would the old European military organization have conquered the disorganized American energies ?

It is always difficult, and indeed vain, to attempt resolving hypothetical historical problems. In any case, it seems to me that any one a little familiar with the psychology of war would doubt whether the Spaniards would have had better fortune in dealing with a land army than with the fleets at sea.

VII

To let one's self be killed is not pleasant in itself: we cannot succeed in dominating, by a simple effort of will, the instinct of self-preservation. Certainly, in a hand-to-hand conflict between soldiers inflamed by passion, by cries, volleys of shot, and all the frantic excitement, a man may be carried away by a species of violent intoxication, under the sway of which he may even find pleasure in feeling his flesh lacerated and cut, and in the sensation of being bathed in his own blood. All spiritual exaltations combine pleasure and pain, confounding them together in that convulsed state of feeling which makes of pain a pleasure.

But a war does not consist solely in these brief moments of supreme exaltations; the real bitterness of a war is not in the desperate tension of muscle and courage required of a soldier at the decisive point of a battle—efforts almost invariably rendered easy by the state of mind in which he finds himself at such a moment. The real hardships of war consist in the long marches, in the long spells of hunger and thirst to be suffered, in the nights passed sleeping in the mud under the pouring rain, in the illnesses to be borne without doctors or medicines, in the discouragement at feeling one's self no longer master of one's own destiny, stripped of all human worth, deprived of the absolute and unconditional right to live. They consist, above all, in the fear which seizes all, even the bravest, the first time they find themselves face to face with the firing, and in the unexpected outbreaks of the instinct of self-preservation, which instinct in the best soldiers is like that of a capricious horse. He remains quiet and docile, restrained by a strong will, in the face of tremendous perils, and then, of a sudden, confronted often by some slight danger, breaks bounds and takes to flight. The real hardship of war, in a word, is in the effort of will a soldier must make to fulfil his duty; for to the humble foot-soldier, who has no responsibility of command, fighting is only an exercise of will. The impulsive faculties count for little in war, everything has to be willed : resistance to fatigue, courage, indifference to death.

Thus, as resolution is one of those faculties of the mind

most capable of education, if we except a few criminals and maniacs in whom the instinct of self-preservation is obtuse by nature, there are no born heroes ; intrepid soldiers are not born, they become what they are by an effort of will. Man is born as cowardly as he is born naked ; the soldier who succeeds in annihilating in himself the instinct of self-preservation is an artificial creation of society, just as a dressed-up man is an artificial being for whose creation many different means have been adopted in different ages and communities.

One means was that adopted in the armies of the Roman Empire, and in which Napoleon placed great faith : of accustoming soldiers to danger by practice. This system, however, can no longer be applied in civilized countries, for wars have become such rare events that a man is seldom called upon to fight more than once. Another method is that of exalting the spirit of soldiers by some savage passion, some fanaticism which drowns the instinct of self-preservation : this is the method which has met with such success in the Turkish army, but which succeeds only with a barbarous race, because civilization signifies reason and moderation in all things. The third system is that attempted by the Spanish Government with its Cuban army : that of placing them between two dangers, of which war is the lesser, and of keeping up their failing courage with the fear of punishment and the threat of the penal code for deserters and cowards.

By one or other of these three systems have been recruited and organized nearly all the armies which have ever fought hitherto, with good or ill luck ; and this is easily explained when we reflect that neither of these systems demands much spiritual *finesse* in the human material to which it is applied. From the most barbarous tribe of shepherds, and the rudest peasantry in the world, an army can be formed by one or other of these systems. Thus the Roman empire recruited from amongst the uncivilized populations in its domains the best support of its decadent age ; thus the feudal Russia of Alexander I. gathered from its rude serfs and mujics the armies which destroyed Napoleon's troops ; it was thus that modern Turkey furnished, from among the most wretched Mussulman peasantry of Anatolia and Syria, the battalions which caused such confusion to the Russians at Plevna. And even in the legions of Napoleon I. were not ignorance and coarseness considered as the distinctive qualities of authentic soldiers, the sign of their superiority over the bourgeoisie ?

But another means—much less common and more modern— by which a people can find the strength to face a great crisis in war is this : that at least its larger portion lives normally under such good material, moral, and intellectual conditions, that it can rapidly adapt itself to the situation of war by a conscious effort of will directed by a moral motive. As Gaetano Mosca aptly observes : [1] "War, like any other dangerous trade, requires a certain degree of habit to be faced with calm and *sang-froid;* when this habit is lacking it can only be replaced either by those moments of orgasm which occur rarely in the life of nations, or by that sentiment of honour and duty which in a small and select class can be roused and maintained by special education."

How did it happen, in the American War of 1861–65, that the armies collected in the Northern States—so disorganized, unbalanced, undisciplined, and liable to the panics of first battles—were transformed rapidly in the course of a few months into armies so formidable for courage, discipline, and

---

[1] G. Mosca, "Elements of Political Science," p. 281 (Turin, 1896).

heroic resolution? Hardly one of those agriculturists, workers, merchants, advocates, and brokers who fought in the rival armies—especially the Northern—knew what war meant either in theory or practice ; and yet, at its termination, all military critics were forced to confess that the ability of the heads vied with the courage and resolution of the soldiers. What force performed this miracle? Neither fear nor habit ; the one was out of the question, for the other there was not time. Thus, more especially, the Northern States would have failed to create any army at all if their citizens had not been excellent raw material, easily transformable into good soldiers. Already, in the year 1848, President Polk had observed, grandiloquently but with considerable insight, the excellence of the material. "Our citizen soldiers," he wrote in a December despatch, "are quite absolutely different from those drawn from the population of the Southern States. They count in their ranks men of all professions and trades : farmers, lawyers, doctors, merchants, manufacturers, workmen ; not only among the officers, but even in the ranks. From their earliest youth they have been used to handling firearms ; many of them are excellent shots. They are men with reputations to be preserved by means of good conduct during campaigns. They are intelligent, and they are developing an individuality to be found in no other army. In battle, every soldier, no less than every officer, fights for his country, and at the same time with the object of obtaining glory and distinction among his fellow-citizens the day he returns to civil life." Raw material, but capable of being moulded in the War of Independence, more especially because the more select portion of the army was composed of educated and well-to-do men who till then had attended to their own business, and who, failing other higher sentiments, were at least sustained

by the pride of showing themselves in no wise inferior to
what was considered to be their worth ; who, with a conscious
effort of will, influenced by diverse ethical sentiments,
succeeded in *becoming* good soldiers in a short time, principally by contracting habits of discipline, and dominating the
instinct of self-preservation.

Is it rash to suppose that an army like the Spanish, composed
of ignorant and indifferent soldiers, fighting only out of fear
of the punishments with which the military code threatened
deserters, could not hold out long against an army of better
educated soldiers, resolved to do their duty, through the
pride of men who will not admit in themselves the weaknesses
of hesitation or fear ? Thus we are led, by another route, to
the same conclusion which is the *leit-motif* of this study, that
in order to prevent the rich and educated classes of a nation
from becoming so selfish by reason of their wealth and culture
as to make use of their power to exempt themselves from the
fatigue and perils of war, and to palm it off on the ignorant
and poor—as happened in Spain—and to make a profit
out of the ruin of their country ; that in order to preserve at
least an *élite* class, who will take part in war without thought
to personal gain, putting all their energy into the undertaking, thus diminishing its risk and fatigues ;—that society
must be governed with a certain degree of justice, and be
founded on principles of liberty, not of protection. Where
a Government is unjust, and the upper classes who enjoy
the fruits of injustice are selfish, the more selfish they are
and the less capable of that plasticity by which in certain
moving times a strong soldiery can be moulded out of a
quiet bourgeoisie, there also the army is composed of
indifferent soldiers, disciplined by fear.

VIII

The Spanish-American War, then, terminated in victory for the people governed with the least injustice; whether this was due to its own merit or chance, it matters little. This war will result in the final pacification of the Antilles and the Philippines, and relieve Spain at the same time from the enormous military expense which their occupation cost her. The Spanish Government, which by its stupidity and tardiness showed itself so unfit to go through with the Cuban War, nevertheless kept stirring up conflicts in Cuba and the Philippines by means of rapacious, indolent, and unjust rule, to which its military incapacity was principally attributable. For the past fifty years insurrections have been periodical occurrences in the two colonies, and it has been beyond the power of the Spanish Government to restore peace; indeed, the military ferocity of its repression merely kept pouring oil on the conflagration. What fearful figures would be reached if we reckoned up all the men who have perished in this long and terrible war!

The intervention of a more civilized, and less military and bellicose Government, has extinguished the long-smouldering fire, and from henceforward both the Antilles and the Philippines will obtain a regular administration that will allow of the natives living peaceably without being in a constant state of insurrection. It is not difficult, therefore, to understand how the work of pacification was accomplished, and how the victory of a juster Government has for a long time liberated that corner of the earth from the sufferings of war.

Now, this leads to the reflection that if the happy termination of the conflict, which had for so long stained Spain and

her colonies with blood, by the victorious intervention of a
more civilized and peace-insuring state between the two
enemies who had been so long at war without either of them
vanquishing the other ; if this were not an accidental and
solitary incident, which occurred once far away in the
Atlantic, but an incident which repeats itself through history,
in all places and ages, under one form or another ; if, in short,
it was a law of social life, could we understand then how the
great war-tempests which fill history are by degrees melting
away into a long period of peace ? The history of the world
would then follow this course : many societies, owing to their
vicious constitution, would be led to an indefinite succession
of wars, injuring each other in turn without coming to any
conclusion ; until one or more states, better or more justly
organized, should interpose and introduce at the same time a
theoretically and practically superior Government. This equilibrium might ultimately be disturbed by defects and vices
inherent in itself, and then would return another long epoch
of war, destined itself also to be finally resolved into peace.

If, moreover, it were possible to demonstrate that the
civilization of the Christian nations of Europe and America
were approaching this phase of pacific equilibrium ; that
there is a general truth, which the particular case of the
Spanish-American War has confirmed—viz. that the countries
which are superior to others in everything, war included, are
the most peaceful, whilst those in which warlike traditions
are greater, are decaying—it would then be proved that this
desire for peace is not merely the idyllic dream of a world of
shepherds, lambs, nymphs, and other similar Theocretan and
Virgilian vapourings, a world in which men would be free
from the pain of wounds and the perils of violent death.
This would be too small and miserable a thing, born of the

D

petty psychological illusion that the physical pain of wounds and death are the greatest misfortunes. Abolish wars, or multiply them as you like, life will still remain full of bitterness ; alter customs, and the physical sufferings of violence between men and nations will be replaced by the moral suffering of those wide contrasts of interests, passions, and ideas. If the numberless ills with which humanity is afflicted are each considered separately, with reference to the subjective suffering they inflict on individuals, and not in reference to their diverse final influence in the eternal game of life, who will not affirm that physical torments are perhaps more tolerable than moral ones ? that a dagger-thrust, which kills in an instant, is not almost sweet in contrast to a delusion which slowly consumes the soul ?   The nineteenth century has seen an increase in suicides, madness, and morbid maladies ; in the injuries and deaths in what are called the bloody battles of labour and civilization, and which, though they are bloodless in the material sense of the word, are not for that less lamentable than those fought with gun and cannon.

The modern significance of peace is therefore something greater ; it is an advance towards justice, a desire for more liberal and equitable, wiser and less tyrannical government. The apostle of peace thus becomes one of the instruments by which a great change in the internal structure of society is being accomplished, which in certain countries has greatly advanced, and in others has scarcely commenced—a change in which the real glory of the nineteenth century consists, and which rapidly tends to strengthen justice in life.   Throughout the whole world there is a slow progress of moral ideas which corresponds to a great transformation in all social relations, from the relation between the production and distribution of riches to the relation between men belonging to diverse religious sects—a moral movement which tends to express the ideal of life in this formula : " To be neither coward nor bully." The peace movement, if the foregoing suppositions are correct, is one of the phases of the general progress towards liberty and justice in modern life.

The object of this book is to prove the truth of this historical law, and to show that the actual condition of the world is such that these things really signify the present desire for peace.

HORDES, OR THE ORIGIN OF WAR

CHAPTER II

HORDES, OR THE ORIGIN OF WAR

I

WHAT was war originally? The briefest and most comprehensive definition of its essence, to my mind, is the following : "War, in the beginning, was an erroneous solution, given by nearly all the different branches of the human race, to the problem of individual happiness."

War took birth in a primitive and violent exaltation of the desire for emotion. The most elementary and vital principle in the human mind is the desire to live. But life does not merely consist in opening one's eyes at sunrise and shutting them again when darkness supervenes ; life consists in strongly feeling our own being in all we perceive, feel, will, and think. No man feels himself alive except in the intimate workings of his own personality, that immortal flame of the inner life which at times flickers and almost expires, and then reasserts itself more brilliantly. Thus in the moments when it is most animated, when the activities of the conscience are more numerous and intense, man feels himself more alive, and therefore, Spinoza would perhaps too rashly conclude, happier. Sensations, sentiments, desires, thoughts, even those that of average intensity continually stimulate the human mind, without intermission feed the fire of *self*, and sink into it, as innumerable fragments of

matter feed the fire of the sun. Not merely for the amuse-
ment and sterile pleasure of man, but to foster the circulation
of a marvellous vital process, does the elation of *self*, produced
by the conscience, excite a new and acute thirst for sensations,
sentiments, desires, and thoughts which in their turn serve as
stimulators ; and thus everything acts on man and exalts his
individuality, and he, thus stimulated, reacts by circumstances
with redoubled energy.   Such is the normal and average life,
to escape from which man is urged by a fierce longing for
happiness, which, to a healthy and vigorous person consists,
at least in part, in those moments of intense feeling which
excite in him unusually strong and energetic thoughts and
sentiments, and kindle the inner flame of *self*, as a breath
kindles the embers which appeared half extinguished under
a thin layer of ashes.   Thus the desire for life excites in men
an insatiable avidity for emotions, which, by reason of their
great intensity, augment the normal sum of life.

Innumerable are the ways by which man satisfies this
longing to augment the sum of his life. They may be
arranged in an ascending scale, according as their nature is
sensual or ideal, according as they demand a greater or lesser
effort of will.   The rudest and simplest emotion is that which
can be obtained from inebriation, from violent and disorderly
bodily exercise, and from very intense sensations.   A good
dose of haschish or alcohol, a wild dance, impetuous music,
create a passing but intense spiritual exaltation in which man
feels, thinks, desires, and therefore lives more intensely than
under ordinary conditions.   This is why civilized men are so
fond of all those stimulants which, without trouble, help him
to augment the sum of life he is capable of living.   Another
means of satisfying the thirst for sensation, and which
demands a certain effort of will and thought, is love ;

because the moral and physical satisfaction it yields exalt the spirit and multiply the physical, intellectual, and moral energy of man and woman. The great collective passions, such as patriotism and religious ardour or fanaticism, belong to a more abstract order, and demand a much greater spiritual effort; and yet higher are the intellectual and æsthetical passions, that arise in a great measure from the desire for emotions and sensations which excite the mind.

But the most abstract manner of satisfying this passion for intenser life, and one which demands the greatest effort—in the majority of cases, at least—is to aim at superiority over other men and things. The knowledge of one's own capacity to overcome obstacles gives the highest of all spiritual exaltations, because the force of one's own being is felt stronger in contrast to other conquered forces, whether human or brutish. Life, then, in its highest form consists in an effort to assert one's own superiority over men and things. In the majority of men, however, this desire for life is mediocre, and easily satisfied by slight efforts of will and thought. But in all countries and in all ages there has existed a small minority of men in whom this desire was a violent passion, who wished to live a life more than humanly intense, almost, I might say, the life of several men; and who, as other men suffer from the thirst for love, suffered from a desire to exalt supremely their own being, and to place themselves above the level of other men.

The few human groups, and the rare epochs in which such men were lacking, have no history; because wars, revolutions, colonial adventures, the innumerable events of private life, religions, sects, philosophies, the fine arts and the sciences, all originated in the sublime discontent of these small minorities who longed for unmeasured lives. These were as the yeast which ferments the soppy and somewhat insipid dough of which humanity is composed ; fermentation thus setting in rapidly or slowly, succeeding or not succeeding, according as the yeast suited the dough and the conditions of the surrounding atmosphere.

The manner in which the greater number of these men satisfied their thirst for life was in the conquest of power and the accumulation of great wealth. If in the world's history some few hundred prophets, artists, philosophers, and saints have tried to rule the human mind by works of great beauty, wisdom and goodness, millions of men, on the other hand, have sought pleasure in power and riches. It is a common opinion that man desires wealth and power to procure more easily spiritual and sensual enjoyment ; but this opinion proves, on closer analysis, to be insufficient. It is proved insufficient, firstly, because power and riches were never free from care and envy, and, in certain ages, also from grave dangers, which were often stronger than the pleasure wealth and power could give ; because in the most numerous class of rich men—misers—the first condition for the enjoy-ment of wealth is the renunciation of all the pleasures it can procure ; because the rich and powerful of all countries and ages have tried to distinguish themselves from the less rich and poor by luxuries and special manners of life, all of them tedious and wearisome ; and lastly, because, instead of using riches and power to wisely increase their own liberty, they have made themselves the slaves of tyrannical formalities and ceremonies, and voluntarily passed the greater part of their existence, not in great or good actions, but in the rigorous and tedious observation of vain, puerile, and senseless social rites.

Riches are earnestly sought after by many men for the same reason that power is sought after : because enriching one's self and governing others is the easiest means of exalting one's own being by the sentiment and exercise of personal superiority and power. There are two essential pleasures in the acquirement of riches and power : the solitary delight which is felt by him who enriches himself or becomes master of the State, and the social pleasure which arises from showing his riches and power, and more especially by the contrast between these and the inferior condition of others. Although some rich men are indifferent to the social enjoyment of wealth and power—in some the attraction of the former pleasure is greater, in others that of the latter— nevertheless, these two are generally the first elements of cupidity and ambition. The solitary enjoyment of wealth and power is the simple and immediate pleasure of feeling himself strong, which man experiences every time he succeeds in bringing any undertaking to a successful issue. The social enjoyment is the complex and indirect pleasure of feeling his power over others, which arises from contrasting his own strength with the lesser strength of others, his own power with their impotence.

Ostentation or dominion : these are the two passions essential to cupidity and ambition, and for this reason they have generally displayed themselves in senseless tyranny and the vanities of extravagant pride, and very rarely in acts of wisdom, beauty, or goodness, and not rarely they have been merged into a single passion.

II

But this insatiable thirst for strong and inebriating emotions, though it is the chief stimulus to action, contains nevertheless a terrible germ of error and ruin, which leads man to perdition whilst searching for happiness. The cause for this must be sought in various vices of will and intelligence innate in the human mind, and principally in the desire to follow the line of least resistance. From this tendency to make the smallest effort possible—which is to be observed in all human actions, but particularly in those of barbarians—springs the lack of power to discern and resist that which is perhaps the most dangerous of illusions, and which is the origin of so many of the evils of life. Thus in destroying or creating, man can procure for himself strong emotions, and persuade himself of his own superiority over things. Two passions have divided the human heart throughout the annals of history: the divine passion for creation, and the diabolical passion for destruction. But since it is easier to destroy than to create, a terrible and universal illusion arose, of which too many nations and men have been the victims, *i.e.* that happiness is more easily to be found in destruction than in creation. Creation, though in reality a benefit, presents itself under a painful aspect, because of the effort it demands; but when this effort is made, healthy satisfaction and lasting happiness follow. Thus the passion for creation can be compared to a delicious fruit enclosed in a thin but bitter peel. Destruction, on the contrary, is an evil which presents itself under a pleasing aspect, because it can cause momentary satisfaction in return for a slight effort, but it brings ruin and death in its train. Hence the passion for destruction is like the nauseous powder concealed in jam.

To a similar illusion of these passions can be traced the origin of war.

Foresight, indeed, is the main virtue which deters modern men from seeking happiness in destruction. The ideal of happiness to a civilized man at this century's end includes, as an essential requisite, foresight for the future. Civilized man does not attach much importance to a lot, however attractive it may be, whether moral or material, if it does not possess a certain stability. Hence any condition, however favoured by fortune, if exposed to the dangers of rapid change, is considered by all but a few fantastical and adventurous spirits, as inferior to a humbler but securer state. Nineteenth-century man may seek after violent and inebriating emotions that permit him to assert his superiority over his fellows, still he tries not to lose sight of the future ; and while attempting to satisfy this desire, he is careful not to expose himself to the danger of misfortunes which would vastly overshadow his immediate satisfaction. To attain this end, he does not hesitate to subject himself to a severe moral discipline, to exercise a rigorous control over his passions, to bridle his imagination, to fatigue his mind in trying to realize so vague a thing as the future. We are so used to this mode of existence that we fail to comprehend how men can be happy otherwise.

But, unfortunately for man, foresight and the habit of restraining his passions with a view to the future are virtues which appear to him unpleasant, because they both imply an effort of will and consequent suffering, lighter or intenser according to the degree of effort made and the strength of him who makes it ; whereas improvidence is an evil which at first appears pleasant, because it exempts man from all mental effort. Hence civilized man is constantly tempted to return to improvidence as soon as the mental effort necessary for providence becomes too great, or his mind is weakened by disease. Is it not true that we are most capable of being provident at a mature age, when in possession of our full force, whilst children are improvident and old men become so? But even a young man may become improvident at times, owing to a species of weariness that comes over him when the difficulties against which he has to fight are so numerous and various that his mental strength is not equal to the exertion.

At such times improvidence and fatalism may become so exquisite a relief to the worn-out spirit that men have been seen to risk throwing fortune, reputation, even life itself unhesitatingly to the winds. In any case, civilized man is constantly encouraged to control his passions in view of the future, and by the thought of great advantages he would otherwise lose. But uncivilized men who live by rude agriculture and pasturage, in a hut easily destroyed and easily rebuilt, who accumulate little wealth, know few luxuries and no intellectual refinement, yield more easily to the temptations of improvidence, and find it more difficult to be constantly thoughtful of the future, since they value so little what the past has bequeathed to them. But from the moment that the usually small amount of forethought which characterizes barbarous peoples is lacking, nothing remains to restrain them from indulging in the pleasure of the maddest and most extravagant destruction, because the momentary satisfaction which constitutes or accompanies destruction is no longer opposed by the thought of its future consequences. War can thus, for a moment, become the passion of a whole nation, because war is a sort of *vie de bohème* to uncivilized man.

It is a sentiment of this character which accounts for the first great bellicose movements of the still barbarous human race, and for the formation of warlike hordes whose periodical appearances fill history from time to time with the roar of a huge tempestuous human sea. The single waves of this ocean bear the names of the Cimbric or Teutonic hordes, of German, Visigoth, Longobardian, Hungarian, Tartar, or Mongolian. These hordes always consisted of great multitudes who abandoned their lands, their work, and ancient modes of life, and descended in tribes of men, women, and children into countries inhabited by other nations. Any event was made a pretext for such transmigrations : a dearth, an earthquake, a pestilence, an eclipse, the predictions of augurs. But their real incentive, at least at first, was the love for an adventurous life, free from thought for the future—the charm of that carelessness which loosens the control over passions ; above all, that strongest of all human passions, idleness ; the desire for wealth easily gained, and for the attainment—by means of the destruction of cities, and the extermination or reduction to slavery of entire populations—of the pleasure born of believing themselves invincible and of domineering over their fellows.

III

To thoroughly understand how this elementary warlike form of society originated, it will be well to consider a modern example, which we can study in detail from documents provided by an eye-witness. Although hordes are no longer formed in Europe, Africa and Asia still offer us living examples of such associations—more especially Africa, where what to us is dead legend, remains there a still living reality. Thus the Soudan has recently seen the formation of a colossal warlike horde, whose rapid and adventurous record is known to us through the recital of many Europeans who witnessed its formation. I allude to the great Mahdist revolution of 1884, known to us as the Dervish movement, which for fourteen years interrupted Egyptian rule in the Soudanese regions.

This uprising has been considered in the light of a religious revolution, due to the fanaticism of certain barbarous Mussulman tribes, incited by incendiary prophets. Religious fanaticism certainly was one of the many factors which contributed to the immense energy of the revolution at its outset ; but its importance was perhaps exaggerated by Europeans, as always happens when they attempt to judge any great event in Mussulman society. Since religion pervades the whole of Mussulman life, Europeans, who observe that many things there bear a religious character which are not religious with us, consequently attribute everything to religion. In reality, however, religion only lends an exterior aspect to events which are really the results of more human and general causes. Thus the Dervish War, which appeared to be merely the conflict of a new Mussulman sect against an elder branch, was in reality a social revolution produced by social and political causes, which determined the formation of a warlike horde.

The Soudan is inhabited by Arabs, Nubians or Negroes, and Berbers, the latter a race born of the crossing of Negroes with Jews and Arians, who dwell between the first and fourth cataracts of the Nile in the districts of Berber. Before the revolution these peoples were a power that could not be overlooked without peril. For example, certain very wealthy, intelligent, and capable slave-merchants had become true military commanders, conquerors, and almost founders of States, such as Zubeir Pasha, lately deceased at Cairo, who, as a young man, when advancing with bands he had enlisted for the purpose of slave-raiding, came in contact with the Sultan of Darfur, whom he conquered and deposed, acquiring thus, in the course of his commercial undertakings, this immense tract of Egyptian land. The Negro population represents the pariahs of Soudanese society. Confined within the remotest regions of the Soudan, they drag out a miserable existence by the indolent pursuit of very primitive agriculture and pasturage. In cities and big villages they perform the meanest services and the most degraded work, both in the public or commercial administrations, or in private houses. Their principal function, however, before the revolution, throughout the whole Soudan, was to furnish, together with the Berbers, the chief material for the slave-trade.

Many were the causes of the violent upheaval of a society so organized. The Soudan at that period belonged to the Egyptian Government, who ruled it by means of functionaries despatched from Cairo. These maintained a purely Oriental administration : indolent, indifferent to the requirements of their subjects, careless of justice, rapacious and corrupt. Into this administration, to make matters worse, there had entered of late years several Europeans and Christians, who had been introduced in the hope of improving matters. These officials, from the highest to the lowest, had no other care than to enrich themselves by means of their authority to extort money ; hence corruption was so deep and universal that the energy of Gordon, sent there twice as governor, if it managed to eradicate some partial abuses, failed to renovate a condition so desperately vitiated. The Egyptian Government, however, was not content to abandon the Soudan to the rapacity of its functionaries ; it wanted to do more, and, in its own interest at least, it wanted to do worse. It wished to concede to itself, in the midst of the general dishonesty—I might almost call it the mortal sin in which it lived—the *bizarre* luxury of an honest scruple,

E

which became the cause of its loss. It wished to prohibit, encouraged by English influence, the slave-trade in the Soudan. The discontent aroused by such an edict can be imagined when we reflect that the richest and most powerful portion of Soudanese society was engaged in this commerce ; that the prohibition, besides the other misfortunes, which its sudden application entailed, threatened to ruin at a blow this very wealthy class of merchants, and to reduce to misery the numerous tribes who assisted in the trade. Nor must it be thought that this abolition of slavery, which displeased the rich merchants and their colleagues, brought the Government into better favour with the negro population from whom all the slaves were drawn. The negro tribes, like all the Soudanese, detested the Egyptian Government for the injustice of its functionaries, of whom they were the victims ; neither could the probability of never again becoming slaves suffice to make them forget the oppression of so rapacious and capricious a Government. Everything —liberty included—has a changeful value ; of supreme benefit to some, it may want much of its value to others. All Soudanese negroes do not appear to have regarded slavery as the greatest evil, since it actually happened that Gordon liberated slave-convoys only to see the slaves returning spontaneously to the dealers.

In any case, these good intentions proved as noxious to the Egyptian Government as its guilty indifference to justice and the dishonesty of its functionaries. The rich and powerful class of slave-merchants turned against the Government, and its discontent, combined with that of all the Soudan, against the oppressive Egyptian administration, prepared a state of feeling and of things favourable to revolution.

Let us add to this religious and class hatred. The

Mussulmans were displeased to see so many Europeans and Christians in the administration ; to know that in Cairo, at the court of Ishmail, the Europeans were heeded better than the Mussulmans ; that much of the money extorted from them flowed into the hands of the numerous Christians, who were working at Cairo with a view to putting into practice Ishmail's dream, which was to make use of Oriental prodigality to forward a sumptuous and innovating administration that should introduce into his states the progressive benefits of European civilization. It was in the midst of such an unquiet and vast society that Mohammed Ahmed, an obscure youth from Dongola, proclaimed himself *Mahdi*, and started to preach a sacred war. It does not appear that this *Mahdi* was a mystic, it looks rather as if he was a rogue, an ambitious man, covetous of wealth, an individual of the most dangerous order, one of those born low down in the social scale, but determined to rise at any cost. He was thus an example of the man thirsty for emotion, whom we always find preceding any stormy events in human history. In Europe he would probably have been a successful political intriguer, in the Soudan he became a religious reformer who, with a certain amount of humbug, which took the form of Divine revelation, and with the pretended performance of some miracles, dared to fan the flame of universal discontent. The effect of this preaching, which was begun timidly at first and amidst poor tribes and the most wretched scum of Soudanese society, was marvellous, owing to the universal discontent. Several tribes readily embraced the occasion to hurl themselves blindly on the strength of a supposed divine revelation, into the pursuit of an existence free from future care and full of violent emotion. Life and the world were to be revivified, according to the Mahdi's prediction, in the form most seductive to these simple minds. The peasant was no longer to cultivate his land, the shepherd was to leave his flock, none were to pay taxes to the Government, or to be any longer subject to the oppressions of omnipotent rulers. All were to live together in the Soudan in a great nomadic tribe, with songs and music to inspire them, fighting and pillaging.

The contagion of this illusion, this great passion, spread like wild-fire amongst the tribes. No one asked himself how long such an existence could endure ; the horde was rapidly increased by contingents from all sides—men, families, and tribes. As happens in all revolutions, the first to hail it were outcasts and vagabonds ; then families who wrung a wretched livelihood from the soil, tormented by usurers, burnt their huts and joined the prophet ; then the inhabitants of entire villages abandoned their homes to follow in his wake ; finally whole tribes arrived with their cattle, utensils, and possessions. They came not as soldiers who leave their homes temporarily to fight in a war of short duration, but as emigrants setting out for some El Dorado whence to restart life. In the course of a few months an immense horde wandered about the Soudan in search of war and prey ; whilst the quieter tribes, those who had resisted the universal madness, continued patiently to cultivate the earth, with the vague presentiment of a huge tempest brewing in the heavens towards the horizon, which must burst sooner or later above their heads.

It is difficult to imagine of what this horde of Dervishes, collected to fight the holy war against Egypt and living by war, could originally have consisted. It is difficult fully to realize to one's self this dense torrent of human lava which set fire to everything along its course. Is it possible to the European of the nineteenth century to imagine a multitude of more than a hundred thousand souls, consisting of men and women, old people and children, who have sacrificed their whole existence to a moment of unutterable exultation, without giving one thought to the morrow—a people of madmen, whose frenzy lasts for months? Yet this was the spiritual condition of the Dervish horde in its initial stage : absolute thoughtlessness, continuous excitement without respite and without pause, fermented by every artifice. The Mahdi and his chief followers never wearied of firing the ardour of the faithful with inspired preachings. When the preachers were mute, the crowd fed its own excitement with wild songs, with dances, and above all with stirring music ; for music, the art whence civilized men demand the most delicate spiritual enjoyment, has ever been the ac-complice of the maddest and most extravagant follies of primitive man. The most intense and voluptuous frenzy was obtained by the extreme violence of destruction, and in the most unbounded extravagances of pride. The only passions which surged in the souls of this terrible crowd were those of ruin and destruction—burning passions which annihilated the slender principles, the fragile moral traditions created by the work of ages, which, as the lava which boils over from a crater raging along the mountain side, effaces the works of man, his furrows and landmarks painfully traced on the earth's surface.

A single example suffices to demonstrate the extent of this madness. The Arab tribes of the Eastern Soudan had followed the Mahdi, with their magnificent flocks, their ancient wealth, the traditional pride of their tribes. When near Khartoum, the Mahdi announced to them that it was a time for fighting, not for pasturing cattle, and exhorted them to kill their animals. These simple and primitive men were immediately prevailed upon to destroy their flocks, and to disperse in a few days the wealth accumulated by centuries of labour, which for ages represented their greatest pride; and this, with the sole object of providing the horde with an orgy of meat for a few days.

Thus in the beginning, and after the first unhoped-for successes, the battles consisted of a species of feasts to which the crowds assembled, thirsting for blood and ruin, drunk with pride, blind and deaf to all peril. A passion for violence fermented in their midst, the courage of impulse proper to crowds excited by fanaticism and the thirst for blood—the boldness of any army intoxicated with victory, and which believes itself invincible. The Dervish horde was chiefly composed of inexperienced soldiers, drawn from pastoral and agricultural tribes, and consequently cowardly, like all barbarians unaccustomed to the perils of war ; of soldiers incapable of resisting the fear of shooting and the hardships of war by a mental effort ; men of no worth, in short, but who, taken together, blinded by fanaticism, intoxicated by a violent and irregular life and by universal excitement, formed an army devoid of fear, because it no longer reasoned—a crowd animated by a formidable impulse which nothing could at first resist.

In the attack on El Obeid, an army of Dervishes, armed only with lances and swords, assailed a fortress defended by guns and cannon. The obstinate assaults are described by Rudolf Slatin in these words :—

" On Friday morning, September the 8th, the seething mass of human beings, armed only with swords and spears, rolled like the waves of the sea towards the town. . . . The rifle-fire of the defenders soon began to play with deadly effect on the crowd, who, utterly undeterred, and seeking only for blood and plunder, continued their advance, swarming into the ditches and up the parapet, and entering the town. At this critical moment Major Nesim Effendi told his bugler to sound the advance ; and the signal being taken up by the other buglers, the soldiers, clambering up on the tops of the walls and houses, brought a murderous fire to bear on the assailants. Slowly the surging mass, under this hail of lead, was driven back, leaving behind them thousands of killed and wounded. Once more they rallied and attempted again to storm ; but again they were driven back with still greater slaughter."

And what frenzies of satisfied pride after the victory ! The Dervishes, like the Huns and Tartars, believed themselves to be, and were believed, for a moment, to be indomitable. Even the humblest and least of the soldiers thus participated, to a slight extent, in the pleasure of having overcome their foes, and of thinking themselves above the common herd, of feeling themselves a little superior to others—an exquisite moral reward for warfare which every member of the horde could procure for himself with little fatigue. To this sense of satisfaction the material spoil must also be added. Plunder, with all its accompanying excitement—the unexpected dis- covery of treasures, the easy acquisition of great wealth, the capricious waste of superfluity, the piquant pleasure of search, and the oppressions over the vanquished—became the ardent passion of the multitude. Everywhere the Dervish horde destroyed what fell into their hands : the Government stores, the possessions of those tribes who had remained neutral, the private treasures of the rich. And since in the Soudan, as in all barbarous countries, the earth is the bank to which men confide their treasures in stormy times, no sooner was a village or a city seized than searches were begun for hidden treasures ; and the conquerors subjected to cruel tortures all those suspected of having concealed wealth. What horrors were witnessed in the Soudan on this account! After the seizure of El Fasher, amongst the many prisoners subjected to torture on suspicion of possessing concealed treasures, was an officer in the Egyptian army, a certain Hamada Effendi. Instead of revealing the hiding-place where his treasures were concealed, he amused himself, even whilst under torture, by insulting his torturers, until the Emir, infuriated by his conduct, ordered him to be flogged until he confessed. For three days he was given a thousand blows, but in vain ; for every time in reply to the demand, "Where is the money?" he answered, "Yes, I have hidden some money, but my secret will be buried with me." After three days of flagellation the executioners were forced to yield before such indomitable determination, and to suspend their tortures, for fear of killing their victim. Major Hamada, whose body was now one huge wound, was then consigned as a prisoner to the Arab tribe, Mina, who, unwilling to relinquish all hope of exacting the secret, subjected him to a new torture, less violent but more ingenious and of longer dura- tion, that of bathing his wounds with a solution of salt water and Soudanese pepper. Slatin, who had known Hamada in happier times, was moved to compassion by his heroism and martyrdom. He wished to come to his assistance, and even managed to persuade the Emir, in whose power he was, to give him into his care. The Emir consented to Slatin's request, but on one sole condition : that if Hamada confided to him the hiding-place of his treasure, he would reveal it. Slatin acquiesced. He had the wretched man carried to his tent, and washed and oiled his wounds. But he soon perceived that his help had arrived too late, and that the victim could not

long survive. Indeed, after four days had elapsed, Hamada
lay dying. Then, having dismissed the servants, he called
for Slatin, and in an expiring voice whispered in his ear—

"'My hour has come. May the Lord reward you for all
your kindness to me! I cannot do so, but I will show you
that I am grateful. I have buried my money.' 'Stop!' said
I. 'Are you going to tell me where you have hidden your
treasure?' 'Yes,' he murmured, 'it may be of some use to
you.' 'No,' I answered, 'I will not and cannot use it; I
secured your release from your tormentors on the one condition
that, should I learn where your money was hidden, I should
tell your enemy. You have suffered greatly, and are paying
with your life for your determination not to let your treasure
fall into your enemy's hands; let it lie unknown in the
ground, it will keep silence.' Whilst I was talking, Hamada
held my hand; with a supreme effort he murmured, 'I
thank you; may you become fortunate without my money.
Allah Karim (God is merciful).' Then, stretching out his
limbs and raising his forefinger, he slowly uttered, 'La ilaha
illallah, Mohammed Rasul Allah,' closed his eyes, and died."

Vagabondage, rapine, violence, thoughtlessness for the
future, a blind indulgence of all the most savage and impetuous passions : this was the condition in which the
Dervish horde lived until the taking of Khartoum. But this
state of excitement could not endure when the conditions which
it caused ceased to exist ; that is, the possibility and hope of
fresh victorious wars and of gigantic plunderings—possibilities
and hopes which could not continue indefinitely. Although
the Mahdi dreamed of conquering Egypt and Syria as far as
Constantinople, he could not fail to perceive, unless he had
gone raving mad, that his empire had reached its furthest
limits, and that victory could not follow him into the heart of

Egypt. Anyway, shortly after his triumph at Khartoum Mohammed Ahmed died of typhoid fever, in the flower of his years and in his full glory as the fortunate conquerer of a vast empire. His death rendered easier and prompter an internal change in the Dervish horde, then very necessary. The Mahdi's successor, the Caliph Abdullahi, a man prudent and little bellicose, realizing the mistake of tempting victory too far, brought the era of great warlike undertakings to a close, and started to inaugurate a new epoch in the confused material of the horde.

At this point that which is the fundamental phenomenon of war began to determine itself in the Dervish horde, the phenomenon which demonstrates how the purely moral arguments against war are far more serious and important than sceptics imagine. He who opposes war on the ground of the purely moral principle which prohibits man to kill or rob, even to-day at the end of the nineteenth century, runs the risk of being looked upon as an imbecile or at best a mere visionary ; because even those who live morally place little faith in the practical value of moral principles, while the great majority of men are always ready to worship vice and crime, when these present themselves with the attributes of power. That morality, even when it appears defenceless, possesses an intimate and organic force of its own ; that vice, even when it is supported by the greatest human force, is in reality hopelessly feeble, this is a truth which men have rarely really believed. Success and power still represent to the poor human mind the justification of the most odious crimes, so ready is man to deny morality the moment vice and crime appear to have gained an instant's victory over virtue in the infinitely varying game of life.

But in reality the words of the Gospel, " He who conquers

by the sword shall perish by the sword," express in simple
form an elementary vital law which can be almost literally
applied to the history of war, because war contains in itself
its own moral sanction, and develops outside of itself the
punishment of the injustice which is its essence. Thus it
happens in the history of hordes that a war, which begins by
destroying other societies, ends with the ruin of the tribe which
gave it birth. By a rapid transformation its deleterious force
towards vanquished societies turns on itself, acting upon the
structure of the victorious society, which undergoes in the end
the same fate as its victims.

The Soudanese revolution was the work of a horde composed of individuals, families, and tribes who had altered
their lives from those of shepherds, agriculturists and labourers
to champions of a holy war. It had been indirectly favoured by
many tribes, who, though discontented with the actual condition of things, did not join it. Its victims were the armies and
property of the Egyptian Government and the tribes which
remained faithful to Egypt, whose riches formed part of
the great booty obtained in the war. This prey was, up to
the taking of El Obeid, divided with fair justice among all the
soldiers, who thus derived no mean benefits from the conflict,
more especially as they had always been used to poverty.
If the Emirs and the friends of the Mahdi apportioned to
themselves a larger share, no one considered this unjust.
And as the spoils were sufficient at the beginning to satisfy
the greed both of the horde and its chiefs, the new Government had no need, and indeed little time, in the midst of the
disorder of war, to impose regular tributes on the tribes who,
without taking any direct part, had favoured the revolution. Hence these tribes, liberated from paying tribute
to the Egyptian Government, and for the moment under no

obligation to pay imposts to the new, were able to delude themselves with the idea that the age of tax-paying had passed for ever.

But of how short duration is human delusion! The Mahdi once dead, power fell into the hands of a ferocious, hard, and greedy oligarchy, which soon converted the conquering army, the horde which governed the Soudan, the faithful who had expelled the impure Turks, into a multitude of wretched slaves, the victims and at the same time the tools of the most humiliating and cruel tyranny which the human mind could conceive.

From the moment that Caliph Abdullahi came into power he had only one object in view : to use every one for his own enrichment and to aggrandize his family. Abdullahi was, indeed, born and educated to be an implacable tormentor of his species. Sprung from poor parents, he displayed no desire to work in his youth. Thus his first life experiences had been bitter : that is to say, those of a poor man who lives in a rude society where there are few rich, but where, through universal hardness of heart, there is little compassion among the poor ; where he who possesses a little likes to increase the small pleasure of possessing by despising the very poor, and impressing upon them their inferiority ; where he who possesses nothing has no rights whatsoever, and is generally ill-treated, the victim of all the contempt and the ferocious caprices of human wickedness. Now, where the rich are malignant the poor are rebellious ; and still more rebellious must have been a poor man like the future Caliph, who cared little for work and possessed great vanity and a desire to enjoy. This poor, ambitious, and covetous vagabond was one of the first to follow the prophet of Dongola. He knew how to curry favour, became one of his intimates, and ended by being appointed Caliph, which signifies in a Mussulman country the successor to power. His greed, suppressed so long by poverty ; his vanity, embittered by so many years of humiliation ; the indescribable exaltation of his egoism and pride, inebriated at a stroke by such a fabulous piece of good luck, which made of the derided beggar knocked about the streets the master of an immense empire and the arbitrator of the fates of so many who had seen him clothed in rags— these combinations of events naturally made of an innately bad man that which he became, to the sinful sorrow of the Soudanese, *i.e.* one of the cruellest, most insolent, rapacious and madly proud tyrants who ever in the history of humanity mounted a throne to torment and chastise mankind. Greed and ambition divided his soul, as they did those of the most powerful members of the horde who shared his empire ; hence the characteristics of his Government were rapacity and tyranny.

IV

Abdullahi and his Government were the scourge of the Soudan ; the terrible expiation which the Soudanese population were condemned to make for their direct or indirect participation in the violence and rapine of the Holy War. No accidental chastisement, let it be clearly understood, which descended by chance on these peoples' heads because ill luck would have it that the Mahdi's first successor should be an inhuman brigand, but an expiation which was in the natural and necessary sequence of events, whose advent was inevitable, through the moral and social condition in which the Dervish horde found itself at the close of the Holy War.

Owing to a very general but little heeded psychological phenomenon, which it is important to keep in view, those few years passed in the midst of war and rapine had left the Dervishes in such a mental condition that they were forced to become, in their turn, the victims of rapine and oppression on the part of a few bolder, more cunning, and crueller men. The fighting over, the half-religious, half-brigand excitement, which had made soldiers of these peasants and shepherds, began to abate by degrees for want of fuel. But the abatement of the fever did not bring back the flocks destroyed in the heat of delirium ; nor did the beautiful cultivated fields return, which the fanatics had left behind in order to follow the Mahdi. The Dervish horde, though formed of uncultured and uncivilized peasants, possessed nevertheless a rudimentary morality which had made of them hitherto a useful element in Soudanese society, owing to their peaceful habits. But, torn from their land and their cattle, they had abandoned their industrious habits, and degenerated into a multitude of armed vagabonds whose only moral impulse was fanaticism. What could possibly become of such when their excitement was passed ? They were as leaves which a tempest had torn from the branch, whirled for a moment, and then, the storm over, left scattered here and there, withered and dried. In the moral world, as in the material, all creative forces are gradual and slow, whilst those of destruction are rapid and instantaneous : they arrive in a moment, and annihilate without allowing time for defence. Does not a forest fire destroy in a few hours the vegetation of centuries ? The habit of regular work, the accumulation of the instruments necessary to do this work, the traditions and principles of primitive morality, —all these, the creations of centuries, the fruits of the labour of generations, were thus destroyed in a few years of idleness and excitement. Nor could they be recreated in a day; as little could a magician replace in the burnt forest the trees which only time could produce. He who has tasted the violent pleasures of a disorderly life, full of factitious excitement, cannot easily re-accustom himself to a dull and monotonous existence. And even those members of the Mahdi's horde who wished to rectify their error, by returning to their former mode of life, were unable to do so, having destroyed or dispersed their means of gaining a livelihood. Besides this, they no longer made any wealth out of the war, because after the taking of Khartoum the Mahdi prohibited the soldiers from appropriating any part of the booty under severe penalties, compelling them to consign it to the *beib-el-mal*, or tax-exactor: that is to say, to himself and his friends, who divided everything among them. In a moment of madness they had voluntarily made outcasts of themselves, and outcasts they were to remain to the end of their days; and, what was worse, they were no longer animated by the fanaticism which inspired them during the war; their barbarous selfishness and cowardice were no longer sustained by any sentiment, however brutal, neither by religious delusion, by the hope of plunder, or by the pleasure men find in a life of adventure.

A multitude of uncivilized men, who possess nothing, who have no longer either trade or laborious habits nor the first rudiments of morality, who have lost the ardour of common enthusiasm, which, however ferocious, is capable of communicating a certain degree of strength to the soul, and thus replace ideals; a multitude of outcasts, with heads yet heavy from an orgie of blood and rapine, they had not the moral strength to resist an oppression exercised by means of systematic terror. They were therefore the easiest victims of a tyrannical oligarchy. There is a great difference between

the blind impulsive courage of a crowd, due to an enthusiasm
which drowns the instinct of self-preservation, and the conscious and reflective courage of men who unite to oppose a
common peril, and combine with a view to the general good,
repressing by a conscious effort of will the selfish instincts
which urge each to look after himself without giving any
thought to future dangers. The lowest class, that which
lives in the extremest moral misery, is capable, on certain
occasions, of this first form of courage ; but only men whose
moral conscience is well developed are capable of the latter.
Thus it came about that those multitudes, armed with spears
and swords, intrepidly assailed fortresses defended by rifles
and cannon, and then, like so many calves, allowed themselves docilely to be coerced by the Caliph and a few Emirs.

The process was most simple by which this tyranny
was established over the warriors who had taken part in
the Holy War, the ancient Dervish horde, as also over those
tribes who had not abandoned their former life, and who had
thus formed the non-military portion of Soudan society
posterior to the revolution. The Caliph summoned to Omdurman, the capital of the new empire built on the banks of
the Nile near the ruins of Khartoum, the Arab tribes of
Baggara, pastoral nomad tribes who inhabited Kordofan,
and were adapted by their life and customs to fulfil the
work Abdullahi apportioned to them. The Caliph, like all
founders of tyrannies, understood that it was necessary to
have round him a small but select and faithful body-guard ;
he felt the need to have janissaries and prætorians ; and in a
society where tribal organization is so strong, on whom could
he depend better than on his own tribe ? Indeed, he was a
member of one of the Baggara tribes, the *Baggara Taisha*,
and these, like the rest, had taken small part in the Holy War.

He persuaded the Baggara to change their rude pastoral life and to become his body-guard ; he ordered them, men, women, and children, to go to Omdurman ; he assigned to them good quarters, handsome salaries, and many privileges ; he gave them almost absolute power over the population, and made of them a troop of several thousand well-chosen soldiers, personally devoted to himself, and interested in maintaining his rule. With this tool he managed to command the remainder of the army, the multitude who had formed the Dervish horde, and which, the Holy War over, he forced to continue in arms, not for the defence of the faith, but for his own defence, and what is worse, not recompensing them in any way. He thus made of these fanatics and warriors who had enlisted voluntarily to fight for or under the pretext of a religious war, a permanent army assigned to the service of his greed, who were under the obligation of lifelong and gratuitous service : in short, a multitude of armed slaves of whom he was the head. How, then, were these soldiers to exist without pay, and excluded, moreover, from any participation in the booty of war ? The Caliph did not care ; he needed them to make up for the generosity he was forced to show to the faithful Baggara. By means of pilfering and exploiting the population, they could not fail to draw an existence, a miserable one, it is true, but which enabled them to live and carry out the expeditions imposed on them by the Caliph. When discontent at this hard and wretched life urged them to revolt, he crushed them down with terrific cruelty by means of his faithful Baggara.

Thus a single harsh and unscrupulous man, assisted by a few Emirs and some thousand prætorians, was able to oppress for several years nearly a hundred thousand armed men ; was able to compel them to render perpetual service

F

without recompense; could employ them constantly in
fatiguing and dangerous expeditions; and yet these men,
who were still the same soldiers who had conquered the
Egyptian troops, never dared turn their arms against their
tyrants.   Does this appear strange?   Those who understand the true nature of courage and cowardice will understand how a wretched and embrutened multitude like the
Dervish horde were unable to resist, when the excitement
of fanaticism was ended, the Caliph's oppression.   The
Caliph, his Emirs and prætorians, were like a single body
moved by a single will to fulfil one fixed idea, which was to
maintain their own rule by terror.   They recognized their
power, and this rendered them even more daring.   On the
other hand, the hundred thousand soldiers were a morally
disintegrated mass, each degraded in his own misery, only
feeling his own individual impotence against the implacable
power of the ruling oligarchy.   They ought to have united
together in a common defence; but they retained too little
of their ancient impetuous courage, and what little remained
only found expression in partial rebellions, the fury of which
soon gave way to make room for abject submission.   And
thus this army of tens of thousands was compelled to serve
for several years a single man supported by a few Emirs and
chosen soldiers—a clear proof that the habit of arms and the
perils of war can be combined with great moral cowardice,
and that an army which can subdue entire unarmed populations may easily be subdued in its turn by a handful of
more resolute ruffians.

V

If the armed soldiers of the horde allowed themselves to be reduced to such a wretched state of servitude, how could the non-military population defend itself from the oppression of those tribes who had favoured, but taken no direct part in the revolution—all that population which continued to labour, and which therefore, whether rich or poor, was the victim of the tyrant's greed? They all found the Caliph's Government, born of the revolution which they had so incautiously favoured, so harsh and covetous a master, that the detested Egyptian in comparison could be looked upon as a *régime* of paternal benevolence. The Caliph substituted for the wars of conquest against the Egyptians, expeditions against the internal or frontier tribes, whose produce went to his benefit; for their flocks and household goods were confiscated, their peoples were enslaved, sold, or employed to cultivate the stolen land for their conqueror's advantage, while their most beautiful women were distributed in the harems of the rich. This treatment was meted out equally to those tribes who favoured the Caliph's Government and to those who opposed it, only the pretext for aggression varied in the two cases; though any pretext, however, sufficed to exploit even the tribes who would have willingly acquiesced in a regular *régime* of taxation : a strange administration whose one object was to reduce all the riches of the Soudan to the patrimony of the Caliph and his Emirs. These latter were, however, only allowed to enrich themselves in order that the Caliph might kill them when they were very wealthy, and confiscate their property. Thus, to give an example, the Jaalin and Dangola Arab tribes lived on their trade

as boatmen, possessing nearly all the boats which navigated
the Nile.   The Caliph, who wished to appropriate the boats,
remembered that in the first days of the revolution, when
he was still at Kordofan, almost all the boatmen had refused to follow the Mahdi, or to favour his attempt.   He
therefore consulted the Council of the Kadis, a sort of
supreme judicial court, to ask whether the boats should not
be considered as "ghanima," or spoils of war subject to
confiscation.   The judges were not of this opinion ; but after
lengthy consideration they concluded that the boatmen were
"mukhalafin," or unconvertible people, and their boats
therefore were liable all the same to expropriation.   The
confiscation was made without previous warning, and thus
suddenly the wretched boatmen were reduced to mendicity,
and all died of hunger.   One of the chief sources of revenue
to the Soudan was the trade in what we call gum-arabic,
gathered in the great forests of the Kordofan by the Gimeh
Arab tribe, and transported by them by means of their
numerous herds of camels.   The Caliph one day took it
into his head to appropriate these herds under the pretext
that the Gimeh had disobeyed his command to make a
certain pilgrimage.   The Gimeh, deprived of their camels, were
forced to abandon the gum-arabic commerce, which totally
decayed in consequence, and no other means of existence
remaining to them, they organized themselves into bands of
brigands.

The ultimate result of these tactics was the rapid social
decomposition which threatened the very existence of Soudanese society, prior to the Anglo-Egyptian re-conquest.
These continued confiscations led to an enormous destruction
of wealth which, though accumulated in the treasuries of the
Caliph and his Emirs, nevertheless got widely dispersed,

whilst the precariousness of general conditions led to a rapid diminution in the number of men capable of work or producing new wealth. Why work when the only recompense for labour was the danger of being robbed, and perhaps killed ? Better become beggars, soldiers, thieves, and brigands. Meanwhile the waste of wealth increased day by day in a *régime* of such violence ; production diminished, thus producing an ever-greater disproportion between production and consumption. This, again, was accompanied by fearful famines which exterminated by thousands the superfluous mouths, like the terrible famine of 1889. Thus the power of the Dervishes, which twelve years ago appeared to threaten Egypt, decayed rapidly, attacked by precocious old age, whose principal symptoms were depopulation and the rapid disorganization of labour. The districts formerly so populous became deserted ; the fields once so well cultivated were abandoned, and nature slowly reasserted her rights ; wild beasts, no longer decimated by men, multiplied and invaded the villages, venturing at times even into the streets of Omdurman, devouring women, old men, children, and even adult men ; work slackened throughout the Soudan, because none felt assured that he would taste the fruits of his labour. Only those professions which depend on the destruction, and not on the production of wealth flourished : brigands, usurers, slave-merchants, soldiers. Every energetic man became by necessity either an Emir or a brigand. The soldiers degenerated into wild and famished beasts, who fought partly out of fear, partly in the hope of eating a little better during the days following the battle, but who retained no permanent traces of their old courage.

This is the typical history of a horde as mirrored in this religious movement of the Dervishes, which succeeded in establishing an immense empire in the Soudan ruled by a narrow military oligarchy of Emirs who collected round that strange adventurer, the lately dethroned Caliph. Rarely has history witnessed so ferocious, selfish, and greedy a tyranny, nor one so implacable in plundering the riches of those territories that fell into his hand. Forty or fifty families managed to devastate a district so enormous that a whole army would have been deemed insufficient to accomplish the task.

Entire tribes were despoiled of their flocks and chased from their land ; industries which provided for hundreds of tribes, that might have been a source of revenue to the Government, were destroyed for the base greed of selling as slaves the men who formerly lived quietly by their work ; the population diminished in an alarming manner in the most florid districts, and the Soudan, devasted by Emirs and brigands, slowly degenerated into a desert populated by skeletons. Terror was the only social bond remaining to prevent the total dissolution of society. The gibbets erected in every village were the only emblems of authority. Having thus consumed their strength, the Dervishes were unable to resist the Anglo-Egyptian army. A society almost ruined by the rage of injustice that flourished in its midst was naturally conquered by an army organized and led by a highly civilized community. The rough and bestial Dervish hordes, no longer sustained by the blind fanaticism of the Mahdi's followers, but fighting merely out of fear of being punished with death, could not long resist the solid Egyptian battalions commanded by superior English officers. The most civilized society conquered, and peace has returned to the Soudan.

At the same time we perceive the reason, or one of the reasons, at least, which explains that terrible phenomenon of history known as tyranny. Why amongst the men called upon to govern their fellows were there so many in whom the passion for emotion expressed itself in greed, in such violent and selfish ambition as to lead an entire society to ruin? This is one of the many-sided aspects of the great problem of evil. Is it possible that so much wickedness should have no other effect than that of tormenting men uselessly and undeservedly? Considering the fate of all the hordes with whose history we are acquainted, how they all terminate in detestable tyrannies, we are able to conclude that the establishment of a tyranny is the inevitable result of the moral degeneration of the majority of society which is the effect of war, and is a secondary evil which springs from the first. But as the debasement of the tribe results from the abandonment of their previous laborious life, from the habits of vagabondage, thoughtlessness, rapine and cruelty contracted in war, thus the tyranny in which it terminates is the punishment of the neglect of certain fundamental duties : an expiation which fatally follows on the sin. The tyrant is an unconscious arbitrator of justice ; his triumphs, which appear its supreme negation, are only one of the most complicated processes by which justice is fulfilled. The tyrant drags his society to ruin by his extravagances ; and also rushes to ruin himself. Never was this justice carried out so rapidly, entirely, or exemplarily as in the Soudan.

VI

Thus, in its most simple and primitive form, war is only an outlet for the instinct of destruction inherent in man, and has no other function than to destroy material things, the established habits of social life and men themselves.

Hordes are a form of society which live in the illusion that the greatest human happiness is to be found in destruction. The masses allow themselves to be induced to abandon modest and monotonous occupations for the greed of wealth, for the pleasures of recklessness, for the vanity of forming part in a body of warriors who terrorize multitudes, and who are considered far and wide as an invincible force of destruction which leaves nothing but ruin on its tracks. All this is entered on in the hope of a life full of emotions and sensual pleasures. The improvidence of primitive men prevents them from recognizing that such a life can but be of short duration, because the material on which to vent their passion for destruction comes to an end, and the inevitable crisis brings painful disillusion. Then follows the tyranny of a few, who, owing to the general state of degradation, are able to use the horde for their own benefit, and to enrich themselves by robbery and exploitation, and rule, not by benefiting but by tormenting others. Greed and ambition become their sole passions, and they satisfy them to the ruin of the entire society. The horde, whose existence is based on this great illusion, traverses a brief period of great prosperity on the way to its perdition.

In horde-life man found for the first time how full of error and peril was the terrible delusion that happiness could be found in destruction ; how much which appears at first to be pleasant proved to be full of pain and bitterness because, after giving a passing satisfaction, it led to permanent unhappiness. This illusion first taught man that life was like an enchanted wood, full of sweet deceits, of beautiful and fatal things. Woe to him who, in the deepest labyrinths of the wood, falls a prey to the intoxicating delights which tempt him on all sides ! Hidden among the trunks he finds delicious honeycombs ; but woe betide him if he yields to the temptation to taste this poisoned honey ! The shade of the fair trees is refreshing and cool in the fierce midday heat ; but he who, unable to resist its invitation, lies down in it to sleep, awakes diseased, for fever lurks unseen in that innocent shade. All the trees bend down their branches laden with delicious fruit within reach of his hand ; but alas ! he who tastes them falls victim to an intoxication which does not pass, and which deprives him in the end of reason. Who can hope to traverse this wood without yielding to its thousand seductions, apparently so full of pleasure ? The austere man who never indulges in voluptuous repose ; he who searches under the surface for the few hidden roots of simple taste, which, in the midst of these noxious delights, can alone increase his strength, intelligence, and health.

But this wisdom and self-control, as we shall see later on, are only the slow work of a long civilization. The Christian legend of the sinner who sells his soul to the devil in order to enjoy the brief delights of this life, symbolizes well the history of the human race, since at every moment we see men paying for an hour's joy with ages of misery, and one thoughtless and ignorant generation destroying, in order to satisfy some caprice, the happiness of their children and children's children.

THE DEFECTS OF ANCIENT
CIVILIZATIONS

CHAPTER III

I

ANCIENT civilizations appear to us as an immense battle-field, a vast cemetery of peoples. Tribes, nations, great empires and small states only emerge in order to destroy the tribes, peoples, empires and states that preceded them, to be in their turn destroyed by other rivals. Nations seemed only born to die a violent death; their lives generally began with a victory and ended with a defeat which entailed, in most cases, not merely the effacing from history of the name of a state, but the physical destruction of an entire society. Every work of art, of science, of politics appears to have had no other object in the distant past than that of fostering war, of covering the earth with costly ashes.

But since these ancient societies were nearly all capable of creating a civilization, an industry, a commerce, a philosophy, an art, it is not rash to claim for the frequency and violence of war that it served some purpose, that it had some influence on life and thought. In other words, it is difficult to admit that war in this case was nothing else but, like with the hordes, the outlet for an instinct of destruction; that it had not a more profound cause is an effect at least partially beneficial. What were its causes, what its object and influences? Let us attempt to solve this question by studying some of the general characteristics and weaknesses inherent in the constitution of ancient civilizations which appear to us to rank among the chief causes of the warlike spirit of former times.

There were four distinct types of ancient society. The rudest were the nomad or semi-nomad tribes, composed of barbarians who, though possessing the first rudiments of agriculture, lived chiefly as shepherds, an unsettled life which rendered it easy for them to unite into hordes for warlike purposes. The tribes were usually ruled under an aristocratic constitution, by a nobility composed of the richest and most courageous families, those who possessed most cattle, lands, slaves, and precious metals. Sometimes a king presided as chief. The best known of these ancient societies were the Gallic tribes previous to the Roman conquest. These possibly represent the highest degree of civilization and stability to which such societies could attain before evolving into that form of society which is really representative of ancient civilization.

Amongst these the most prosperous in Asia were the military empires, such as the Assyrian, the Babylonian, the Egyptian, and the Persian. These empires extended over vast territories, but their chief seat of government was generally centred in a town built on the banks of a river and situated in the centre of a continent. They derived their power principally from their dominion over the land ; the greater number of their soldiers were drawn from the peasant class. It was, therefore, to the interest of these states to encourage agriculture by fostering those great public—and especially hydraulic—works which ranked among the chief glories of Oriental monarchies, and to which are due the first great attempts at irrigating the Nile, the Tigris, and the Euphrates. The social constitution of military empires was in some cases aristocratic, in others democratic. In the first case—as, for instance, in the Assyrian Empire—the high civil and military posts were reserved by legal and hereditary privilege to a certain number of families who formed the nobility ; in the second case, as we see from the eleventh Egyptian dynasty, they were bestowed by means of examinations and promotion, without regard to birth, to professional functionaries ; men of all social conditions being admitted even to the highest places. A sovereign—almost always hereditary—presided over the administration and nobility. He lived in a magnificently luxurious court, he was resplendent with precious gems and metals, and governed his nation despotically with the help of the great functionaries. The army, composed chiefly of peasants and vanquished populations, was generally recruited by force, and kept together by terror. The empire consisted of vast lands cultivated by the peasantry, and a few big cities, sometimes one only, grandiose according to the taste of the period, in which were accumulated riches, provisions, and luxuries—ranging from precious metals to the books of the wise, from industry to the fine arts.

Industry and commerce, not agriculture, were the chief sources of the prosperity of such mercantile towns as Tyre, Sidon, and Carthage. These were situated on the sea-coast, and were governed by a rich oligarchy, who were at one and the same time capitalists, ship-owners, and merchants, possessing large fleets but no armies. These vessels they used ordinarily for commerce, but in case of need they employed them also for warfare—turning their commercial fleet into a military fleet.

These oligarchies did not aim at conquering lands, but at possessing the knowledge that should enable them to be the masters of distant markets.

The agrarian-commercial states of the Italo-Græcian order, where a class of landowners and merchants contested and divided power, were more complex and original. Power was exercised by magistrates elected by the citizens. The militia was no compulsory service, to enter it was regarded as a high privilege of citizens ; and whether peasants, rich proprietors, artisans, or merchants, they alone had the right to take part in war. The cities were ruled now aristocratically when only the richer portion of the population were in power ; now democratically when all, or the greater part of the citizens, participated in the Government ; in both cases, however, the Government was an oligarchy, for the citizens were only a portion of the population, outside of which there existed numerous clients—foreigners and slaves who had no political rights.

II

These various forms of society, both barbarous and civilized, had one great defect which prevented them from rising above a certain level of ferocity and brutality, although able to conceive moral philosophies of extraordinary perfection. This defect was the principal cause why ancient civilizations were so unstable and wars so frequent : *i.e.* the difficulty they had in finding new productive employment for accumulated capital, a condition of things which was partly the cause and partly the effect of the unlaborious habits of the population.

The facility of productive investment for capital is quite a recent development, due partly to the great scientific and technical progress of our times, partly to the abundance of accumulated riches and of men ready to work, also to the vast unexplored and uninhabited territories that have come into our possession. Owing to these fortunate conditions, outlets for human energy are varied and multiplied daily, for since, as there is an excess of supply, men are able to turn their vigour to the production of new things, with the result that an unprecedented abundance has been rained into the earth, rendering it possible for all to produce and consume. These conditions have altered our mode of life, and introduced the habits of continued and methodical daily work. The love of labour is always proportionate to its difficulties and to the liberality of its recompense. Hence in our civilization, where work is easy and fruitful, it tends, with the increase of population, of consumption and civilization, to become every day more universal and intense. The characteristic type of our age is the busy man, always anxious to produce and consume as much as possible. In this wise the productiveness of work increases, as it were, geometrically.

This was not the case with ancient civilization. The only productive employments for capital—either in the hands of individuals or the state—were the following :—

1. The construction of cities, roads, bridges and hydraulic works which served for agriculture and communication.

2. The acquisition of lands, tools and slaves, to plough and cultivate the same.

3. The acquisition of slaves required for domestic work, to serve their masters, wear his clothes, make his furniture and build his house ; to do all the roughest work and to serve as sailors, stablemen, and crews.

4. The construction of land and water vehicles and the acquisition of goods for trading. The most profitable commerce in the ancient world was done by sea, and speculated upon the great differences of price that prevailed

G

in countries between which communication was difficult and in which the degree of civilization—that profound factor in the value of goods—was so diverse. In fact, the object of commerce anciently was to buy objects from barbarians who could not appreciate them, at a low price.

5. The acquisition of the simple instruments used in the industry of the period for weaving, mechanical work, etc.

Population was never very dense in ancient times. This rendered the cultivation of the land more difficult; great expanses of land had to be abandoned owing to scarcity of hands, or on account of the solitude and wildness of their situation, rendered impracticable through forests, marshes, and wild beasts. The very limited agrarian development which resulted indirectly restricted the progress of industrial labour, for many industries cannot exist without a large class of agriculturists to provide the raw material in exchange for the products of industrial work. Industrial employments were only practicable for small capitalists, because they were always exercised by free artisans who provided themselves with their own inexpensive tools. Any extensive industry, carried on by great capitalists with the aid of numerous workers, was an unknown thing in the old world, excepting in the mining industry. Mines worked by great capitalists with multitudes of slaves were common things, but other more refined industries, such as the mechanical and manufacturing, carried on by capitalists in large offices, with numerous employees, whether free or serfs—of this we only find some trace in the history of Athens in the fifth century. Commerce offered the possibility of medium gains, greater, that is to say, than industry and smaller than agriculture. A man who owned sufficient money to build himself a ship, buy a few goods and some slaves, could try his luck in trade. We read in Plautus that commerce was the resource of young men who had ruined themselves with excesses. When they found themselves on their last legs they collected what little money remained, bought a ship, and tried their fortune. But it was not usual for a merchant, who had once enriched himself, to invest his gains in new ships in order indefinitely to extend his business. Commerce in those times was too risky a matter ; besides, the development of trade was not rapid enough to justify this course. An enriched merchant bought land, houses, etc., and sought to become a *rentier*.

In short, the only good investment for large capitals was in agriculture, though even this, in comparison to modern civilization, was very restricted.

III

The consequence of all this was that the ancients lived in small communities, and contented themselves with working and consuming little. If some fine morning an ancient Egyptian, Assyrian, or Greek, were suddenly reanimated in Oxford Street, preserving recollections of the world in which he lived, at the sight of so many people hurrying in the same direction he would imagine that something extraordinary was happening in London : a catastrophe, a festival, a procession, the return of some victorious king. It would never occur to him that all this bustle was a daily occurrence, representing the urgent desire and need of numbers to reach in time their day's work, which rarely lasts less than six or seven hours. The ancients, with a few exceptions—such as the slaves in the mines, who were overburdened till they nearly died of exhaustion—worked little, both the higher and lower classes.

The rich and powerful (whose riches were derived

principally from lands and cattle), when they were not busy with state affairs, had no other care than to pass their time in the midst of dissipations: hunting, feasts, balls, spectacles, gallant adventures; consuming the rents of their estates, which they left in the hands of agents and rarely visited. Thus the chief characteristic of the higher classes in these societies was idleness, the lack of any profound and serious habit of work: such can be observed even in their particular kind of work, politics and war. What deliberateness in ancient combats and politics! Sieges and wars lasted for years, months were wasted in bringing about some small state reform, or concluding simple diplomatic treaties. Their administration and diplomacy resembled very closely that of modern Turkey. The men at the head of the state were good fellows, who wanted to enjoy their lives like every one else, consequently matters of great urgency were frequently postponed in order that they should not interfere with some festival or other entertainment. Only in the extremest moments, when face to face with imminent danger, did the habitual indolence of these *régimes* give way to a frenzy of activity capable of immense efforts. In ordinary times it was hopeless to expect of them the continuous alacrity, always on the watch, of the well-governed states of our day, because in the habits and character of the ruling classes of that period there was a little of that indolence which nowadays we only find in *viveurs*. In ancient states, even those at the head of the social hierarchy were characterized by the indifference of men who work little and abuse pleasure, like our dissolute rich, who, in the opinion of contemporary morality, are the most despicable portion of the modern upper classes.

Antiquity does not afford the phenomenon of the busy

man. Great and small merchants, ambulating vendors, and shopkeepers were more anxious then than now to pass their time lounging about their shops, gossiping with their customers and passers-by. A merchant's work in olden times had nothing in common with the drudgery of our modern tradesmen, who every day has to conceive new projects, direct the execution of contracts, and resolve the innumerable difficulties which continually present themselves. The merchant of old was capitalist and privateer in one, who invested his moneys in ships, and generally navigated his own vessel when he set forth to exchange his goods in various ports. His life was thus hard physically, but not mentally. He had to put up with the fatigues of travel in an age which ignored sleeping-cars and transatlantic liners ; he had to face the perils of seafaring in a fragile boat, and the dangers of commerce with barbarians in an epoch which knew neither consuls nor state protection in foreign lands. But the nature of his business scarcely ever varied, or did so very slowly. He had to deal with scant competition ; his commerce demanded little culture—the result of study and fatigue— but considerable cunning, which is a natural gift, and he had not to worry his brain further than to find some new trick for deceiving his clients.

The populace willingly followed the example of their betters. Factory inspectors were not needed then to insure artisans and peasants against overworking or unsanitary conditions. Unwittingly they applied the most perfect hygienic rules to their work, exercising that precaution not to exhaust their strength, which is displayed by primitive men, when working, not under a severe master, but under the stimulus of their own zeal. Virgil describes, in his " Georgics," the life of the small Latin proprietor, which he holds up as an example of austere industry to the proletariat, who idly lounged about the theatres and forums of Rome. And yet how sweet was that life in comparison with that of a modern workman ! The small proprietor only had to apply the traditional agrarian practices which descended from father to son, no inventive effort was demanded of him to better his technique. All the agriculture which Virgil describes is so simple that the peasant could easily achieve it with ordinary industry during the spring and autumn months. The heaviest work consisted in sowing and reaping the corn, and even this was done by the peasant, not under the harsh direction of a master, but under the far sweeter stimulus of his own zeal and the consciousness of his own interests. Autumn, moreover, ended in the vintage festivals, and winter was nothing but one long repose, an uninterrupted merrymaking and hunting season.

> " Mutuaque inter se laeti convivia curant ;
> Invitat genialis hiems curasque resolvit."
>
> (i. 301, 302).

Still idler, perhaps, was the life of the town worker, men whose laziness was encouraged by the numerous amusements and attractions the city offered. Political and religious festivals were innumerable in ancient society, and they all formed an excellent excuse for both rich and poor to pass their time in lounging about, and in amusements of all kinds. For certain peoples—such as the Athenians—politics were an extra distraction, because when the tribunals sat, or assemblies of citizens were convoked, shoemakers, iron-founders, dyers, and carpenters left their work or shops to take part in the meeting of one or other party ; to attend some noisy trial in which the speeches of celebrated rhetoricians of the hour were to be read. In any case, as ancient industry was chiefly composed of artisans who worked in their own homes and then sold their goods to wholesale merchants, their labour was necessarily far less hard than that to which modern factory workmen are condemned, because it was much less disciplined. A free artisan works when he likes ; he varies his working-hours every day according to his inclination ; he is not obliged willy-nilly to slave a certain number of hours, and to overcome his weariness. Those days when he feels disinclined for work, he is not subjected to the tedious discipline of time-tables and overseers charged to convert all his energy into a useful product. What a difference there exists, in hardship and productiveness, between ancient and modern labour, even considered independently of the instruments which served in the two cases !

IV

Consumption and production were alike small. Ancient living was poor and simple in comparison with ours. The ancients were not acquainted with tobacco, coffee, tea, sugar nor alcohol. They were used to simpler food than we are, excepting when they viciously abandoned themselves to inexcusable orgies. They dressed much less, so that neither hats nor shoes were objects of ordinary use, even in the most prosperous periods ; they lived in small houses, and had most imperfect means of transporting goods and communicating thoughts to distant countries ; their technique was simple, and therefore inexpensive. Ancient life was totally lacking in comfort, in all those numerous little objects that render modern existence so expensive, and which have became so necessary to men who have to work as hard as we do. Subject, as we are, to continuous mentally exhausting work, we need to recuperate every evening the nervous energies spent during the day; we could not exist in dark unheated houses, go out semi-nude, abstain from all nourishment which stimulates the nervous system, nor sleep on hard beds like the Romans under the Empire. The house of a well-to-do London merchant of our times consequently contains more comforts than did that of a Roman senator. The houses of the rich, more especially the Roman, used to be true works of art, with their ebony ceilings inlaid with ivory, with their fine marble pavements ; their frescoed walls and halls adorned with splendid statues, either original or copied from the Greek masterpieces ; their rich and precious furniture, their silver or gold plate. Even the kitchen utensils, pans and saucepans, in grand houses were frequently *articles de virtu* worked and engraved by skilful hands. And yet these sumptuous dwellings were badly illuminated, because that ingenious arrangement of windows and skylights, to which we owe our good lighting, was lacking in Roman houses. The means of defence against cold were still more meagre ; the richest Romans might eat at a silver table from a golden service, but they did not possess any machine resembling those comfortable stoves which a modest bourgeois, living in town, possesses to-day. Noctural illumination was practically not existent. It appears that Rome under the Empire was the only city of the ancient world where any attempt was made to light the streets, the custom being for every one to carry lanterns. As to the illumination of houses, if an ancient millionaire were to come to life again now, he would consider even the little petroleum lamps as something magnificent. The Romans conquered the world, and built the Coliseum, but they did not know how to make artificial light.

The following little fact is even more curious. The Roman senators only began to make use of cushions in theatres in the era of Caligula. Till his time they had sat on bare and hard wooden benches. Therefore these masters of the world, these rich men of the Empire, did not attend spectacles in greater comfort than the workmen of our time who frequent the gallery.

Wealth in olden times, in short, was generally combined with a large degree of slovenliness : personal slovenliness, slovenliness in the houses, slovenliness in the streets, slovenliness in towns.

Washing appears to us to be an elementary principle of life ; and yet a long time passed before men took to the habit sufficiently to feel its need. It is true that in some societies bathing was a universal practice ; but bathing with the ancients was quite another matter to what it is now : it was rather a voluptuous passion than a cleanly habit—a vice which, in a certain degree, corresponded to our modern vice of smoking, unknown in those times. People did not bathe themselves then for the sake of cleanliness, but as a means of passing the time, for the pleasure of splashing about in tepid water, and of artificially varying the temperature of their bodies ; sometimes with the object of complicating the lasciviousness of love. So true is it that cleanliness had very little to do with this passion for baths, that it frequently happened in the Thermæ for several people to bathe together in not very large tanks, where the water necessarily soon became very dirty. The bath was as much a voluptuous gratification as dancing, music, wine, or women ; consequently, at that period, when sensual enjoyments so easily became morbid passions, there was a true sybaritism of bathing, and there were people who abused bathing, as others abused wine and women, taking five, six, seven, eight a day, eating, reading, or sleeping in their tubs.

This is proved by the modest cinderella station held in the world of *toilette* in all military civilizations by soap, which now reigns supreme. Formerly the post now occupied by soap was held by perfumes, substances capable of affording sensual pleasure. Both men and women always scented their entire bodies ; they perfumed their clothes, their beds ; they burnt incense in their rooms ; they even scented their food and drink. The number and variety of their perfumes, almost all imported from the Orient, were infinite, wherefore the modern world would strike a man of that period as a world without perfume. Thus odours formed a great article of commerce in the ancient world, whilst of the industry of soap-making there is scarcely a trace. It would seem that the Romans were acquainted with soap in the days of Pliny the Elder, deriving their knowledge from the barbarian peoples of the North.

V

The three principal vices of ancient civilization were : the small opportunity for increasing the riches and productive power of capital, the universal lack of industry, the poverty and simplicity of life—cause and result of the previous factors. On the other hand, habits of simple and poor living where little is consumed generate a species of resistance and psychological aversion to augmenting the products for consumption. Men nowadays augment these products and easily contract fresh habits because they are used to this constant change, and find pleasure in it. But this is a custom artificially acquired, for man is naturally a misoneist, and tends to persevere in habits once formed. Thus the very simplicity of living, which was partly the effect of the small productiveness of capital, rendered the development of labour in its turn, more difficult.

Neglect also has its torpid pleasures, its inert delights, which men addicted to hard work cannot understand, as a lazy man cannot appreciate the keen satisfaction of activity. What represents supreme happiness to one, appears to the other as intolerable tedium and suffering. The principal difference between ancient and modern civilization is, perhaps, to be found in this diversity in the ideal of happiness. But although in the ancient world the possibility and desire to multiply the products of labour were small, the commonest form taken by the thirst for emotion—greed—was not lacking. In ancient times, as in modern, there were always a few thoughtful and learned men amongst those who ruled states, but the majority—then as now—consisted in men who sought to satisfy the strongest human passion, that of power, by accumulating and increasing wealth. It is a common observation that the desire for riches grows with the possession thereof: that wealthy men are never satiated, because acquirement facilitates further acquisition, and this facility is a new incentive to covetousness.

What is true of the modern man is true of the ancient, with this variation, however, that owing to the different constitution of society, these indefinite possibilities of greed were formerly a great factor in the dissolution and ruin of society. In an age like ours, where productive investments are innumerable and always on the increase, those minorities anxious to enrich themselves who are at the head of society can find satisfaction, not by diminishing but by increasing the wealth of the whole community, employing their money in speculations, in industrial, commercial, and banking schemes, all of which, with the exception of a few of which we shall speak of later on, are beneficial to all. This possibility of investing to good advantage results in the rich using only a small portion of their wealth in display, the bulk is put to better use. In other words, the increase in individual wealth is derived from and promotes the prosperity of the entire community.

But in a society in which the development of industry was very slow, and productive investments for capital few, the enrichment of minorities could only proceed at the cost of society. As the sum-total of riches remained stationary for long periods at a stretch, the enrichment of one man was necessarily accompanied by the loss of another. Nor was this all : owing to the difficulty of finding investments for large capital, the accumulation of wealth depressed its productiveness, and consequently the enrichment of a few not only impoverished a few, but the whole of society, by diminishing production. And this happened in various ways.

VI

The rich men of antiquity must necessarily have wasted a great part of their wealth, owing to the difficulty of finding good investments for large capital.

Nowadays, thanks to the great facilities for investing money at interest, even millionaires own a relatively small amount of bullion. They invest all their fortune in lands, edifices, industrial, banking, and commercial undertakings. But in an age in which fertile land was limited in amount, commercial and industrial investments few, and when the general conditions of society were much less secure than they are at present, men naturally desired to hold metal more than they do now. Of all those desirable things which do not satisfy the elementary requirements of life, gold and silver are the most desirable ; because they do not wear out, because they can easily be hidden, saved from fire, kept intact underground for centuries together, or transported from place to place. Also, if so desired, they can be made a show of. In short, they easily provoke that sentiment which we have named the "social satisfaction of wealth." True, these metals are of little utility when locked up in safes or converted into plate, true that besides satisfying the sentiment of vanity they are only useful as a reserve of wealth in case of necessity. But at a period when even the needs of the wealthy were few, the very rich were able to invest a part of their property in precious metals without depriving themselves of any of the material satisfactions offered of their age. Hence the ancient world was travailed by a perfect thirst for gold and silver. Commerce was not carried on, as nowadays, almost entirely by the exchange of certain goods and services for certain other goods and services, but by exchange of the precious metals. The poorest and rudest men loved to decorate themselves with shining metals ; barbarous tribes exchanged their wares for gold wherewith to mount their arms or make bracelets and trinkets. The Gauls walked the world semi-nude, but they never would forego the gold necklace, which the Greek sculptors of the Rhodian school never failed to reproduce in their statues. The emblem of power and position in their chiefs was the amount of golden ornaments and vessels they possessed. While the barbarians were thus in the habit of accumulating metal, the houses of the rich in more civilized societies overflowed with splendours difficult for us to realize. The temples were frequently depositories of gold and silver, whether in money, bullion, or objects. The whole of Athens in the time of Pericles was probably not worth one parish of London for wealth, and yet its temples and public monuments were full of gold and silver-plated statues, some indeed of them of solid metal, for the like of which we should search London in vain. Oriental monarchs, however, were the chief accumulators, compelling their subjects and vassals to pay the greatest portion of their tributes in precious metals, which they horded in vast quantities in their palaces.

Had they not withheld from circulation a great part of the capital necessary to the maintenance of civilization, these stores would have been useful because they would have implied a good reserve of capital in case of need. But the greed of the rich, especially in an era when social experience was limited, did not apprehend, and therefore could not respect, their subtle limit ; so that at times the states of the ancient world decayed for want of the capital accumulated in idle treasures or vain pomp in the houses of the wealthy. Commerce languishes and loses its agility if forced to return to the practice of barter, the value of goods diminish, as also the wealth of those who depend on the products of the land and industry. Agriculturists, small proprietors and artisans are impoverished through no fault of their own ; there is a falling-off in all those more delicate branches of work which require a convenient medium of exchange—only usurers and the owners of precious metals thrive. One of the most deep-seated causes of the internal decay of the Persian Empire at the time of Alexander's conquest was the stagnation of precious metals stored at the court, which had deprived industry of a considerable part of the necessary capital, sown misery through-out the nation, and disorganized the public administration.

The scarcity of circulating capital was a constant drag.   This
was felt more acutely in moments of crisis, as for example
during the two last centuries of the Roman Republic.   The
rich Romans accumulated gold extorted from all parts of
the empire.   This they converted into objects of luxury and
squandered in all manner of ways, till the wretched peoples
they had vanquished found themselves without the where-
withal to pay the tributes and taxes imposed on them, and
saw the value of their harvests and produce diminishing in
consequence.   One of the chief drawbacks to the economical
progress of the ancient world, moreover, was the scourge of
usury, the rapid increase in the value of the metals that
formed their medium of exchange, which originated in the
scarcity of capital.   But this scarcity was not due to any
inadequacy in supply to meet demand, but to the fact that
the rich horded the precious metals for the satisfaction of
their vanity and love of pomp.

VII

Precisely the same thing happened with the land.   The
minorities who governed ancient states, and who desired to
increase their wealth, naturally aimed at possessing much
land, more especially as agriculture was the only investment
then possible to large capital.   Thus we constantly observe
in the ancient world that the system of small properties (the
most productive *régime* then known) was always of short
duration, being rapidly ruined by a greedy set of land mono-
polists, who cunningly or violently concentrated them into a
few large holdings.   Sometimes the method adopted to attain
this end was violent : a minority acquired political power,
and arbitrarily expropriated the small agriculturists.   But

usury was the usual instrument. An easy-going life without
much hard work frequently led the small proprietor into
habits of extravagance. They took to dissipation, games of
chance, intrigues with the courtesans of neighbouring towns.
Opportunities for getting into debt were not lacking, nor
temptations to neglect business. A man could consider himself lucky when he had only spent his all, so long as he did
not get into debt. But if he was overtaken by a war, a
famine, a flood ? He then found himself reduced to beggary,
and had to raise loans, at a heavy interest, since capital was
not abundant. And since he was frequently incapable of
augmenting the products of his land by his own zeal, and
thus of repaying the loan, one debt followed on another
until the proprietor found himself expropriated by his debtor.
Thus the usurers became the big proprietors.

By this means the two finest systems of small agricultural
holdings known to the ancient world were ruined. Greece,
in the fifth and fourth centuries B.C., was almost entirely
divided into small properties growing principally corn, barley,
and olives. The population was at its densest at this period,
the country at its richest epoch, and the intellectual and
political life of Athens in its full glory. Aristotle arrived in
time to find Greece in this condition, which he with reason
considered as the best possible ; he observed that, wealth
being well divided, there were few people absolutely destitute.
But the social decadence of the third and second centuries
was accompanied by the total ruin of small properties.
Frequent wars had devastated Greece : these, combined with
the improvidence of the landowners, had reduced the whole
rustic population to an almost inconceivable state of debt and
misery. Debtors were innumerable in Thessalonia, Etolia,
the Peloponnesus and Attica ; a few usurers who had known

how to accumulate capital were expropriating the majority. The population was rapidly diminishing, decimated by misery, whilst vagabondage daily increased. The disputes about debt were of such gravity that they formed the basis of all the political struggles of the century. The enemies of Rome, more especially Persius, attempted to make themselves popular with the masses in Greece by raising hopes of a general abolition of debt.

The same thing occurred in Rome after the destruction of Carthage. The enrichment of Rome, the extravagant manner of life adopted, the hopes of great gains to be made in war, the passion for gambling and dissipation, resulted in the agriculturist abandoning the land on which his forefathers, during the intervals of peace, had long led a rough but laborious life, according to the austere ideal of Virgil. With the new requirements came the passion for distant expeditions ; the relaxing of the duties entailed by marriage and paternity, debts, and with debts the expropriation of the small proprietors by usurers. Moreover, Rome was falling into the hands of powerful factions who in turn dominated the state, whose chiefs, covetous of riches, espoused this opportunity of expropriating others and enlarging their own *latifondi*.

Still large properties were much less productive in the ancient world than small ones. This was another reason why these accumulations were noxious to the development of society. A large capitalist possessed no perfected machines and instruments to apply to his land, he could not augment his produce in comparison with a small proprietor, without capital or machines, like a rich farmer of our times. Indeed, these properties were less productive, because their owners—with the indolence and indifference of the age— entrusted them entirely to bailiffs or slaves, who profited by

H

the absence of their master to work as little and rob as much as possible. The only object of landlords was to draw their rents—whether large or small. They did not wish to be troubled about their property, living far distant from it in large cities, there to idle away their time, occupied in politics or literature, or indulging in libertinage. Thus we understand how it was that all the great writèrs, from Aristotle to Pliny, were in favour of small holdings ; how the land, robbed from these small owners, rapidly degenerated; how the country grew depopulated and decivilized, making of it a convenient haunt for brigands—another of the scourges of ancient civilizations.

VIII

The mania for accumulation had another result : the diminution of the third factor of production—men. With the increasing difficulty in exchange and diminution of work, men found it more and more difficult to live up to the standard of life to which they were accustomed, and hence they resorted to the first economy which civilized man attempts when society is impoverishing : abstention from children. The ἀπαιδία due to infanticide and celibacy was a scourge of ancient civilization in times of crisis. We find it in Greece in the third and second centuries B.C., in Rome after the fall of Carthage—when the great fecundity of Roman families suddenly ceased,—in Gaul in the time of Cæsar, when infanticide was a common practice. But this diminution aggravated matters instead of improving them, because diminishing the number of producers and consumers in a society which nominally did not possess too many, ended by decreasing the force necessary for production and restricting still further, for the survivors, the possibility to live and work.

Owing to these three fundamental vices, ancient society was unable to maintain an equilibrium between the three factors of production : capital, land, and men. Several societies managed for a brief period to maintain a sufficient poise ; and this was their brief moment of greatest glory and power. But this equilibrium rapidly broke down : capital stagnated, land accumulated in the hands of a few and became less fertile, population diminished. The impossibility of angmenting productive investments, owing to the poorness of their technique, to scientific ignorance, to the universal prevalence of indolent habits and content with poor and simple life, caused those efforts made by energetic minorities to increase their wealth invariably to terminate in the ruin and progressive decomposition and disorganization of society.

We shall see, in the following study, that the chief reason for wars in ancient times is to be found in this law of rapid and periodical decomposition, to which all old civilizations were subject owing to their very constitution.

MILITARISM IN THE ANCIENT
WORLD

CHAPTER IV

MILITARISM IN THE ANCIENT WORLD

I

FOR various reasons war was necessary to the development and progress of ancient civilization, and this must account for the numerous and terrible conflicts of antiquity.

Civilization does not develop beyond certain bounds unless it possesses a fair quantity of circulating capital in the form of metallic coin. Precious metals when coined, or used as coin, have the virtue of facilitating the most complicated exchange, regardless of distance or time; of increasing the efficacy of human work, and of endowing it almost without men's knowledge with a broader object than the immediate benefit of individuals. So, if it is going too far to say that civilization could not develop without the use of precious metals as money, it is anyway certain that, after fire and the alphabet, it has been man's best friend since the beginning of his history.

In the ancient world the essential function of war was to provide civilizations, which were on their road to progress, with sufficient capital.

We have seen that these precious metals, owing to a vice innate in ancient civilizations, were periodically withdrawn from circulation to stagnate in the houses of the wealthy, where they served no other purpose than that of vain display.

Wars served to force this capital into circulation and to send it where it could be of some profit. Nowadays, when capital is only accumulated in order to find a profitable investment for it in some portion of the civilized world protected by laws, customs, and international ideas, a nation desirous of raising its standard of civilization can easily procure the necessary money by borrowing it from richer nations, so that financial difficulties are among its least important drawbacks. They were, on the contrary, the gravest difficulties in the ancient world, where a people could not procure this capital without plundering, in a fortunate bellicose undertaking, the riches hoarded by other nations in their temples, wealthy houses, and palaces.

II

Thus the wars between civilized states and nomadic, or semi-nomadic tribes, were in the ancient world essentially struggles for the conquest of capital and for its better employment. These were among the most terrible wars of ancient history. Civilized states were like oases in the desert of barbarism. How many attacks from the Gauls Rome and Greece had to resist! Carthage had fallen, and yet Rome—mistress of a vast empire—again saw Italy threatened by the Cimbric and Teutonic hordes, from which it could only free itself by a ruthless extermination. But Oriental states were more subject than others to such wars. Assyria was constantly at war with the Cimmerii and Scythians in the north, with the Medes and Persians in the east, with the Arab tribes in the region of the lower Euphrates and Southern Syria. The Egyptian state was constantly threatened by the Asian and Nubian nomad races. The fragments of Oriental history which have come down to us strike us as the history of an interminable chase that was far more terrible than the lion and tiger-hunts partaken of by the Assyrian kings, so splendidly represented on the bas-reliefs in the British Museum. When empires were young and strong, they endeavoured to forestall the danger by bearding the ferocious tribes—these human tigers—in their dens, in the wilds of the Steppes, and in their mountain gorges. The Asiatic Empires exterminated large numbers with their arrows, while the remaining clans lurked in inaccessible retreats. But empires grew weary of chasing these innumerable and indomitable beasts ; the hunter aged, and at the return of the hunting season began to lose his interest in penetrating into the heart of the forest in order to decimate these human animals. Then they multiplied in their lairs, took fresh courage, and finally turned out in vast hordes, invaded the land and attacked the hunter's flocks. Hearing their cries, the hunter would arouse, and in an impulse of fury, he once more found his original vigour, left his tent and seized his bow and arrow. But it was too late. The tigers had become too fierce and numerous, the hunter's arm too weak —he fell, and was torn to pieces by the beasts.

The periodic attacks of these tribes were probably caused by the same motive—excluding religious fanaticism—which led to the formation of the Dervish horde in the Soudan, amongst which the strongest was the greed for precious metals. Gold and silver were more desirable for their own sake than as a means of exchange to the ancient barbaric tribes, whose requirements were small even in comparison with the modest ones of ancient civilized peoples. But the barbarians' desire for the possession of these metals greatly exceeded their capacity to procure them by trading, because they were lazy and ignorant, producing, and consequently selling, little. Moreover, a thoughtless, adventurous and uncontrolled warlike existence was attractive to their primitive and violent minds. Tacitus has described the Germans as passing from periods of abject indolence to attacks of savage excitement. Thus from time to time the combination of various nomad tribes formed great hordes which attacked the wealthy cities of civilized states, appropriating furniture, carpets, cloths, and above all precious metals. Some of the gold and silver was divided amongst the soldiers, but the greater part was appropriated by the strongest and most cunning warriors, who thus became the tyrants of the swarm.

Civilized states were led, in their turn, to counter-attack these barbarous tribes, partly in order to forestall future assaults, partly to become masters of their wealth. Even the poorer clans possessed relatively large quantities of wealth lying idle. On the battlefield where the barbarian warriors had fallen, and in the villages razed, the conquerors were able to collect large booty of precious metals. Thus the wars of barbarians against civilized states aimed at accumulating capital for ostentatious display, and those of civilized nations against barbarians, to replace this gold and silver in circulation for a higher object. Much of the progress of Roman civilization was rendered possible by spoils thus taken ; the first great aqueduct, for instance, which after a more modest attempt initiated the great Roman hydraulic constructions, was built in 272 B.C. with the booty taken in the Pyrrhic wars, while the first public library was founded in Rome by Asinius Pollio with the spoils taken in 40 B.C. from the Dalmatian tribes who lived by piracy.

The same thing, on a smaller scale, happened in Athens. By wrenching it forcibly from less civilized peoples, who

would have used it merely for show, the Athenians procured
the capital necessary for creating the splendid Periclean
civilization, for constructing the Parthenon, and for re-
munerating Phidias. Athens was able, moreover, to construct
the Salaminian fleet with the silver of the Laurian mines ;
and by means of these vessels, and the glory of their Persian
triumphs, they forced the Ionian cities to conclude the Delic
confederation, and to pay them a tribute sufficient to maintain a great army capable of defending the coast against Persia.
This tribute, later on, served not only in part to construct the
navy, it also helped in a great measure to beautify Athens,
to maintain artisans, painters, and sculptors, to increase the
pay of the Athenian workers in State service. The tribute
was at first fixed at 460 talents ; but this was by degrees
increased, until, in the time of Pericles, it formed more than
half of the Athenian revenue, so that in the end it was no
longer so much a voluntary contribution to a military ally as
an obligatory tribute to a work of civilization, whose remains
we still venerate as almost divine. The sailors of the Athenian
fleet, who obliged the Ionian cities, weary of the league, to
continue paying their tax, were unconscious collaborators
in the architecture of the Parthenon, in the works of Sophocles,
Aristophanes, and Socrates, because they contributed to maintain artists and writers on the one hand, and on the other
that happy class of citizens who, without being rich, were
intelligent, and had a passion for beauty and discussion :
men whose chief office was to form an appreciative and
encouraging public to that extraordinary generation of
artists and thinkers who existed in a unique moment in
the intellectual history of the world. Strength, beauty, and
wisdom had united to found together the reign of intellect
in a small Grecian town.

III

We have seen that the equilibrium between the three factors of production—land, men, and capital—was of short duration in ancient civilization, owing to the difficulty of finding productive investments for capital, and that wealth had a tendency to stagnate uselessly when the moment of highest prosperity in a civilization was over. War, by replacing capital in circulation, imparted new life to decadent societies.

The social work of Alexander the Great was to conquer by arms the immense treasures lying dormant in the Persian and Egyptian courts. With this money, which was thus made to move, he founded cities, opened roads, organized states and stimulated the energy, the inventive genius, and the greed of innumerable Greeks. In short, he provided Greece with the funds necessary to conquer Asia, to organize fresh fields for commerce, to found new centres of study, and to prepare the Orient for the coming of Christ.

The chief results of the Roman conquests were not only to replace in circulation the wealth accumulated by the semi-barbaric Alpine, Gallic, Spanish, and Illyrian peoples, but also that of the civilized Asian states, which, since the days of Alexander, had had time to re-accumulate and stagnate, using them for the advance of a new type of civilization. From the conquest of Carthage up to the time of Julius Cæsar, Roman politics were directed by a crew of financiers whose sole object was to appropriate, by fair means or foul, the wealth lying dormant in the provinces. These were the *publicans*, who belonged to the order of knights, and formed a high financial bourgeoisie, a class of rich bankers, who organized commercial societies similar to those of our time, in which any one in Rome who possessed a little money— a soldier on his return from some campaign, or a rich senator —could buy *partes* or shares. The societies had a director called a *magister*, a sort of administrative council, offices, and employees ; they supervised the collection of taxes in the provinces, the working of State mines, military transports, and the construction of public works. Their *partes* were sold at prices varying from day to day. Well-provided with money, counting among their shareholders the most powerful persons in the empire, these societies were practically masters of the State, and could be as overbearing and violent as they chose in the provinces, in order to extort money from their victims to carry to Rome and divide among the shareholders. At critical moments, moreover, they did not lack the support of high-placed politicians and celebrated orators to defend their interests with the State, just as is the case in our own days where big financial schemes are concerned. Cicero's speech, *pro Lege Manilia*, is a warm defence of the shareholders of the Asian publicans when threatened with ruin by the war of Mithridates, who had invaded the tract in which the society extorted tribute. The great orator exhorts the people to provide quickly for war expenses, describing the anxiety of the shareholders, who feared losing capital and interest.

Even Augustus, who commenced the work of consolidating the empire, used Cleopatra's treasures as a capital for the foundation of his imperial civilization. This was, perhaps, the last great reserve of wealth remaining in the Orient after the Roman depredations, which accounts for the zeal the latter displayed in subjugating Egypt after the battle of Azio. Augustus did not merely desire to conquer the future granary of Rome ; long wars had exhausted his treasure, and Rome at that moment suffered from a scarcity of circulating wealth. The accumulating greed of the Ptolemies, their uncontrolled passion for luxury, had unconsciously prepared the remedy. Augustus obtained Alexandria and the royal treasures of Egypt. He carried them to Rome; he coined a great part of the metal; he employed this money to found new colonies with his veterans, to re-organize the army, to make roads and bridges, to provide, in short, the most urgent requirements for the restoration of that civilization which was his work.

IV

Another motive for war in the ancient world was the accumulation of land, which reason we have already traced. This amassing frequently conjoined with the stagnation of capital by decreasing agricultural production, reduced a portion of the rural population to forced idleness, and indirectly impoverished the town labourers. Thus the ancient world, like the modern one, was tormented by the evil of the unemployed, with the difference, however, that men then refused to use certain hard but salutary remedies which we have proved to be efficacious; and the remedy was sought, instead, in war.

It was a difficult matter, then, for the expropriated small proprietor, or the unemployed, to make a living by other work, because antiquity was poor and did not know how to augment and vary men's labour and consumption. To this cause we must add the unlaborious habits of the age. The people's requirements were few: a handful of olives for dinner, a little material for clothing purposes, a ray of sunshine for warmth, any sort of shelter for the night, a friend to chat with, some *gratis* entertainment, and the Athenian or Roman plebeian was content. These elementary needs could easily be satisfied by beggary or theft when work was short. It was an age of improvidence and lightness of heart, because there was not present that gaoler who now watches day and night over society, over offices, fields, and workshops, rendering the multitudes docile to the hard discipline of modern work —*i.e.* hunger. The ancients were in danger of periodical attacks of universal famine ; but in periods of abundance no one—not even professional vagabonds—needed to go without a piece of bread and a handful of olives or figs. It never happened, as it does now, that in the midst of great and continuous abundance an improvident or unenergetic man risks dying of starvation. This fact explains the co-existence of lazy multitudes and slaves. Slave labour, as Cairnes demonstrates, costs more and produces less than free labour. How was it, then, that in such poor times, when lack of work was so prevalent, free men were not employed for the work generally performed by slaves ? Because for very tiring work, such as mining, transporting heavy weights, turning grinding-mills, ploughing uncultured land, for work which interfered seriously with personal liberty, such as serving in rich houses, free men could not easily be found, and it was necessary to coerce by force. Free men preferred mendicity to such hard work, or parasitism on the rich, a feature highly developed in the ancient world; or, when occasion offered, they chose rather to impose themselves forcibly on others. Hence the reason why ancient colonizations so frequently assumed the character of military conquests. Emigrants did not contemplate inhabiting new countries and ploughing the land ; they only submitted themselves to such hard and ungrateful work when absolutely forced by circumstances.

They rather sought to conquer land already cultivated, and to disperse its original possessors. Some have tried to explain ancient colonization by increase of population ; but this is only possible by supposing a greater analogy than really existed between ancient and modern civilization. Population could not increase rapidly in those days, especially in nations of a certain civilization who countenanced infanticide, since, besides this artificial means of destruction, there existed others not less efficacious : wars, epidemics, famines, and the absence of hygiene—so fatal, more especially to children. But even without supposing a rapid increase of population, it is easy to explain the prevailing desire to conquer new countries. The instability of small properties must have been one of the primary factors. Even in moments of great prosperity (for reasons we have already explained) a certain number of small proprietors got into debt and were expropriated. When they were overtaken by a crisis, debts and expropriation combined ended in the complete ruin of the small rural class, to whom all hope was thus lost of living by work in their native land. The acquisition of other cultivated lands on which to settle, or some way of existing by means of war, was their only resource.

Thus we see Athens, even in the height of her glory under Pericles, sprinkling with *cleruchies,* or colonies, many islands of the archipelago, the shores of the Chersonese, the Black Sea, and even the coast of Italy : colonies whose object was to occupy land already cultivated by getting rid of its original owners. Many of these emigrants were Greeks from various regions, but Athenians were not numerous in these colonies because, at that period, the prosperity of the small Attic proprietors and Athenian artisans was at its highest, and work was abundant for all. But in the years of Athenian and Greek decadence—the third and second centuries B.C.—when the great ruin of small holdings occurred, innumerable Greeks emigrated as artisans, merchants, soldiers, counsellors, writers, artists, tutors and priests into the Asian states founded by Alexander the Great.

Greece became depopulated and impoverished, its culture declined, the land became massed into a few immense properties, capital lay idle. Side by side of a few insolent and extravagant rich men, there lived a nation of debtors and mendicants who dragged out a wretched and angry existence. Fortunately, a military genius had thrown open to the Greeks the fabulous expanses of Asia. He had made accessible immense territories, occupied by gigantic states, abounding in wealth, blessed with a grandiose but formless and stationary civilization which had for long alarmed and disquieted the Greeks, habituated to their small poor country, their tiny states, and to the exquisitely harmonious proportions of their civilization. Had it not been for the Greek social crisis of the third and second centuries B.C., the conquests of Alexander the Great would have lost much of their importance. Thanks to this, the Greeks emigrated to Asia by the road the Macedonian arms had opened to them ; and here their genius lost much of its equilibrium and serenity, replacing its loss by the gain of an ardent energy.

Expropriated proprietors also played a great *rôle* in Roman history. Rome's more ancient wars against the populations of central Italy aimed at seizing their enemies' cultivated lands. In the same manner the main object of the conflicts waged during the two last centuries of the Roman Republic was to provide for the ruined class of small landowners. After the conquest of Carthage, small Italian farms went down under the pressure of hard times, the expropriated

I

owners moved to Rome, became soldiers, lived by elections, or passed into the provinces to fight or become usurers lending at high rates of interest the moneys acquired from their share of the booty. Now this class of professional speculators on war required a constant supply of such conflicts, more especially as they rapidly squandered in times of peace the money then gained. Hence the small expropriated landowners formed in the Roman assemblies a public opinion always favourable to war. When towards the middle of the first century B.C., through the multiplication of foreign and civil wars, the world was much impoverished, and that definitive crisis which was the beginning of the empire, was imminent, the land question became a stimulus to war in yet another fashion. The poor Roman plebeians flocked round the standards of the heads of factions, not through enthusiasm for the contending ideas, but because they hoped to receive cultivated lands in return for their services, lands on which they could live, helped by some slave, without the fatigue of labour. The lands which the veterans hankered after were already prepared to give fruit and harvests, so that the heads of parties, more especially after the death of Cæsar, were compelled to proceed to those expropriations of small Italian proprietors, which threatened the total ruin of Roman society. When Augustus came into power, in order to restore peace he bought, instead of robbing, the lands to distribute to the veterans, who, establishing themselves in the various cities, were thus enabled to satisfy the principal desire for which they had taken up arms, *i.e.* to live without working, like a modern *rentier* on the income of the lands received.

The last motive for war in the ancient world is to be found in slavery. We have already seen why slavery was necessary ; but if the slaves were procured in small numbers by legal artifices, such as the sale of children and the loss of liberty to insolvent debtors, they were obtained in much larger numbers by violence. Man-hunting was a regular trade. No sooner did the State relax a little of its vigilance on the coast, than remote creeks became the haunts of pirate ships, forests and mountains the resort of brigands; the first attacked navigators, the second travellers, whom they then sent, by means of merchants, to distant markets, more especially to Delos, which for many centuries was the great slave-market of the Græco-Roman world. How numerous were those whom this fate overtook in the ancient world! Many great men—Cæsar not excepted—ran this risk. But countries in a state of war were able to carry on this commerce on a larger scale. The prisoners who to-day are an expense and nuisance to the victors, then formed part—and no mean one either—of the booty. They were sold as useful merchandise for industrial purposes, and to serve the rich in diverse countries ; and the results of the sale largely repaid the conquerors for the expenses of war.

V

War was consequently a necessary factor in the progress and spread of ancient civilization ; it was able to provide nations, who desired to develop with the requisite capital, land and men by seizing them from barbarians or from civilized states in decadence. Hence war was a struggle for civilization, because without it nations could not emerge from barbarism, or raise themselves from periodical decline, owing to their ignorance and lack of industry. This explains how it came about that great warriors were regarded with an admiration that almost amounted to worship, and why Alexander was considered of superhuman greatness. The warrior was not merely a soldier, he was also the capitalist of the ancient world, the administrator of past and future wealth, the great architect ; the protector of religion, of art, of literature, of knowledge ; the arbitrator of the future in the decisive moments of history. The means massed in his hands were immense, his power unlimited, his practical responsibility nil, his historical responsibility was enormous. He had to understand, or at least to divine, the necessities of the future, because for centuries to come men would inhabit, pray, and study in the places and manner indicated by him, would travel along the paths he traced. A single error on his part might become a calamitous matter for ages.

And yet war, even in the ancient world, though so necessary to civilization, contained such an active element of destruction, that its services were always accompanied by grave perils. In this respect it was similar to fire, which is man's best and most useful servitor, but woe betide him if its destructive forces once break loose ! Now, the destructive qualities of war in the ancient world were much more difficult to control than those of fire. Man is stimulated to every action by some need or reason, but in the performance of this, certain sentiments and passions arise which may, in their turn, have great influence on his life. Though war originated in the causes given, it generated pride, overbearingness, ferocity, and all the desires of destruction in the people. These passions, and above all pride, became a fresh and terrible incentive to war ; while greed, on the other hand, its first stimulus, developed a larger appetite after every nourishment, and grew in ancient oligarchies as their fortune in war increased.

For this reason it was impossible to ancient states to keep

war within those bounds which alone would have enabled it
to be useful to civilization. And even when reduced to its
purely beneficial essences, it was an expensive matter, because
the capital and land, seized by force, cost the ancients much
more than it costs us to borrow money, buy land, and
remunerate men for their services. War cost then as it does
now : it cost directly for the arms and apparatus required, and
for the men and property it destroyed. It cost indirectly,
through the immense waste it caused, the destruction of
harvests and the devastation of fields, the burning of villages
and cities, the dispersion and loss of funds.

It is therefore easy to understand how ruinous war became
when some ruling oligarchy allowed itself, blinded by the
pride of victory and greed, to multiply wars, provoking
enemies on all hands, consuming all their reserves, so that
their first defeat fatally entailed ruin.

Such is the history of nearly all ancient states, which were
incited by a first military victory to be more and more masterful with others, to increase their plunder, augment their armies,
until ruin almost unexpectedly overtook them. For instance,
the empire of those Assyrian kings of whom one was able
to write : " I passed like a devastating hurricane. I transported to my country Su-Zub, king of Bab-Ilu, him and
his family. I destroyed his city and his palace, from its
summit down to its foundation I delivered it to the flames ;
I devastated the ramparts, the altars, the temples, all the
works in brick in his empire I ruined at a blow." As an
immense tower which reaches nearly up to heaven is suddenly
flung down by an earthquake and reduced to a mountain
of ruins, so Athens, after she had killed the Persian giant
with her short sword and her light armour, grew covetous
and overbearing when seated on the throne of Greece and

mistress of the sea. By her pride and cupidity she provoked a conflict with Sparta, in which she obstinately persevered, always attempting new military undertakings, till after the Sicilian campaign she found herself ruined and undone. Alexander uprose shortly after, and led Greece to the conquest of Asia ; but at the height of his might he lost his reason and heaped madness on violence. After his death the empire was divided into large kingdoms, whose heads for two centuries waged terrible wars in the hope of gain. Another nation meanwhile was rising in the west : Rome, a strong, bellicose, and austere people, who for centuries waged long and wearisome wars with the other inhabitants of Italy, and engaged in a protracted and terrible duel with a city of proud and greedy capitalists, Carthage. But having conquered Carthage, the vices of her enemies seemed to enter into the soul of Rome. All the treasures of the Orient no longer satisfied her greed, the world seemed scarcely big enough to contain her unmeasured ambition and her appetite for plunder. Then Rome herself fell, ruined in her turn by war, and became involved in the most alarming anarchical disorder. Woe to her, if in the last century before the Christian era, a strong military nation had survived !

In this wise, ancient history was one great chain and succession of wars, a panorama of contending nations. An equal degree of civilization, the similarity of religion, race relationship, did not suffice to maintain peace.

War was necessary to civilization, and it ended by destroying civilization. To this contradiction is due all the tragic grandeur of the ancient world. It scattered everywhere haphazard the germs of life and death in almost equal proportions, so that the two combined were at the root of many things, and much which appeared strong and full of life was destined to be of short duration. War introduced that element of fragility to the older society which renders its remains so pathetic. Its greatest monuments have only reached us in a ruined state, despoiled of their marble facings and artistic friezes ; their sculpture appears to be the field of a terrible battle, strewn with mutilated bodies, with headless and limbless trunks ; their books have many of them been lost or reached us in fragments, damaged by fire from which they only escaped by chance. Not even genius could subdue the element of decadence in ancient society which originated in war. Under the ruins of Rome the masterpieces of Phidias, the greater part of Aristotle's books lie buried ; and those few things which have survived this universal ruin, only cause us to realize the better what an immense conflagration of precious things was entailed by the ending of the ancient world, and what innumerable treasures were then reduced to ashes.

And yet this decay was a necessary coefficient of greatness. In the ancient world it was not possible to live well except by living briefly. A great life was fatally a short one : a tragic law essential to the fundamental vices of ancient civilizations. It is possible for us moderns to realize with precision to what interminably long and shameful decadence ancient states were subject, if no great wars came to reanimate their sinking life, when they had reached the period of concentration of capital, land, and depopulation. We can realize this, because barbarous tribes to this day furnish a mirror for the past history of civilized races. There still exists a nation whose slow death shows us what life too much prolonged signifies to a society in which exist the vices proper to ancient civilizations : I refer to Turkey.

THE DEATH-THROES OF A NATION

CHAPTER V

I

IN many respects Turkey resembles ancient societies, because in it we find their three cardinal vices: lack of industry, simplicity of life, and ignorance, with the accompanying difficulty for the productive investment of capital. The Turkish people consume little and work little. Turks do not find happiness in the morbid activity of Europeans and Americans, which appears madness to them. Their ideal, on the contrary, is a quiet life of absolute repose, idleness comforted by coffee and tobacco, *chief*. Europeans have only managed to introduce their goods into Turkey on a small scale. Tobacco to the whole nation, coffee, and a comfortable harem to the rich, are their goals of luxury. The Turks are conservative in their mode of living, and slowly alter or augment their requirements. Great industries, business and capitalism on a large scale, are unknown quantities to them. Europeans trade with Constantinople—that is to say, they buy there the many things required in Europe—but the Turks and Mussulmans, who form the ruling class, only desire to be agriculturists, soldiers, officials, or priests; they only wish to exercise those traditional professions which demand neither hard nor long work. To cultivate the earth in accordance with accepted precepts, to idle in barracks, to smoke and snooze in offices and mosques, writing a letter once a week, or occasionally murmuring a prayer—this appears to the Turk as the only life worth living.   To live in this manner he is frequently forced to put up with poverty, to practise every possible economy ; but this is of little moment to him, because, like the ancients, the Turk prefers the pleasures of idleness to those of an active existence.   In this sense, Islamism is still the best representative of the ancient spirit, for this reason it is vain ever to hope to introduce great capitalistic industries and modern civilization into Mussulman countries.

The result is that in Turkey ambitious minorities seek to satisfy their desires by plunder, as happened in the ancient world.   Turkey finds herself at present in a period of stagnation.   We may presume that the Persian and Egyptian empires found themselves in an analogous condition before Alexander's conquest.   Only as the Turkish Empire is suffering from this disease at the end of the nineteenth century, in the midst of universal peace in an era when no Alexander turns up to put a stop to this stagnation of wealth, this decay slowly continues, corrupts society, lowering the people to a state of odious barbarism, ruining everything in the vast empire.   Without periodical wars, or the possibility of invasion by some outside nation, this society, which represents the old world in so many of its characteristics, is decaying, and exhales miasma like stagnant water.

II

Turkey presents four distinctive symptoms of decay, viz.—

1. The dispersal and concentration of capital, and the uncultivated state of the land.

2. The dissolution of the bureaucracy.

3. The mania for persecution displayed by the government.

4. The social dissolution consequent on usury.

The present crisis in Turkey is largely due to the waste and concentration of capital which culminated during the reign of Adbul Azis, the uncle of the present Sultan, who was deposed and assassinated in a domestic revolution in 1876. From the beginning of his reign a demoniacal mania for waste characterized the ruling oligarchy of the empire. The enormously increased taxes no longer satisfied their greed ; and the Turkish government got into debt to the extent of £120,000,000, negotiating the famous Turkish loan, of such painful memory to all European bond-holders. Public funds were squandered, not for the public good, but to maintain senseless court extravagances and large swarms of parasites who, on various pretexts, managed to live in luxury. It is calculated that in the Sultan's palace there were 1200 odalisques, 6000 servants and 800 cooks, and that 1200 oxen were provided for the Sultan's kitchen every day. "All the sultans," writes Kesuin Bey,[1] "have a passion for destruction. The European is dumbfounded at the sight of these immense palaces, modest enough in their exterior, but marvellously luxurious inside. All these palaces are deserted and so neglected that they are all falling into decay. They were built to satisfy some caprice, but the caprice died with the builder, and sometimes even before his death. All along the shores of the Bosphorus are sprinkled these chiosques (from the Turkish word *kieuchy*). The whole country is rich in imperial residences, which prove, on inspection, to be all in a state of ruin. Nothing is more funereal than these splendid buildings, which stand out solitarily in the midst of desert plains, half ruined, like the relics of some ancient civilization."

[1] Kesuin Bey, " Le mal d'Orient," Marpon e Flammarion, p. 10.

The high officials imitate the example and luxury of their sovereign ; they bleed the treasury so as to make a grand display, to collect a select harem, to accumulate gold and maintain large retinues of servants, who form a proof to the public of their power and wealth. A Turk who desires to grow rich has no other means than that of preying on the state, with all the violence or cunning of which he is capable. It is a well-known fact that many pashas amassed great wealth during their time of office, that the Sultan is one of the richest sovereigns in the world, and his court a vast store of precious metals. It is said that he possesses gold, silver, jewels and lands to the value of over £40,000,000 ; but whether this calculation be correct or not, it is anyway certain that Abdul Hamid is as great a hoarder of precious metals as the Oriental sovereigns of old. Thus in Turkey, as in the ancient world, the small ruling minority, covetous of wealth, accumulates capital and withdraws it from circulation.

III

This evil naturally leads to others, amongst which the most serious is the agrarian crisis.

Asia Minor, the ancient seat of so many civilizations, the granary and orchard of Europe, from which came corn, peaches, prunes, apricots, myrtle, and a thousand other necessities and luxuries, appears to-day to have lost all its former fertility. Turkey no longer produces sufficient grain for its own consumption, and Constantinople would be reduced to a state of famine if the export of corn from Russia and Hungary were suspended for a few days. The country where the splendid Syrian race of horses was bred, now only pastures a wretched, mangy breed, so that the

Government has to provide the army with steeds from
Hungary. The land is rich in pasture, and yet the breeding
of cattle is almost unknown ; a considerable number of
beasts for slaughter are imported from abroad ; milk is
expensive, and butter is sent over from Italy. Asia Minor
was very rich in trees, and possessed fifty-two varieties of
oak alone ; but now combustibles have become so scarce
that the peasants burn manure to warm themselves. Immense areas of land lie uncultivated, and supply every day
grows less adequate to demand, so that Turkey could not
exist without the produce of poorer countries. This un-
productiveness increases so rapidly, that the Mussulman
peasant, thick-headed and apathetic as he is, is beginning
to feel a vague sense of alarm. He can remember hearing
his old people say that the increase of the sowing was twenty
times, while now it never renders more than seven.

And yet this land, which every day becomes poorer, is
nearly all possessed by the Government, and tilled by the
Turkish-speaking Mussulman population. With the exception of a few Armenian districts, the land is never cultivated
by Christians ; they practise professions and engage in commerce, whilst the possession of the land, participation in the
government, the wielding of arms, and propagation of the
official religion are the four signs of Turkish supremacy.
But though the Turks have conquered by force a great
variety of nations, their pride has been curbed by this
obstinate caprice on the part of the land constantly to
diminish its produce. The earth has rebelled against its
masters ; it renders life in the conquered regions every
year more impossible, making vain the conquests of
these marvellous regions. The disciples of Mahomet
have forced by the sword the gates of this paradise, full of

all the magnificence and sweetness of nature, which should have been reserved for the most elect members of the human race, and lo! the paradise is slowly degenerating into an uninhabitable desert, in which the conquering nation cannot exist.

Now, all this indicates, and at the same time punishes, the iniquity and injustice of a nation. In the most terrible moments of history, man has always asked himself this question : "What will happen when the cup of iniquity overflows?" He has pictured sudden chastisements which descend on the human race like thunderbolts hurled by some superior power, which readjust at a blow the unstable equilibrium of justice! In his infantile simplicity and impatience, he has always allowed himself to be seduced by the image of these resolving catastrophes, and has not realized that not from above, but right in front of him, was a slow but infallible Nemesis, a force capable of re-establishing justice in the relations between men: the very nature by which he lived. To keep the destructive forces of nature within bounds, to cultivate the earth without ruining or exhausting it, is a delicate work which all manner of men have attempted, but in which only men of refined customs and long-standing civilization have succeeded. The warlike Ottoman race, in its life of brigandage and strife, was certainly not best prepared for this sacred work ; but what could happen when the Mussulman peasant, already unfit for this mission, was still more barbarized by the oppression of a scoundrelly Government?

The dishonesty of the high officials, anxious to enrich themselves, necessitated a foolish increase in taxation. The taxes on agriculture were so raised as to reduce to misery a large portion of the laborious population, whose distress was embittered by arbitrariness and caprice in the methods of exaction. Even to-day the Turkish peasant, after having paid the tithe of his produce to the tax-collector, has been forced to submit to the exaction of the *vali* or governor, those of the *mutusarif*, or prefect, of the *caimacanor*, sub-prefect ; and if anything escapes the rapacity of all these officials, the wretched peasant may yet come in for a regiment on march through the country, to whose nutriment he has to contribute. The agriculturists, ruined by taxes and usury, finally go to swell the ranks of mendicants, who form the base of town populations, or they seek the post of servant or parasite in some rich house, whilst the boldest become brigands in the wildest and most deserted regions. For some time past brigandage has flourished in Turkey, and has been one of its greatest scourges. It has grown so much in strength and audacity, that the brigands now venture under the very gates of Smyrna and Salonicus, and plunder the environs of Constantinople. But the brigands, like the usurers and officials, are a class who live in a great measure by extorting taxes from the peasantry.

Exploited by publicans, brigands, officials, and usurers, the Turkish peasant gradually degenerates, without resistance or complaint, into a state of careless resignation. Of wonderful sobriety, he contents himself by producing that little which suffices to keep himself and his family in existence, and to procure an occasional pound of tobacco, smoking which, he is able to indulge in the voluptuous inertia of *kief*. *Kief*, which signifies absolute idleness, the entire inertia of body and soul, represents to him the height of human bliss. He avoids, therefore, every species of effort ; he does not work hard, but barely scratches the earth, and has reached such an incredible degree of indifference and improvidence, as to have

K

quite forgotten the use of manure. The Mussulman peasant appears to ignore the fact that the fertility of land diminishes with long cultivation, and so he does not trouble to enrich his soil : he uses manure as a combustible.

With the falling-off in the productiveness of the soil the population decreases. From time to time, as happened in 1876 and 1878, terrible famines overtake the land and make fearful gaps in the Turkish peasantry ; in normal times, chronic hunger and disease silently decimate this people, destined to disappear. Entire villages have vanished in the interior of Anatolia. Turkey is not a nation given to statistics, and so it is impossible to calculate with precision this decrease in the population ; but there is no denying the truth of the fact, in face of the unanimity of all writers who affirm that the rustic population of Turkey decreases every day decimated by chronic poverty, famines, administrative ill-treatment, and no less by the burden of military service, which weighs on the Mussulman peasantry to the entire exclusion of Christians. Christians take no part in war ; and thus wars, whether fortunate or not, have one certain result : that of diminishing a class of men, who, owing to the extreme misery in which they exist, are never able entirely to recover from their continual losses.

Thus the conquerors and rulers, whilst oppressing the people of whom the fortunes of war have made them master, accomplish a slow suicide. In these military countries, which remind us of ancient societies, war ends by destroying the victors with the vanquished ; it mingles their ashes under the earth once vainly defended by one, vainly conquered by the other, and, summoning another race to live there, it settles for ever the disputes of ages. Do I hear Rome named the Eternal ? Her walls certainly, if not eternal, have made

a long resistance ; not so her men. In the century of the
Antonines not a single pure Roman, perhaps, existed ; not
a single descendant, that is to say, of a single family of those
which had combated the Samnites. The true Rome which
founded the Empire perished centuries before, while the
Rome which benefited by the Empire was composed of the
descendants of the conquered. The first wore itself out in
the gigantic efforts of dispersing and destroying so many
races, so that at the moment when its work neared con-
summation it went to join, in the void of things that have
been, Carthage and its other victims.

IV

The other symptom of decay, the dissolution of the bureaucracy, is another effect of administrative wantonness. The
Turkish treasury was unable to withstand such wholesale
robbery, and in the end was forced to stop payment. The
State, in consequence, could not remunerate its functionaries,
more especially the middle and lower ones.

This is the condition of the Turkish bureaucracy of to-day
—only the high functionaries are regularly paid, the others
are only paid when the Government finds it convenient.
Thus it is calculated that on the average an official, captain
or major in the Turkish army, does not receive regularly and
directly more than one month's salary a year, or at the best
two months'. The arrears frequently accumulate for years.
The arrant selfishness of the court and bureaucracy, who,
being hard up, think only of their own interests, and abandon
the lower and medium officials to their own devices, has
made of them a body of blackmailers who live by oppressing
and exploiting the population.

All those who have visited or written about Turkey: journalists, travellers, English consuls, repeat the same complaint regarding the corruption of the high Turkish officials— one of the plagues of Turkey, as it has been named. Judges sell their sentences, police officials imprison innocent men, and make them buy their liberty at a high price by means of threats ; the tax-collectors raise or lower the duties at their own discretion, gaining on the concessions they graciously make to debtors ; the officials who have to deal with Government contracts make profit out of them ; those charged with any sort of supervision take bribes from the supervized ; all, in short, make use of the small amount of authority conceded to them, to terrify their subjects and extract money. No remedy for this evil is possible, because the small officials have no other means of living, and the higher ones set the worst possible example. A governor, Bahri Pasha, who till recently was *vali* at Van, in Armenia, reached such a depth of villainy as to excite the Kurds to attack, rob, and burn the harvests of the Armenian peasants, so that corn should not sell too low in the markets of his *vilayet*, and he be able to make a larger profit on the tithes which every peasant is compelled to pay the Government.

Indeed, State disorder has reached such a degree that corruption is no longer so much an evil as a vital force, without which the Turkish executive would collapse ; it never moves in any matter except when the officials see some possibility of making *bakshish*. To give an idea of the incredible impudence and audacity displayed by the Turkish Government, it will suffice to recount the affair of the railway which was to have been constructed between Brussa and Mudiana. The Turkish treasury assigned about £6,000,000 for this purpose, nearly the whole of which sum it disbursed ;

but not a single yard of the railway was constructed, because
the money was all swallowed up in bribes. The funds collected, the Minister of Public Works hastened to order in
Europe the locomotives and material necessary, in order that
the big officials could make considerable sums out of the
contractors, and this ready, it became necessary for the
engineers to get out plans for the proposed line, out of
which job no tips could be extracted. The engineers, in
consequence, did nothing at all ; the goods which had been
bought were allowed to rust at Mudiana, in the vicinity of
the spot where the railway was to commence, and for long
after, nothing remained of the railway but a report in which
the Minister of Public Works informed the Sultan that the
line was nearing its completion, and in which he described
the construction, route, and stations.

Later on, indeed, the railway was entirely constructed, the
rails laid down, the stations built ; but only to be left severely
alone, as no train was ever run there. To-day the stations
are falling to ruin, the rails are rusting, the locomotives sleep
in their depôts. The neighbouring peasants rummage amongst
the ruins for unconsidered trifles ; and Angoran goats "with
splendid fleece, calmly browse on the long grass which grows
in the waiting-rooms of the stations."[1]

V

Having finished with the recent symptom of decadence in
a military empire, the dissolution of the bureaucracy, we will
now consider the third : the mania for persecution. When a
great man is at the head of a decaying state, the gravity of the

[1] Kesuin Bey, *op. cit.*, p. 59.

danger may rouse him up to heroic defence. But it is almost an historical law that for every sovereign of superior mind and heart, there are always ten weak, inane, and selfish ones. Now, only very superior minds are able to maintain their balance in face of serious peril ; weaker ones are often roused to great egoism by fear. Fear has the most possible influence on a weak character ; it frequently happens that men, not bad by nature, but merely weak and stupid, are led under its sway to acts of cruelty which the most inhuman of tyrants would not have committed.

Such is the state of things prevailing in the royal palace at Constantinople. Abdul Hamid, according to those who have known him, is a weak and consequently selfish man rather than a downright bad one, whose natural egoism has been increased by the life of unbounded pleasure which a man in his condition is almost forced to live ; he is a man in whom the instinct of self-preservation is so strong as to raise in him at times paroxysms of fear and outbursts of fury, vain fears and mad rages. His counsellors, the better part of whom are astute and cunning, but currupt, greedy and ambitious, instead of trying to correct these painful terrors in their lord, make use of them to augment their authority. " The imagination of the courtiers," writes Kesuin, " never wearies of inventing new alarms and plots, and of multiplying espionage. Even the great men of the empire are not insured against these calumnies. . . . Such and such a pasha is growing too powerful ; . . . another has relations with Europeans ; . . . a third receives papers from Paris, the hot-bed of universal socialism. . . . By means of these alarms they succeed in keeping the Sultan in a continual state of factitious excitement, which paralyzes him for any good." [1]

[1] Kesuin Bey, p. 91.

Thus to the Sultan's ears the buzzing of a fly sounds as formidable as the crash of an earthquake.

What a torment such an existence of terror must be ! Only Shakespeare, perhaps, could adequately describe it. The Sultan lives at Yeldiz Kiosk, in a monumental palace resembling a rock surrounded by granite ramparts, guarded by huge barracks, in which reside an army ready at any moment to rush to the assistance of their master. And yet in the heart of his fortress, protected by an army, the Sultan trembles night and day ; and in company with his friends he constantly plans new schemes of defence, now violent and tragical, now puerile and absurd. Thousands of spies swarm everywhere in Constantinople. All importation of explosives is prohibited by the Government, so that the peasant cannot even buy sulphide of carbon to protect their vines from phylloxera. Telephones are prohibited, so frequently are fireworks. Some years ago, in consequence of the Sultan receiving several threatening letters posted in Constantinople, the internal post of the town was completely prohibited. The Sultan scarcely ever dares leave his palace on the *plateau* of the Yeldiz ; but even so, he does not escape the torments of fear. Yeldiz, a few years ago, was still a solitude overrun by weeds on which a royal, and many other superb, palaces, were erected, thanks to the water conveyed there by means of an aqueduct constructed by a French company. But this company risked having to abandon the work, and being ruined, because a zealous functionary insinuated to Abdul Hamid that his enemies would be able to use it as a mine in order to secrete dynamite. The Sultan, terrified like a child at this idea, ordered the immediate suspension of the work, and nominated a commission to inquire into the facts of the case. The commission, composed of high court officials, made an examination, and, thanks to the astute corruption of the society, concluded that there was no danger.

A trifling anecdote, but one which reveals well the mental state prevailing at the Turkish Court, determining the internal politics of the Ottoman Empire in its minor acts, no less than in those infinitely tragical episodes known to us as the Armenian atrocities that horrified Europe during the last few years. The Sultan and his environment constantly see the sovereign's life and the welfare of the empire threatened by internal foes. To defend themselves from these, they multiply cruel and futile persecutions, and, while neglecting all real dangers, create new ones for the State.

One of the worst forms taken by this oppression is seen when a province, considered tainted with dangerous agitation, passes from the Ministerial Government to that of the Sultan. The provinces are governed in ordinary times by the Sultan's ministers, to whom he delegates his power. But it does not appear that he places much confidence in his representatives, possibly because he has learnt from his country's history that all former plots against his predecessors were originated by their ministers. Consequently when the Sultan is more than usually disquiet, he orders that some province, which appears to him in an exceptionally threatening state, should be placed under his direct supervision. From that moment only those orders which come straight from the palace are valid, and the officials act under the Sultan's direct orders, and to them any complaint against the functionaries must be directed. It can easily be understood how, under these circumstances, any control over the officials, however feeble, is lost, how the law forfeits even the small influence it boasts in normal times, while the people are entirely abandoned to the caprice of unscrupulous bureaucrats. For instance: the police arrest a man as a suspect, or as being concerned in a political offence. The provincial court before which he is brought absolves him, but the police keep him in prison as long as they choose, because he is considered to be imprisoned by the Sultan's orders, so that no provincial court has power to order his release. The complaints of the victim never reach the Sultan, who, after throwing thousands of families on the mercy of a tyrannical and unscrupulous administration, abandons them to their fate, callous to the injustices and iniquities committed in his name, and satisfied with the thought that he has thus averted an imminent peril from his throne.

VI

Arrests *en masse*, the secret execution of suspects and those accused of conspiracy, the Government of terror, in short, as arbitrary and ferocious as it can be in a country like Turkey, such are the tactics of this oligarchy of madmen and scoundrels. These oppressions are the work of the bureaucracy; but besides these, there is another infamy in which the whole Mussulman population is accomplice. I allude to the Armenian massacres, whose consideration leads us to the study of the fourth phenomenon of Turkish decadence.

The " Armenian atrocities " have been very widely discussed during these last years. The European press had described its most terrible episodes, and the general opinion seems to be that their sole cause lay in the innate brutality of the Turkish population. And yet even Turkish ferocity is not without some incentive, motive, or at least excuse : even a Turk, unspeakable as he is, does not amuse himself by wallowing in Christian blood as a mere pastime. The Armenian

massacres are not merely a new chapter in the history of
fanaticism, a religious war ; they are the convulsions of a dying
nation, a last desperate and ferocious struggle between two
societies, embittered by all degrees of cruelty ranging from
fanaticism to greed.

The Armenian crisis is connected with a phenomenon
common to the decadence of all military empires : usury.
The usurer, that shady character who in modern times has
degenerated into the hidden accomplice of the dissipated sons
of rich families, used to be an historical force, and he fulfilled
at certain moments the solemn and terrible office of social
executioner to a corrupt society.

This is now happening in Turkey. The bureaucracy, drawn
for the most part from the Mussulman population, lives on
what it can extort from the workers, and, though forming the
highest class in Turkish society, is by no means rich. If we
except the high State dignitaries, the majority of the officials
live poorly, are badly paid, and display no aptitude to save.
The economy of a family of Turkish functionaries, whether
situated high or low in the hierarchy, is as follows : When
there is money, to spend it recklessly ; when funds are low, to
live as circumstances best permit. To save or accumulate
are two things of which a Turkish functionary is incapable.
Thus no one knows how to make use of those strokes of
fortune which, in the midst of such general administrative
chaos, befall many officials, and which would enable him to
put by a little store. Everything is rapidly dissipated in
luxuries, presents, and generosities, because a well-to-do Turk
is fond of spending liberally, not only for his own satisfaction,
but for that of others. A little pleasure which a Turk with
some money to throw away always allows himself, is that of
buying small loaves to distribute among the innumerable

dogs which haunt the streets of Constantinople. A great part of the bureaucracy live in very straitened circumstances, enlivened occasionally by some orgy or dissipation, the result of some more than commonly generous bribe.

The Armenian, on the contrary, who has abandoned his native plains and mountains because unable to cultivate them, is an industrious man of business, gifted with sobriety, providence, and those miserly habits which go to build up large fortunes. Whilst the Turk spends, the Armenian hoards; a conflict ensues between the pair, in which the former represents need and the latter money, arms, and usury. The Armenian merchant in large Turkish towns is generally by necessity a usurer, whether on a larger or smaller scale, whether avowed or dissimulated. The Turkish Government, by administrative depredations, systematically reduces the wealth of society and contracts to the minimum the productive investment of capital; it discourages any industrial enterprise by heavy taxation; it renders commerce impossible by the utter neglect of public works in the provinces. Under these conditions the Armenian's capital, which in a more industrious and productive society would be accumulated in banks and help to develop the immense latent natural wealth of the empire, has to seek a usurious investment, which, owing to the indolent habits of the Turkish population, proves far more profitable than any industrial or seriously productive speculation.

To illustrate how far the Armenian, in his character as money-lender, aids in the dissolution of Turkish society, and fattens and prospers on its ruin, as the bacilli of phthisis flourish by the slow death of the being upon whom they live, it suffices to cite a single one of these usurious speculations, which, in the Ottoman Empire, are a purely Armenian monopoly.

This is the speculation of the *seraf*, or money-changer.
·We have seen that the Turkish civil and military officials
rarely receive more than one month's salary in the course of a
year. It might therefore be supposed that the Turkish army,
administrated with such a rigorous system of economy, would
cost but little to the Government. And yet the Turkish army
costs as much in proportion as any other European regularly
paid force, because the Turkish Government disburses, however tardily, the sum fixed for the salary of its officials ;
but the greater part of this sum, instead of reaching these
officials, finishes in the hands of the rich Armenian *serafs*.

Here is the strange administrative process through which
this is accomplished. The Turkish functionary who is
embarrassed and has saved nothing, and who is consequently
in need of money every month to send to his family, sells the
payment-orders for his salary to a rich Armenian *seraf*, who
buys it at a rebate of 60 or 80 per cent. When he has bought
for £800 or £1000 several payment-orders to the value of
£4000, he goes to the minister on whom the functionaries
depend—to the Minister of War if he has been dealing with
officers—where he has friends in the highest ranks, and by
the distribution of bribes he manages to get his orders
paid at a reduction of 20 or 25 per cent., thus making
an enormous profit out of the transaction. Thanks to this
state of things, a large part of the revenue goes to enrich
Armenian speculators and the ministers in league with
them, and together they manage to make money out of the
universal ruin of the Turkish Empire. They find, indeed, that
there is so much to be made out of this business that they do
their best to prolong the conditions which render it possible :
the delay in payment. It oftens happens that the treasury
has money in hand to pay the salaries punctually, but the

ministers delay just the same in order to force the poor officials to treat with the Armenian usurers, who later on give them their share of the profits. If to-morrow a reforming Sultan wished to re-establish punctuality in the payment of functionaries, he would be met with violent opposition, more especially on the part of the higher dignitaries.

This is a typical example, but the entire commerce of the Armenians is of this order—usury exercised on the careless and indolent Turkish population. An improvident Turkish peasant finds himself in need of funds. An Armenian merchant from the neighbouring village will lend him money at an exhorbitant rate of interest, for which the Turk always has to deliver the better part of his harvest to the Armenian. An official, after a brief period of good luck, finds himself forced to sell his furniture and jewellery. An Armenian immediately turns up to buy them for a mere nothing. In every conceivable manner, in short, the Armenians accumulate capital in their hands, withdraw it from circulation, hide it away as a reserve, and employ it, not to enrich society, but to expropriate the population by usury, collaborating with the higher functionaries to produce that stagnation of wealth which, by slow degrees, is disorganizing and ruining the Turkish nation.

Putrefaction is the laboratory of life, said Karl Marx. Now, putrefaction is the work of microbes, who are thus life's most active agents, because death is a necessary condition prior to life. The Armenian usurer is a microbe of putrefaction, the most active agent of the decay which, by degrees, destroys the corrupt body of the Turkish nation, and prepares, by dissolution, the materials for a new and better society.

VII

The financial power of a small group of Armenian usurers is, moreover, only the expression of a more general pheno- menon : a continual increase in the number of Christians in the Turkish Empire. Masters as they are of commerce, more capable of capitalizing, exempt from military service, and therefore from war, they multiply and constantly increase their social power, under cover of the humble servility of subjects. They exploit the poverty of the poor and the vices of the rich ; in a certain sense they keep the executive under their thumb, preying on the salaries of the lower officials, dividing the spoils of their villainy with the highest, who thus become their accomplices. They are contractors to the Government, and can teach both Turks and Europeans a thing or two in the matter of fraud, thus working towards the ruin of the Ottoman Empire more effectually than any army.

They do not derive this power from the fact of being Christians, but from having exercised certain qualities under oppression and in servitude—stinginess, industry, and thrift ; from having excelled in ingenuity and cunning ; from their Job-like patience ; from having lost, moreover, in the course of their terrible struggle with their oppressors, the last vestige of moral scruple. The Turk, on the contrary, is always liberal, improvident, and idle, and, when he has not been demoralized by bureaucratic life, is a simple and good-natured man. He only wishes to be priest, soldier, official, and agriculturist because he naturally prefers repose and pleasure to work. As agriculturist he confides in the benignity of his land ; in the character of official he smokes and idles in his office ; as priest or soldier he snoozes in his mosque or barrack. Thus the power acquired by the Christians is merely the victory of ingenious energy and greed over indolent thriftlessness ; a victory which was inevitable, and which no human power could prevent, as nothing can prevent the fine point of a diamond penetrating the softer rocks.

This tyrannical military bureaucracy, in the midst of its slow consuming disease, is subject to attacks of fury, during which it thinks to save itself by resorting to the prime instrument of its power : force. It is difficult to imagine the state of mind in which a Turk finds himself when watching nearly his whole salary disappearing into the safes of a rich Armenian banker—this interested assistant of his misery. Everything induces him to regard the Christian as his enemy and exploiter, the cause of his poverty. And since hatred is the most communicative human sentiment, and the one most easily generalized, hatred against the Armenian usurer, by a very common psychological process, of which history affords many examples, easily develops into hatred of Armenians and Christians in general ; not only of the city Armenian merchant, but also of the Armenian peasant in Armenia—a poor wretched being dragging out a miserable existence, who neither enjoys nor, frequently, knows anything of the wealth accumulated by his lucky compatriots in distant towns. Thus, through fear and the spirit of imitation and solidarity which exists in evil, this hatred passes from the bureaucracy, the principal victim of Christian usury, to the whole Mussulman and Turkish-speaking population : it becomes a national and religious hatred.

This does not explain, however, why this hatred has expressed itself of late years in periodical massacres, almost overtly the work of the Government, and perpetrated with the sanction of the authorities. It appears that this fearful

tragedy is due to the encounter between the popular Mussulman hatred—embittered by the sufferings of which they are
the victim—with the sanguinary mysticism of the man who
is now Sultan and Chief of the Faithful.

Abdul Hamid is not the frivolous, indolent sultan, cruel at
moments through the impulse of passing caprice, so frequently
met with in Islam history. Unusual as it may appear in
a Turk, he is a methodical and highly persistent worker ; a
most diligent administrator of his own wealth, who both
accumulates and spends freely. Always shrewd, and with
a distinct object in view, he supervises and controls every
detail. He is a tyrant whose cruelty is not impulsive but
reflective, arising, not from passing caprices of mood, but
from well-considered and matured determination. This man,
however, who has the solid temperament of a merchant, is
governed at the same time by the demoniacal power of a
mystical and atrocious dream, through which he has yielded
to the fascination exercised by great violence over the
imagination. This dream is not exclusively his own. Many
years ago a governor of Aleppo, desirous of ingratiating himself with the Sultan, sent him some rare gifts chosen among
the most precious Syrian curiosities : otto of roses, ostrich
feathers, exquisite coffee. To this he wished to add a still
more *bizarre* curiosity : a dervish (a species of Mussulman
monk, addicted to mystical practices) of the name of Abul
Huda, who lived in Aleppo as astrologer, prophet, miracle-
worker, and preacher.

Shortly after his introduction to the Court, the Aleppo
mendicant held the keys of the Sultan's heart ; he became
more than the sovereign's friend ; he was the master of his
mind, already so well prepared for the seductions of gigantic
pan-Islamistic schemes, through the education received at

the hands of the Cadrish dervishes, who had habituated him to lengthy meditation on Mussulman greatness. Abul Huda tempted and mastered that proud and fantastical man, metaphorically raising him by the magic of his ardent mysticism to immense heights of imaginary greatness, informing him that one of the greatest kingdoms ever offered to man lay at his feet, that the infinite multitude of Mahomet's disciples, reunited and animated by a pan-Islamite propaganda, were prepared to worship him as the head of Islam, restored as in the grand times of Omar. The poor astronomer told the sovereign that the stars had destined him to be the greatest of caliphs ; he persuaded him to use his treasures for the pan-Islamite propaganda fanned by the Senussi, of which he was a member, a society which tried to rouse in Mussulmans, all the world over, from Sudin to Africa, an ardent fanaticism.

Overcome by giddiness, on the edge of the abyss of greatness to which the magician had transported him, Abdul Hamid persuaded himself that he was the champion of pan-Islamism. "The bed-rock desire of this man," writes the anonymous author of an article in the *Revue des Revues*,[1] " so modern in his business dealings but who spiritually lives in the seventh century, is that of reconstructing the Mussulman Empire as it was in the age of Omar—an empire, that is to say, divided into two classes : the believers, who form the government and army, and the *rahai* (plebs) who by *manual* work maintain the former in luxury. . . . The *rahai* can rise from their servile state by becoming Mussulmans, but if they

---

[1] " Le Matre et les serviteurs d'Yeldiz " (*Revue des Revues*, 15th August, 1st September, 1897). These two articles, published anonymously by a man who must be well acquainted with Turks and their ways, are a vivid picture of the Turkish court.

L

attempt to raise themselves on their own account by their own effort . . . they must be crushed down by massacre."

The Armenian massacres appear to have sprung from this political conception, matured by Abul Huda and communicated by him to the Sultan. Abul Huda, indeed, at Trebisonde, personally recruited and maintained the emissaries charged with preaching massacre in the Armenian districts. The Armenians are the most numerous and powerful Christian population inhabiting Turkey, taking a first rank as regards number, tenacity, and fortune. Thus the victims of the sanguinary attempt of the Aleppo beggar, and his slave and lord, were directed against those who, being absolute subjects, were more defenceless than other Christian populations, such as the Greeks, who are protected by special international treaties. The Armenian massacres are the execution of a political programme, whose object is brutally to thrust back into the degradation and poverty, from which they escaped by patience and ingenuity, a people who, in the midst of Turkish decadence, grows every day more powerful, to cow them by the terror of slaughter, and impoverish them by systematic robbery. To effect this work, the emperor has summoned as chief collaborator a sanguinary brute, Nazem Pasha—the son of a Kurdish brigand and a Syrian mother—who, having inherited his father's instincts, was best suited to the post he now occupies as head of the police. Nazem organized two years ago the terrible massacres in Constantinople that lasted three days, during which he accumulated £160,000 worth of booty : spoils found in the ransacked shops and on 12,000 Armenian corpses. He has made an instrument of the police by which to receive by force from the Armenians the money they had extracted by cunning from the Turks. Armenian merchants, professional men, and artisans are

arrested by the thousand every year, and kept in prison until
the police have succeeded, by various means, in extorting
from them all they possess : then they are sent back into the
world as poor as when they entered it.

Fearful convulsions of a dying society ! Abdul Hamid and
this Aleppian have been able to conceive and perpetrate
these horrible things because they happen to have been born
in the decline of the Ottoman Empire. They are the expression of a social necessity, the impersonification of an
epoch in history ; of the epoch in which a nation of believers
feels that its power, established by arms, is giving way, and
attempts to rebuild it by multiplying violences ; a society
which feels that European civilization is threatening it, and
turns recklessly back to the past which gave it birth.

For this reason the man whom Gladstone named " the
great assassin," will long live in the memory of the faithful ;
he will be regarded by them as the last hero of Islamism, the
worthy descendant of the great Caliphs, who attempted to
preserve by the sword what his predecessors had conquered
by the sword. The European philosopher, on the contrary,
sees in this tardy saviour of I slam and in his counsellor, who
let loose in Turkish society the extreme violence of fanaticism, two terrible agents of dissolution. To burn, plunder,
and massacre, all signify to *destroy*, and it is not by destruction and ruin that a decaying nation can be reconstituted.
As the writer in the *Revue des Revues* says : " Such a *regime*
necessarily leads to anarchy. The Oriental Empire might or
might not be a harmonious combination of Mussulmans and
Christians. The oppression of the Christians re-kindled the
religious war, the death of 300,000 Armenians ruined
commerce, industry, and agriculture. The official sanction
of theft, espionage, and the sale of Government appointments,

has broken all social bonds between individuals. All the conditions necessary to the maintainance of a state have ceased to exist. Nothing remains but armies ; when these are crushed by a Christian power, Turkey must perish. If they continue to conquer, the present anarchy will increase."

This means that Turkey will continue to live in the midst of fanatic convulsions and violence, of massacres and atrocious hatreds ; wealth will diminish, administrative disorder will increase ; the small remains of Christian honesty will perish with all that survives of Mussulman good sense ; the earth will daily grow more niggardly, and men will be decimated by natural and social scourges : famines, epidemics, earthquakes, chronic misery, wars, murder, rapine, madness, and the spread of unnatural vices. No human power will be able to stay this inevitable chastisement, and then the Sultan's conduct will be revealed in all its senseless folly. He tries, by multiplying outrages, to re-animate the worn-out vanity of the Mussulman empire ; but in vain. The sacrifice of human blood cannot give life to dead things, as certain barbarous superstitions suppose ; the Turkish crisis, born of the fundamental vices inherent in Mussulman and ancient societies, will end in the extermination of a people. When the Turks shall have succeeded in extirpating the Armenians, will they be freed from the financial oppression of a more ingenious and industrious people, will they be able to acquire and preserve a social superiority which is beyond them ? The place of the Armenians will be filled by the Greeks ; the Greeks exterminated, the Germans and English will step in, because wherever in a society that has few productive investments there exists a class of rich merchants beside a parasitical and indolent bureaucracy, the former will always rule and exploit the latter.

VIII

" Quam brevis est risus quam longa est lacryma mundi ! "
Thus wrote an English copyist of the fourteenth century on
a manuscript of the *Magna Charta*, preserved in the National
Library of Turin. The Turkish crisis, which originated in
the stagnation of capital, the decay of agriculture, and depopulation, is similar in its general features to all crisis
that periodically tormented and ruined ancient societies, and
especially those founded on hatred of work, simplicity of life,
and ignorance. The Turkish crisis is terrible because that,
thanks to the almost universal state of peace, it may last
a very long time ; it may resemble a slow disease, which
does not kill its victim, but allows him to drag out a
miserable and stunted existence. If the end of the nineteenth
century were an era of great and frequent wars, the Turkish
Empire might be destroyed by some younger state whose
Government was more civilized. This would possess itself
of the Sultan's treasures and the wealth of the mosques in
order to repair streets and bridges, to improve the executive ;
in short, to give fresh life to the dying state. Asia Minor,
indeed all the Turkish territories, suffer from the lack of war
and the absence of conquering nations. They are perishing
because peace abandons them to the gradual aggravation of
the ill-being, from which they suffer, without any hope of
a probable recovery. Left to its own devices, there is no
future for this nation ; the Christians will not destroy the
Mussulmans, nor the Mussulmans the Christians, and so long
as the Mussulmans are in command, Turkey will remain
what it is : poor, simple, idle, conservative in habits, the prey
of usurers and powerful pashas. European civilization will

be unable to penetrate. Only a war, by abolishing the oligarchy now in power and substituting another more desirous of progress and civilization, could remedy the present evils and rehabilitate that portion of Asia in the history of the world.

We shall see, in the following pages, that frequent wars would be a great impediment to the progress of European civilization. Turkey, on the contrary, is slowly decaying owing to the long peace which now reigns over such a large portion of the world. This fact demonstrates the main difference that exists between Christian and Mussulman civilization, which is at the same time the essential difference between the modern and the ancient. Without war, ancient civilization could not have existed, the Iliad would never have been composed, Plato would not have philosophized, the Roman jurisconsults would not have elaborated the law. We shall see that modern society, on the other hand, would be destroyed by war.

NAPOLEON AND HIS WARS

CHAPTER VI

I

ON the threshold of this century stands a figure of colossal grandeur: Napoleon. He is certainly the man of our age about whom most has been said, written, and investigated. Many believe him to be the greatest personage of the century, and attribute to him the miracle of having created much out of nothing—the victories of his armies, his own extraordinary career, the glory, power, and wealth of France, the end of the feudal system, the inauguration of a liberal movement in every European state.

Napoleon is certainly the greatest problem which presents itself to him who would study the causes and functions of war in this century. Was he in reality the greatest man of our times, the last of the great? Does his career resemble those of the warriors of old? and was he, by the power of his works, an Alexander or a Cæsar?

None would deny that he was a man of genius; but that his importance raised him to the rank of a demi-god, I do not believe. He possessed great gifts and energy; but chance led him to perform a vaster work than that which he had consciously intended, nor were there wanting in his character many weaknesses and a terrible lack of balance. He resembles too closely a great barbarian, Attila, to be the greatest man of the nineteenth century. In fact, between the two warriors, Attila, as described by the historian Priscus, who saw and spoke to him, and Napoleon, described by the many who knew him, there is a curious resemblance ; that is to say, they resemble each other in their personal character as men, not for the part they took in history. They are alike because the fundamental trait in their characters is the same : selfish and unmeasured pride, an inextinguishable thirst for eminence, an insatiable desire for superiority and dominion over their fellow-men. As the central nerve branches out in a leaf and sustains the whole structure connecting the various parts, so in every human character one single sentiment connects various qualities, and stamps the man. Pride was the backbone of these two characters. Thus these two leaves which grew on the tree of life at such very different epochs, and under conditions so diverse, almost seem to belong to the same year. Wrathfulness was common to them both, violence and insolence of manner, as well as the desire to domineer over other men, more especially by ill-treating them, sometimes with genuine anger, sometimes with feigned. Napoleon's rages were of terrific violence. On one occasion, for instance, he kicked the Senator Volney in the abdomen ; at Campo-formio, impatient of the delay of an Austrian ambassador, he smashed a porcelain vase of great value. When in anger, he behaved with extraordinary brutality towards dependants, whether simple servants, clerks, or the highest functionaries, and at such moments he was wont to give such extravagant commands, that his *entourage* were at a loss to know how to induce him to withdraw them. This irascibility—in part assumed—he preserved even in his relations with the punctilious diplomatic world. During a treaty at Dresden, in 1813, when his power was already on the decline, he brutally

asked Metternich how much he had been paid by England
to play his part. At Wilna, in 1812, whilst in conversation
with the Russian envoy, Belatcheff, he abused Alexander's
counsellors, calling them the worst names he could think of—
vauriens, debauchees, and *viles personnes*.

Now it is curious to read in Priscus, that Attila's diplomacy
was equal to Napoleon's for ceremony. The embassy to
which Priscus belonged wished to negotiate with Attila about
the Hun deserters, whom the emperor declared to have all
returned, but of whom Attila maintained that many still
remained in the Roman's power, which matter seemed to
highly irritate the Hun king, to judge from the manner in
which he received the ambassadors. When these had saluted
him with the greatest deference, "May all that the Romans
wish me, befall them," answered Attila, and turning to Vigilus,
the head of the embassy, he called him an impudent fool,
asked him how he had dared come before him, knowing as he
did what the terms of the peace were when he accompanied
the preceding embassy from Anatolius ; and added that no
other ambassador would have dared to make his appearance
before all the hostages had been returned. Vigilus attempted
to make some reply ; but Attila, growing more and more
enraged, loaded him with abuse, and, howling with fury, told
him that it was only thanks to his quality of ambassador that
he refrained from crucifying him.

As anger and violence were common to the two men, so
also were obstinacy of ideas, insufferance of advice, the desire
to be surrounded by mental dwarfs reaching no higher than
their knees. Priscus recounts a conversation held with the
members of another embassy, sent this time by the western
emperor, who for a long while had tried to persuade Attila to
renounce certain of his absurd pretensions. He asked them

whether they had any hope of success. " No," they answered ;
" it is impossible to make Attila change his mind." And
Romolo, one of the ambassadors, added, " Fortune has given
him a great empire, and he has become so proud in consequence that good counsel no longer has any influence with
him, so that he only believes his own caprices to be right."

Fourteen centuries later Chaptel repeated nearly the same
words, in speaking of the Attila of the nineteenth century.
" From the moment that he had formed some idea on political
matters, whether right or wrong, Napoleon consulted no one.
He wished for servants, not counsellors." And Mollien
added, " Napoleon considered himself as a superior being,
created to govern and direct every one according to his
own ideas."

This similitude can be observed also in small details which
might appear valueless to too serious a psychologist.   One of
the ways in which proud spirits seek to satisfy their ambition,
is by despising all that is prized by others.   By remaining
unmoved by what is generally sought after, a man displays
an essential difference from his fellows ; he flatters himself
that he shows himself superior to the common horde.   This
is the reason why the nobility always affects contempt and
scepticism, and consider it vulgar to enthuse too much, even
over anything well meriting enthusiasm.

Napoleon, partly by nature and partly by affectation, was
a past-master in the art of magnifying himself in the public
eye by paying no attention to what most men loved.   His
face always appeared absorbed and impassive to the public ;
it was difficult to amuse or distract him at theatres ; he was
bored and yawned at court fêtes, and at Fontainebleau he
appeared abstracted, a colossal being whose head reached the
clouds, and whose thoughts were intent on other things far

removed from the little men who grovelled at his feet. He
spoke little, as though fearing to appear too familiar. On one
occasion at Saint Cloud, in the midst of a distinguished circle
of gentlemen, Varnagen heard him repeat some twenty times
this single phrase : "It is hot." So that the court was "silent
and cold," as Madame de Renuisat put it; adding picturesquely,
"Both intentionally and by inclination he never relaxes from
his royalty."

Attila also was of a nature that "never relaxed from his
royalty," not even in the midst of the barbaric freedom of
court banquets. Priscus recounts a solemn feast which the
ambassadors attended. After the dinner two bards sung war-
songs, which moved the auditors to tears ; then a fool cracked
a lot of jokes and comicalities which made every one laugh ; a
Moor made a long discourse in a mixture of Latin, Gothic,
and Hun. But in the midst of all this merriment "Attila
alone," writes Priscus, "preserved always the same counte-
nance. He remained grave and immovable ; he did and said
nothing to reveal the slightest desire to laugh or amuse
himself. Only when they brought him his youngest son,
Irnach, did he look at him affectionately and pat his
cheek."

Again, in speaking of this official banquet, Priscus gives
another curious particular : that Attila distinguished himself
from the others, not only by the gravity of his manner, but
also by his sobriety in eating and simplicity in dress.
Amongst all the court magnates, he was the most moderate
eater, and donned the simplest attire. "He had prepared for
the barbarians and for us," writes Priscus, "all manner of
viands, which were served on silver platters, but Attila ate
nothing but meat on a wooden dish. He displayed great
simplicity in everything. Whilst the guests drank out of gold

and silver bowls, Attila used a wooden mug ; his clothes were simplicity itself, and distinguishable from those of the other barbarians by being of one colour and without ornaments ; his sword, his shoe-laces, the reins of his horse, nothing about him was adorned with gold and precious jewels as in the other Scythians.

Even in this simplicity of taste Napoleon and Attila were alike. Napoleon always dressed unobtrusively, like a fairly well-to-do officer, without displaying any of those showy ornaments which amongst soldiers are still in favour. It is a known fact, moreover, that he was wont to chaff Murat on his pompous clothing, on his plumes, decorations, damascened weapons, for his love of glitter.

II

Simplicity and pride : an apparent contradiction by which we must not allow ourselves to be deceived. This external modesty is only the surpreme form of pride, which, in its most intense degree, finds no other satisfaction than in the contempt of the outward attributes of power. Attila and Napoleon despised display because they believed themselves to be, and wished to appear, so infinitely superior to the rest of humanity as to have no need to excite admiration and respect by all those material vanities whereby mediocre men attract attention.

Thus Napoleon's chief characteristic was pride : the pride of an Oriental sovereign, of an Assyrian king. But whence did Napoleon derive this pride, and how did he nourish it? In part it was certainly innate. A military conqueror is always a man born to command others. We already find germs of this pride in the young officer who, poor and obscure, dreamed of offering his services to the Sultan to undertake great Oriental wars ; the vague romanticism of an active and ambitious spirit, in which the insatiable avidity for greatness that was to torment him all his life, was fermenting. But only the first grandiose and unexpected successes of his Italian campaign gave form to these vague, ambitious dreams ; converting these youthful fantasies of future might into a virile pride, conscious and unlimited. Napoleon himself confessed that the flame of his ambition burst forth after the battle of Lodi ; that before then he only thought of becoming a fortunate soldier. After it, "the idea struck me," he himself writes, "that I might become an important actor on the scene of politics."

This psychological phenomenon, moreover, is so simple that it does not demand elaborate explanations. None of the men whom fortune has raised to the summit of power have ever begun their career without entertaining wild shapeless hopes ; none of them have been gifted from the beginning with the superhuman lucidity of foresight and self-confidence necessary to specify exactly the degree of greatness to which they would attain, nor the exact date for the said elevation. The youth destined to become the boldest and most self-confident of men is easily discouraged ; he vaguely mistrusts himself, as can be observed in the indecision of his ambitious dreams. Notwithstanding his extraordinary latent force of character, Napoleon, still young and obscure, had not the courage to believe what turned out to be the truth : that he should become the general of a conquering army at twenty-six years of age ; he scarcely ever dared to dream that one day he would be a great Oriental warrior, perhaps the head of one of those distant empires. Maturity of character cannot be measured by the extent but by the precision of its ambition, hence the young officer who dreamed of distant glory whilst walking the streets of Paris had to experience victory before his ambition could conceive the plan of making himself master of Europe and crowning himself emperor.

Victory was necessary to give shape to the ambition of one who was already inclined to consider himself made of other clay than that of the common mass of humanity, and well-established good luck to definitely persuade him that he was a unique man, destined to succeed in everything, and to rule mankind. Men are so easily overcome by the intoxication of power : how could this man, so proud by nature, resist, when raised to immense Himalayan heights, from which he could see half the world at his feet and nothing but the heavens above his head ? But if war roused Napoleon's innate pride into madness, pride rendered his passion for war still acuter. The pleasures of pride are perfidious, the more we drink the thirstier we grow, till we can drown even our reason without finding satisfaction. As the mental and physical vigour of the general who had fought the Italian campaign declined, Napoleon's desire to re-taste the violent emotions of victory, to re-animate in himself the inebriating consciousness of his superiority, increased—little matters it whether this be in part illusive—the immensity of his power, which had no other limit than in his own will and in the materiality of things, not in the will of other men.

III

But as Napoleon's faculties got more and more absorbed by war, and as his pride by degrees increased, we observe a transformation in his intelligence, wherein lies one of the most curious phenomenon in his history.

Every man who lives in society, and has friendly or hostile
relations with his fellows, should be capable of understanding
external life, of comprehending men and the world in which
he lives and moves ; more particularly if his relations with
others are close or difficult. Now the chief phenomenon in
the moral history of Napoleon, that to which the principal
events of his life are attributable, and on which the political
history of Europe for fifteen years depended, is this : that by
degrees, as he advanced in years, the work of war absorbed
and exhausted him ; as his pride fed by victory grew more
extravagant, he progressively lost count of the realities of life,
until in the end he became involved in a world of imaginary
chimeras.

Napoleon's intelligence possessed from the beginning a
great quality and a great defect : extraordinarily active as it
was, capable of immense efforts of prodigious variety, it was
much less capable of perseverance and continuous effort.
This explains why he was such a great general and such a
poor politician. Taine has splendidly analyzed the prime
quality of Napoleon's intellect : the unmeasured *ensemble* of
such diverse things which he could conceive in a single
thought ; the lucidity with which he perceived the minutest
details in a moment. This quality made him a great leader
in his early years, when his mind was still fresh, because of
his facility to realize, with precision of detail, those minutiæ
which a general, directing the operations of a campaign,
has to keep in mind. But he possessed in a very minor
degree the genius for slow synthetic creation ; the capacity
to understand a complex matter in its aggregate by studying
its particulars one by one, by a persevering and patient effort
of mind to reconstruct the whole body, so to speak, from its
separate parts. Thus, for instance, although he had so long

M

inhabited Europe, known so many people and dealt with so many states, Napoleon never succeeded in forming a precise idea of the social conditions of European countries, in attaining a deeper understanding of the various European nations, of their latent forces, of what was maturing in each. This can be clearly perceived from the triviality and superficiality of many of his expressed political opinions, and which for the most part are mere journalist's phrases, paradoxical crackers let off by a man who always desired to astound his fellows, even when enunciating a political judgment ; such as when he said, " Constantinople is the capital of the world," and " Europe in a century will be all republican or all Cossack." Napoleon never really foresaw what would follow after his death : the end of the chronic wars of invasion ; the application of the energies formerly expended on war to home interests, and the development of trade ; in short, the apotheosis of the bourgeoisie. He believed—and the most curious proof of this is to be found in the conversation he held with Lord Ebrington in the Island of Elba—that nations would continue to wage war with one another through ambition for rule and rivalry for glory. For this reason he aimed so earnestly at creating a new nobility in France, founded on the remains of the old, because " I felt," he says, " that France was in need of an aristocracy." He felt this great need—so lacking was he in the historical sense—on the eve of an era when the aristocracy, as such, was to lose in all Europe, but more particularly in France, all social importance. This man who had a lynx's eye in war, was blind in social life.

Napoleon's intellect, in short, was of the flashy order, not of those which cast a steady and continuous light on everything. His intellect was rather intuitive than reflective ; his mind understood in a flash or misunderstood, penetrating the truth all at once or understanding nothing at all.

Now this is the intellectual temperament which renders difficult the maintenance of that just equilibrium between ideas and external truth, in which reason consists. It is true that the intellectual energy and will of Napoleon was such that, despite this defect, he might have reached a deep comprehension of life, repressing by an energetic effort of will the caprices of his imagination, disciplining his natural impulsiveness. He would then have become one of that class of great thinkers and artists to whom Shakespeare and Hegel belong. But for this he would have needed the peace of a quiet life, the long and severe discipline of methodical work. War, on the contrary, by distracting attention with a thousand hurried cares, gradually increased the fundamental defect in his character. War acted on Napoleon's intelligence in much the same way as journalism acts on that of many writers: it exercised many of his qualities up to a certain point—his rapidity of ideas, for instance, the precision in his perception of details, his withstanding intense work, his capacity for great efforts; but it tired him out at the same time, it diminished his capacity for self-concentration, and for labour which demands deliberation. Intuition is the essence of genius; but in some it remains in its native rawness, while others refine it by education and discipline. Such is the genius of Darwin, Goethe, Stein, and Julius Cæsar, to whom we owe great and lasting creations, who, having received the intuitive revelation of genius, did not give their ideas to the world in their first crudity, but refined and tempered them. But for this to be possible one must be capable of long brooding over an idea without growing weary, nourishing it like a fœtus, with one's own blood—a tremendous effort, to which many keenly intuitive intellects succumb. This faculty can only be acquired by sustained effort in view of one single object. Napoleon was a genius by nature, so intuitive as to be absolutely impulsive ; how could war discipline this extraordinary being ? War, by diverting the mind to a thousand different objects which demand rapid solutions, could only increase this defect, and thus could only leave the most powerful of geniuses in a crude state, rather than facilitate the refinement due to slow reflection. Indeed Napoleon, in the course of his agitated career, always occupied with transitory details, lost this capacity for synthetic creation by continuous effort, which alone creates the enduring in politics and art. He acquired the habit of rapid conception. Even in his political relations we see the man of the camp, satisfied with resolving every difficulty in a superficial way, content with the hand-to-mouth policy, consequently he became every day more unfit to realize the ultimate consequence of things, and therefore to act coherently. From this arose the entanglement of his politics in ever more inextricable knots, in which at last he found himself entangled.

IV

This intellectual degeneration, exercised by war, was intensified in Napoleon by the increase of his pride. Pride isolates, removes from reality, concentrates the mind on contemplation, not of the outside world, but of its own greatness. What is experience to a proud man in comparison with his own ideas or plans ? By degrees, as his pride grew almost to a belief in his own infallibility, Napoleon lost all count of reality ; he lost himself—and this was his punishment—in a gigantic hallucination in a world of imaginary phantoms in which great creative ideas merge with the phantasies of a madman and the ingenuousness of a child.

The first and second facts were aggravated by another malignant influence, exerted by a life of war : intellectual fatigue and exhaustion. War is always accompanied by violent emotions—anxiety, impatience, triumphant excitement. Now all things which cannot be accomplished with a serene mind, but demand tension of thought and agitation, are those which weary the most. Moreover, war is a species of work which does not allow of methodical application ; during a campaign, those moments in which a general can give himself up to diversion, are capriciously alternated with moments of intense mental strain. Work is more fatiguing when it does not demand methodical effort. Now, variety of mental efforts augment fatigue. This renders war one of the most exhausting of human occupations, to which even the strongest succumb. Moltke did not exhaust himself, because, in the whole course of his career, he only fought in three wars, each of few months' duration, with long rests between the first and second, which he passed in the quiet and methodical occupations of a military bureaucracy. Napoleon insisted on waging almost uninterrupted war for twenty years, opening a fresh campaign as soon as a preceding one was completed ; and he wore himself out in the effort.

The psychology of Napoleon in his later years is that of a wearied and exhausted man. Not only did he become more and more intuitive, but his intuition grew constantly more analytical, whilst the *ensemble* of things grew more remote and his mind became more subjective and less controlled by the conscious observation of exterior life. In order to understand external life, observation and criticism are necessary : a fatigue for which Napoleon grew more unfit as years passed by, and he was prostrated by mental fatigue. His attention was less capable of restraining his formidable imagination ; extravagant and chimerical ideas hustled excellent ones in his brain. Nor could he separate them ; his conduct became incoherent, almost like that of an hysterical subject.

The Russian Campaign is the most terrible proof of the state of mind reached by Napoleon owing to the concurrence of these three causes induced by war : growth of pride, the disintegration of the synthetic faculties, and brain exhaustion. At last nothing remained to him but the capacity for details ; every now and then he organized a manœuvre, directed a battle, ordered a march with his usual ability ; but the *ensemble* of the conditions among which he lived escaped him. He was blind to what his generals had seen from the outset : that the Russians aimed at enticing the French army into the interior in order to wear it out by slow stages. Indeed his marshal's opposition to the advance was only a fresh motive to Napoleon to proceed. At times he agreed with his generals that this was the plan of the Russians ; and yet he acted as though his real conviction lay in the contrary direction, as though some force drew him towards the abyss. At Wilna he already began to realize the danger he would encounter through the expedition he had commenced ; but he declined the proffered peace because, after so many preparatives, his prestige would be diminished by a war that finished in anything but a great victory. At Vitebsk he resolved to stop and pass the winter ; then he thought that Europe would consider that he hesitated, so he was re-animated by the desire to end the whole affair with a master-stroke. He asked the counsel of his generals, who advised him not to advance. At this he grew angry, abused them, and ordered an advance to Smolensk. During the battle of

Borodino his generals observed with terror "le calme sourde, la douçeur molle sans activité" which he displayed. At Smolensk, in a moment in which he foresaw his imminent ruin, he offered the Czar that peace which he refused at Wilna, but the Czar made no answer. Irritated by this insult, he desired boldly to advance, and ordered the march to Moscow. The Russian general, Kutusoff, admits that Russia would have found herself in a difficulty had Napoleon followed his contemplated plan, to winter at Smolensk and await the spring to recommence hostilities ; but Bonaparte was still the general of Italy, used to rapid campaigns with a succession of repeated assaults and great battles ; and he sought in the vast plains of Northern Europe the booty he had collected wholesale in the valley of the Po. A vain illusion, which urged him on to Moscow in the pursuit of an ever-vanishing enemy! At Moscow, when his generals informed him that the army was diminishing every day, he set himself obstinately to prove that it was not true ; that fact pointed to the contrary. After the Moscow conflagration, in the midst of the first symptoms of his army's dissolution, when ruin was suspended above his head, Napoleon lost his time in inertia and puerile etiquette ; he passed his evenings finishing the regulations for the *Comédie Française ;* he discussed literature with his intimates ; he ordered the great cross to be removed from the tower of Ivan Velihi in the Kremlin and transported to Paris. This man, so sober formerly, wasted his time at table, as though seeking to stupefy himself with drink ; though previously so active, he now passed long hours in bed brooding over some book, as though he had entirely abandoned himself to Fate. Moscow was burned ; his army began to suffer from hunger ; Alexander made no reply to Napoleon's letters. One morning, the 22nd of

October, Napoleon arose, irritated after a sleepless night, and
summoned a council of generals.   He expounded to them an
elaborate war-plan he had matured during the night, viz. to
march through Twer to St. Petersburg in mid-winter.   And
the master of the world had not thought of the single difficulty
which immediately occurs to Davout, *i.e.* that in a day three
hundred peasants could render impracticable the road from
Twer to St. Petersburg, which ran for a hundred leagues
through marshes capable of swallowing up the whole army !
The first snows fell and the retreat became an urgent
necessity ; the generals awaited this order.   Napoleon did
not give it, he could not make up his mind to let the word
" retreat " pass his lips in the presence of his generals.   He
adopted a circumlocution which salved his pride, saying that
in twenty days the army should be in winter quarters.
When at last he resolved to issue the order, it was found that
the horses did not suffice for the transport of the artillery.
And yet he persisted in his desire to carry everything with
him, even at the cost of postponing the retreat, for fear the
Russians should retain anything as a trophy.   When the
army neared the Beresina, a colonel of the advance-guard
arrived with the terrible news that the Russian troops of
Moldavia had reached the Beresina and occupied the whole
of the passages.   Then an extraordinary scene was witnessed.
Napoleon, enraged, ground his teeth and waved his stick
threatening to strike the messenger, roaring, " It is not true—
it is not true !—you lie ! "   Blinded by fury, he raised his fist
to heaven and broke out into terrible oaths.   And in this
moment, when all appeared lost, in which it did not seem
possible that either he or the relics of this army should escape
imprisonment, the conqueror wept in the presence of his
generals.   His conduct, in short, was so strange that all

around him vaguely felt that almost superstitious horror and
anguish which a man, struck by the dark and immutable
sentence of Destiny, inspires. " It is incomprehensible,"
writes Labaume, "how Napoleon could have been so blind
and obstinate as not to abandon Russia when he perceived
that the capital, on which he had counted so much, no
longer existed, and that winter was approaching. . . . It seems
as though God had stupefied him as a punishment for his
pride." Carnot declares that he no longer recognized,
physically or morally, in the aged emperor the general of the
Italian Campaign. " He used to be thin, suspicious, and
gloomy, now he is fat and jolly, but always sleepy and disinclined. He—the man of rapid decisions, who took offence
at every counsel proffered—is now constantly talking instead
of acting, and asking every one his opinion." " The Napoleon
we used to know no longer exists," added General Van-
damme at Waterloo. And General Wolseley concludes a
recent study on the downfall of Napoleon with these words :
" No, during the campaign of 1813, Napoleon was no longer
the man of 1796 and 1805. The extraordinary vicissitudes
of his life appear to have persuaded him, not only that he
differed from the rest of mankind, but also that victory was
his guardian angel, that he was the conjurer of Fortune."
To such a state was his intelligence reduced by pride and the
exhaustion of war.

V

Napoleon has always been celebrated as possessing a deep
knowledge of men, as being an able practical psychologist.
Even this quality has, I believe, been much exaggerated by
his admirers. In order to understand mankind, it is necessary

not to despise it and to consider one's self as vastly superior.
Napoleon was too egoistic, too deeply persuaded that he was
made of better clay. He possessed a special psychological
ability in things concerned with war; he knew how to inspire
respect and fear in his generals, how to encourage his soldiers
and give them confidence, how to dishearten enemies ; he
was, in short, a past-master in that simple game of elementary
passions which constitutes the practical psychology of war.
He had a rare power for understanding the special, I might
almost say technical, capacities of men ; the portraits of his
generals, for instance, which he has given us, are little
masterpieces of psychology.

But a comprehension of the human soul in its entirety, full
of those complicated and contradictory passions which build
up real character, he did not possess.   Napoleon was a one-
sided psychologist, who only grasped a few elementary
qualities of the human mind.   Used, as he was, to imposing
himself by force and fraud, to seeing himself always surrounded by men governed by fear, greed, or vanity, led by
his pride to consider this as the natural condition of mankind,
because it best served his passion for power and flattered his
sense of superiority, this man naturally formed a pessimistic
and contemptuous conception of humanity.   He regarded man
not only as a being replete with base and brutal passions (and
in this he was right), but—and here he was mistaken—as
possessing *nothing* but low and brutal qualities, stupid into
the bargain, and easily deceived by gross impostures.
Examine, for instance, all his proclamations to his soldiers,
the observations he has left on social and psychological
phenomena.   It is obvious that the whole scale of human
psychology is composed of three notes only for Napoleon :
fear, greed, and vanity.   Hence arose his brutal manner of

treating his fellow-men, which was *partially* good, but which applied by him as *absolutely* good, was among the causes which led to his ruin.

In none of those formidable wars on which he embarked did Napoleon make any account of the nobler passions. Force was to conquer all; where force did not suffice he employed deceit and corruption; above all, deceit, rude, simple, and into which these fools of men—so thought this man intoxicated with pride—must always fall. His system often met with success: that of force succeeded in Italy, where the higher classes, easy going and addicted to a quiet life, accepted his dominion, almost without resistance, after their armies were destroyed; that of fraud in Poland, where he deluded the flower of the Polish youth into following him by the forged proclamations of Kosciuzko. But he did not understand the psychology of the Spanish peasant and the Russian mujic; he never imagined that the soul of a people, offended in its rude pride and religion, could be roused to a fearful outburst of courage, energy, and desperate hatred—to a sentiment of anything but interest, in short; he believed that, the armies beaten, everything was at an end, and that the vile multitude would submit to his conquering yoke without ado. But the armies beaten, he found himself, on the contrary, enveloped in the flames of a terrible conflagration that burst from underground, from the depth of the peoples' souls, where a more violent passion had extinguished that brutal cowardice which, according to the fortunate warrior, was the elementary sentiment of mankind.

Nothing could better depict this ingenuousness of Napoleon's, his incapacity to understand the strong energy of the human soul, than that which he contemplated and did in the Russian campaign. In order to ingratiate himself

cheaply with the Russian people, he falsified a hundred
million rouble notes. These he counted on spending liberally,
bribing and buying souls and goods, thus gaining men over
to his side through the vile passion for money. But this
idea, which in any other country would have been regarded
as a shameful perfidy, resulted in ridicule in Russia. Between
those who concealed themselves, those who burnt down their
houses, and those who fled before him leaving nothing but
ruin behind, those who persecuted with petty skirmishes his
retiring army, he found no hands outstretched to receive
his money. Thus—Napoleon himself confessed it to Lord
Ebrington—nothing surprised him more than the Moscow
conflagration, that unexpected and tragical *dénoûment* of the
1812 campaign. This burning was partly due to the chance
disorder of a city abandoned by its inhabitants and occupied
by an undisciplined soldiery, but in no small part also to the
patriotic and religious mania of a few fanatics, who set fire to
their dwellings rather than see them inhabited by the enemy.
An abyss of fire suddenly opened at the conqueror's feet ;
and his surprise at the event which compelled the French
army to retire, and condemned it to destruction, was so great
that he expressed himself literally in these words to Lord
Ebrington : " It was an event which I could not have foreseen,
for it was without precedent in the world's history."

Napoleon in his later years was worn-out and ill. Was it
a caprice of chance which insinuated the germs of dissolution
in the structure of this colossus ? No ; he carried in himself
the law of his own ruin, which no human force could avert.
War, to which he owed his rise and the glory of his first
successes, slowly undermined his intellect by exhausting
work, and by developing that pride which exiled him from
the world to the solitudes of an arrogant might. This ruin

was not the work of chance, or individual malady, but the natural development of a germ of decay innate in the man's character.

He was not a man who created by his genius a unique condition of things in history ; he was a man who, through pride and selfishness, abused a most extraordinary good fortune, and made of it a tool for his own destruction. Napoleon does not represent that victorious force of will and human genius which subject and dominate reality within the limits of reason, but the moral weakness of genius which knows not how to resist the folly of pride, and squanders all its energy to satisfy this weakness. He is a monstrosity rather than an example of human greatness, his power consisted principally in extravagances and violence.

VI

But if such was the man, must we conclude that all his political and warlike deeds were mere ambitious caprices, the result of unmeasured and criminal vanity ?

That personal egoism and pride were among his political motives is certain, as it is certain that the devotion of his generals was in a large measure proportionate to the high salaries he paid them. In the Emperor's view, many of his wars were merely the caprices of an Assyrian king ambitious to refresh the terror with which his name inspired the world, as in his generals' views they were mere plunderings by which they stuffed their pockets at the expense of their victims.

But in history the results of a man's deeds frequently far surpass what he had contemplated, as a ball, thrown by a strong arm, frequently goes beyond the destined limit. Thus the Napoleonic wars, without the cognizance of their author, contributed to a social work of great importance to some of the conquered countries : those which were Catholic ; that is to say, a work which is the explanation, and in part the justification, of those fearful slaughters.

Napoleon was a Jacobin ; the most coherent and energetic, and therefore, at the same time, the most useful and dangerous of Jacobins. The Napoleonic wars, so far as they were not merely the bloody manias of a conqueror, but useful historical events, were the decisive victories of Jacobinism ; and, as such, they were necessary and beneficial episodes in the struggle which waged for three centuries between the new spirit of liberty, elaborated by European civilization, and the Oriental spirit of universal spiritual dominion by which the Catholic Church exists. The Catholic Church was not merely a religion, that is, a theological doctrine and system of rites dealing with the worship of divinity, it was, and still is, a state which aims at directing, in accordance with certain ideas, the whole of society : the family, education, law, the State, charity, art and science. The fact that it has never possessed political power, except within a very narrow limit, does not detract, nay, rather adds to the power and originality of this singular theocracy that aims at being a universal spiritual empire higher than all national states. A grandiose ambition —perhaps the greatest that history has ever witnessed, and one corresponded to the perfection of the organization and energy, stronger than time.

This ambition for dominion over the minds of men is indeed Oriental and mystical, this desire which the Church has always displayed to subordinate to itself all the intellectual forces of education, science and art; Oriental and mystical also is the negative conception of life which is considered as a painful expiation rather than as a thing to be enjoyed.

Mystical and Oriental, further, is its fundamental moral theory, that perfection consists in the capacity to annihilate will and personality. The result has been that for centuries, as the human mind and European civilization evolved by degrees, men felt an ever-increasing need for liberty, and discovered that many direct or indirect Church regulations could be greatly improved upon, that many Church institutions, such as monasticism and celibacy, were injurious to society as a whole. Then commenced the struggle against the Church, resolved to defend its institutions and ideas, a struggle to which many nations gave a religious solution by reforms, substituting other churches for the Catholic, sects whose institutions were weaker, whose moral and religious theories were more plastic. Thus in Protestant countries the various and diverse churches, all of whom are weak, were never able to acquire much social and political importance, and remained subordinate to the State, which was thus freed from the rivalry of that other state—the Catholic Church.

But in those countries where the Church managed to quell the movement for disestablishment, it took courage to reform itself, as in the Council of Trent, and with the Jesuit movement. But these reforms only affected its internal discipline, and not its ambition for spiritual dominion and its rigid conservative spirit, which indeed, lent it fresh strength. The Jesuits took a large part in this movement. But, during the eighteenth century, Catholic societies began to find irksome this mental coercion which partly assisted and partly opposed the lay authorities. The more enlightened men of the times considered the influence of the clergy and monks as pernicious. Thought and science advanced in Protestant countries and felt the need of intellectual liberty in Catholic lands, a need which the Church refused to recognize. With the spread of

knowledge, a part of the community began to regard the
gross superstitions born of ignorance with a species of disgust ;
but the clergy, more especially its more ignorant members,
spread them far and wide among the people. The tenacity
with which the priests and monks sought to work their way
into families and sow discord, led to grave discontent. All
political, fiscal, and judicial reforms, which the superior men
of the times attempted to introduce, went counter to the views
of the Church. Finally the need was felt for more wealth
and the better use of it, and all the remonstrances addressed
to the Church terminated with accusing it of accumulating
and abusing riches, with employing both the immense properties belonging to it, and wasting what little money they
possessed, in maintaining prelates in luxury, monks in idleness, and beautifying churches with gold and precious stones.

Jacobinism was essentially a political solution of the
problem of the relations between modern civilization and
the Catholic Church. The Church, during the last century,
obstinately opposed all social and political reforms which a
minority of intelligent men demanded as necessary. How
to quell this opposition was the question. These minorities
could not give the problem a religious solution such as
Protestantism, nor oppose smaller, less ambitious, conservative and powerful sects. They held no beliefs, or at best a
very vague one in theism ; thus they could not put themselves at the head of new creeds and attempt to reform the
religious ideas of the masses. These, moreover, were satisfied
neither with the incredulity nor the vague belief which could
only find favour with cultured people. The masses, for want
of a better faith, remained Catholic, and a political rather
than a religious solution had to be found for the problem.
The Church was allowed to continue the profession of its

Oriental ideas, and its authoritarian conception of society ; but in order to diminish its influence, the Jacobins organized against it a strong State, that made itself master of the country, and proposed to regulate in accordance with its own views the life of the whole community in frank opposition to the views of the Church. Such was the Jacobin State founded on a democratic executive. It conceded to the country all those liberties which could counteract the power of the Church and first of all the intellectual liberty to discuss dogmas, to profess atheism and agnosticism. It despoiled the Church of its landed property, and enriched itself by taxes, and, through money, it tried to gain that ascendency over the middle class which the Church had attained by money, substituting the bureaucracy for the monastery, offering, by State employments to the sons of middle-class families, the means to raise themselves above the masses, which were formerly offered by the ecclesiastical grades and convents. In everything else the new Jacobin State entered into competition, so to speak, with the Church. It organized secular in opposition to religious education, State philanthropy in opposition to Church charity ; it sought to encourage profane art and science ; it established civil marriage and, in some countries, even civil baptism. The Jacobin State, in short, wished to replace all the social functions of the Church in a new secular spirit ; a condition of things special to Catholic countries, and not to be met with in Protestant, where the State does not consider as enemies the various sects under its power.

Napoleon gave the finishing touch to this grand and, in a certain measure, extravagant social renovation of doubling the functions of the State, a work which the Revolution had commenced, thanks to the Jacobins and the Convention.

N

By organizing the administration which still rules France, Napoleon only completed the work of the Convention ; with the difference that the former destined the executive to be the tool of a democratic oligarchy, opposed to both Church and Monarchy, and Napoleon intended it as an instrument of his own military despotism. But in this case, also, ultimate results went far beyond human intentions. The Jacobins and Napoleon disappeared ; the administration remained, the apparatus of a new conception of government matured by the French people in opposition to the Church, an instrument destined to save France from theocratic despotism. This revolution, brought about in France by Napoleon, was commenced by his invasion of other Catholic countries : Italy, Spain, Austria, Belgium, the Ticino Canton. In these countries, more particularly in Italy, feudalism and spiritual tyranny were decomposing in the eighteenth century ; the decadence of the aristocracy and monarchy filled society with misery, corruption, and disorder, whilst only a small minority of cultured men realized the necessity for great political and ecclesiastical reforms. But the Church, strong in the blind support of the masses, opposed these energetically. Hence these minorities felt too weak to break the alliance that bound this ancient constitution with feudalism. Then, just when they found themselves discouraged and disgusted at their own impotence, Napoleon and the French invasions came to their aid, and in a few months were wrought the necessary reforms which they had been unable to obtain in opposition to the allegiance between the masses, the Church, and the bigoted feudal aristocracy. The Gordian knot which they had so long struggled to untie was suddenly cut by the sword of a warrior, by his victories in Catholic countries. Napoleon assured the triumph of Jacobinism over the Church. What matters it, for instance, if, after 1815, Italy appeared to fall again into the power of the Church? The Jacobin spirit introduced by the conquests had fermented, and finally broke out in the revolution of 1859-60, creating out of the ruins of the ancient state that had docilely served the Pope the new Italian secular and Jacobin Government, destined, like the French, to rule in the name of an ideal opposed to the Church.

Such was the true useful result of the Napoleonic conquests which it would be as unjust to deny as it would be unreasonable to attribute all the merit to Napoleon and his genius. He was merely the violent and impetuous executor of the Jacobin programme, using it as a pretext for his extravagant ambition. Moreover, it is not to be denied that the number and proportion of his wars was too great in comparison with the partial utility of their results. What a gigantic waste of life and property he caused throughout the whole of Europe, with the effect of aiding the social evolution of a part! Napoleon helped in the work of human progress, but not by opening up large and easy routes through a new and desert region; he rather constructed a frail bridge across a deep and terrible abyss full of perils. He wasted all the timber of an immense forest in order to construct this little bridge, and he did not mind sacrificing a large number of workers during its construction. His proud and tremendous hallucinations contained a small element of truth and reason, and through his misty dreams he caught a vague glimpse of the future.

VII

These things being true, how are we to account for the lively admiration for the man that has so revived of late years ?

May I be allowed to say it frankly : the Napoleon-worship is to the higher classes what brigand-worship is to the lower. The upper classes always believe themselves to be superior to the masses, not because they have fewer vices, but because they are able to satisfy them in a more refined manner. Thus the cultured classes in Europe read with avidity the history of Napoleon for the same reasons that the working classes devour brigand tales. One of the greatest intellectual pleasures, felt by men of all conditions, lies in the perusal of books of adventure, describing life free from all the laws which render ours so secure and monotonous. A simple and uneducated man finds this pleasure in reading about the bold bad brigand. A better educated man needs more delicate food for his imagination ; and this order of literature can offer him nothing more exciting, nearer to our times, or more dramatic, than the Napoleonic story. What is it in Napoleon's history that proves so seductive to youths who vegetate in the monotony of contemporary life ? The inexhaustible surprises, the miraculous changes of fortune, and the romantic existence led by the chiefs of the Napoleonic horde—those corporals who became generals in a few years, those sons of innkeepers who became dukes, kings, and millionaires ; that romantic life of reviews, marches across Europe, battles, triumphant entrances into conquered cities amidst the excitement of applauding men and women who pelted them with flowers ; this panorama of perils and excitements, of gallant adventures and unforeseen fortunes, which formed the existence of the chiefs of the Napoleonic adventures, and which we imagine were common to the time, without reflecting that if a few enjoyed a great feast, many were forced to pay the expenses.

The history of Napoleon affords yet another pleasure to educated people, just as that of a brigand does to an uneducated man. It is the pleasure which springs from admiration, the ideal pleasure felt in witnessing the affirmation of a striking individuality. One of the greatest of human pleasures lies in dominion, the imposition of our will over others. In order to enjoy this in real life, a strong will and the material possibility to rule are necessary, just as to enjoy a life of adventure great force of character is required to bear up against times of adversity. The power of the great is much reduced nowadays, for the conflict of interests tends to establish an equilibrium of power, and few possess sufficient energy to be able to support a life of adventure. Men, therefore, seek an ideal satisfaction in the perusal of the histories of brigands and heroes. For the ignorant and the educated, the pleasure is identical ; the sense of admiration roused by the contemplation of their hero is like a reflection of the pleasure they would derive from ruling themselves, or from pursuing a prosperous life of adventure and pleasure.

But he who fully considers the case will not allow himself to be seduced by the illusion cast by time. Napoleon was a mighty warrior, who lived at a singular period of the great struggle between the Catholic spirit of dominion and the spirit of liberty, between the Asiatic spirit represented by the Church, and the European as represented by the Revolution. Fate made use of this second Attila, of this proud and violent man, as a temporary tool in the great social struggle which for three centuries had tormented Europe. War was able to be useful at that moment, and Attila appeared, summoned by the need of the age. But this Attila, although engaged on a partially beneficial task, always remained at bottom a warrior—a destroyer. He fulfilled his task, but with terrible loss and waste, ruining many great and beautiful living things for a comparatively small result, finally ruining himself and his genius.

MILITARISM AND CÆSARISM
IN FRANCE

CHAPTER VII

MILITARISM AND CÆSARISM IN FRANCE

I

To the query, "What is France?" comes the answer, " A Republic." But "republic" is a word signifying many and diverse things. We must, therefore, overlook superficialities and seek under the surface if we desire to understand the military policy of the European state which has waged the greatest wars of the century, and has played, and still plays, such an important part in the political events of the world.

France is a parliamentary and democratic republic, founded on universal suffrage. But the republican constitution to-day is what the monarchy and empire were in the past, a mere bark whose nature has changed, but which still covers its original trunk and pith ; that is Cæsarism. France is still the country of surprises and enigmas : a little-known and misjudged land, admired or contemned at hazard, because the real nature of its Government is generally ignored. The study of French militarism serves to acquaint us with the life and structure of this social system.

Essentially military ideas are still most popular in France, more especially with the cultured classes. Although, owing to an increase in the sentiment of justice, war between civilized nations is coming to be considered by many as only tolerable

when urged in defence of some principle, the general sentiment amongst educated Frenchmen is favourable to war, and
little tempered by moral considerations.   They deem it a
great thing, *per se*, for a nation to conquer ; political and
military supremacy are regarded as the first factors in the
superiority of a civilization.   Hence, a conquered nation that
has not yet taken its revenge must necessarily consider its
civilization in decadence.   The policy which aims at the
annexation of fresh territories, in Europe, Asia, or Africa,
is considered excellent in itself, as by increasing the area
of an empire, its glory and power is also increased, wherefore the cost in men and money is held of small account.

That such is the opinion of educated France well appears
from what follows ; for the time being I wish merely to
remark that this is not due to chance or to any special disposition on the part of the French, who are not born possessed
of devils or a passion for fighting.   The collective ideas and
sentiments occupying the minds of a people during an entire
historical epoch are never without some meaning, they are
not created out of nothing; their existence is always connected with some special social structure, as a musical sound
is connected with some instrument.   A blind man, on hearing
a piano played, might imagine that the sounds vibrated
in the air independently of any metallic cords or sounding-
boards ; but when some idea or passion possesses the minds
of a nation during a whole period, we are blind in spirit if
we imagine that it exists of itself without being connected
with some social structure, as music is connected with an
instrument.   The social structure at the base of French
militarism is the Jacobin lay State created by the Revolution
in opposition to the Church.

II

I must repeat here what I said in speaking of Napoleon : the Jacobin State represents a political solution to the problem of the relation between Catholicism and modern society, and was created by a cultured and unbelieving minority to be the bulwark of a society founded on liberty ; but an indissoluble contradiction presided like an unlucky star at its birth. We might almost name it the original sin of the modern Latin nations, and more especially of France and Italy, to which their greatest misfortunes are attributable. The opposition to feudalism, and the spiritual theocracy of the Church, originated in the general weariness of tyranny grown morally and materially insupportable. In France, during the last century, public opinion came to consider it as unjust that certain men should pretend to possess power without control and truth without discussion. The theory of popular sovereignty was founded in opposition to absolute Monarchy. It was affirmed that authority, as a human institution, should be wielded by the numerical majority of that society which controlled it, and that it should be discussed, criticized, changed without difficulty, and subjected to such control and restrictions as would prevent it from degenerating into a tyranny. In opposition to the Church was affirmed the divinity of human thought, capable of great deeds when freed from the trammels of superstition. It was said that men and nations were capable of governing themselves, recognizing no other authority than that of reason, and ignoring those who named themselves the ministers of God, and who were in fact His enemies, and desired to keep the world in ignorance for their own interest. But the advocates of liberty were a small class

composed of the enlightened men of the time, of the discontented and *déclassés*, of the middle class, of the turbulent
portion of the working population of large towns, who rose
to power, not through the force of their ideas, but because
the ancient *régime* was so far advanced in decay, and the
Government so little capable of governing, that a small and
bold minority was able to make itself master of everything.
The greater number remained voluntarily under the control
of the Church, and, therefore, showed themselves hostile to
the new ideas of liberty, sometimes in a fanatical spirit, sometimes merely passively. The result was that the liberal
minority in France during the Revolution and the Empire
were forced, in order to maintain their authority, as happened also later on in Italy, to impose a liberal *régime* tyran-
nically by means of force, and to enter into competition with
the Church, imitating it in many of its authoritarian ways.

We have observed, in our study of Spanish and American
society, that true liberty can only exist where the educated
classes lead a useful existence. Despotic societies, on the contrary, are found to be based on the spirit of protection. Now,
the Catholic Church, after the Roman Empire, was the greatest
State ever founded on protection. It was, indeed, essentially
a gigantic system of protection, organized in barbarous times
to assure men, through the fear of God, against those perils due
to the poverty and ignorance of the age. The great wealth
it has always aimed at accumulating, the culture it has sought
to attain, were the tools with which it hoped, and perhaps
still hopes, to rule the minds of men. Its gigantic hierarchy,
whose highest posts are attainable by men in all conditions,
was always a means whereby the intelligent members of
the poorer classes could become rich and powerful, even in
an age when, owing to the prevalence of poverty, ignorance,

and disparity of fortune, it was more difficult to rise. The Church exercised in the past an able patronage over all those studies not dangerous to Faith. It received into its ranks, by providing them with a modest but sure livelihood, many of those "intellectuals" who, as long as they were able to attend to their studies without worrying, material cares, willingly renounced the vanity of wealth and power. By the monastic system, moreover, Catholicism organized a splendid scheme of charity which benefited all social classes. To unmarried women and widows it offered a shelter in convents ; to the poor fathers of over-numerous families it gave relief by accepting a son among the monks ; to all those who found themselves *de trop* in social life it offered a refuge. By obliging the rich, in an age when the sentiment of social solidarity was feeble, to give money to the poor through threats of hell, it found a means of assisting the indigent. They made one of their principal arms of this system of charity at the cost, it is true, of encouraging idleness. Every church and convent was a fountain of charity, both to the genuine poor and to professional vagabonds. In short, the Church was a reserve of spiritual and material assistance for all human weaknesses and improvidence ; it assured the nobility the hereditary transmission of the father's wealth to his first-born by making monks and priests of the younger sons ; it assisted the intelligent and ambitious members of the lower and middle classes to overcome the drawbacks of humble birth ; it persuaded the rich to sacrifice part of their wealth, which it distributed amongst the poor, thereby alleviating their sufferings and conducing them to remain obedient and docile.

The Church was indeed what it professed to be, the *Santa Madre*, the universal protectrix in the rude and barbarous ages which gave birth to our civilization. Owing to the difficulty in augmenting wealth due to the scarcity of capital, education, and civilization, many would have dragged out a fearfully degraded existence without her benevolent influence. This vast protective system had, until the Revolution in France, and in Italy until 1848 (though in a somewhat modified degree), formed practically the backbone of society, consequently it necessarily exerted an immense influence over ideas, institutions, and customs. It encouraged amongst the masses a tendency towards idleness and ignorance, an impetuosity of affection and simplicity of mind that pertain to savages, a servile reverence and humility towards those whom they considered as benefactors. In the middle classes it developed political passivity, indifference to public affairs, social egoism, devotion to the powers that be, and the need to be protected. In the highest class it encouraged idleness, bigotry, vanity, and the ambition to distinguish itself, not by benefiting society, but by piety, by ostentatious charity and almsgiving.

Now, these habits and traditions, which in the course of centuries had penetrated into the very marrow of society, could not disappear in a day. No wonder they found a terrible impediment to the establishment of a genuinely free *régime*. The Jacobin State, whose object was to give liberty to France, grew rapidly entangled in a grave contradiction, for it was compelled to establish a new protective system analogous to that of the Church, in order to raise itself from the condition of a feeble governmental minority engulphed in the midst of a vast hostile community. French society, accustomed for centuries to universal Church protection, would have found itself, when the Church was stripped of wealth and power, as though deprived of some necessity of existence, in a terrible position, whose dangers can be apprehended if we study that agitated period of French history from the proclamation of the Republic to the establishment of the Napoleonic rule. Napoleon's reign saved France and the work of the Revolution, by definitely organizing, on the lines traced out by the Convention, the new universal secular protection of the Jacobin State in place of that formerly exercised by the Church.

Thus the French Government took the middle class under its protection, and offered to it, by means of the bureaucracy, the same advantages which Catholicism had offered by churches and monasteries. Such was the origin, and is still the function, of those 400,000 governmental and 127,000 county and communal officials, who receive together in salaries 637 million francs (or about 25½ millions sterling) a year, to which, if we add the £8,000,000 which goes in pensions to the veterans of the bureaucratic army, amounts to a sum of nearly £34,000,000. This civil and military bureaucracy, whose origin can be traced back to the reign of Louis XIV., strengthened and amplified by the Convention, by Napoleon, and successive Governments, is renewed from among the bourgeoisie, but is occasionally reinforced by some recruit from the aristocracy or the people. It is ruled by a competitive system of promotion, in which intrigue plays as important a part as merit ; but which in recompense is democratic, for no privilege of birth is recognized there. Notwithstanding the fact that the larger part of this bureaucracy is not handsomely paid, middle-class families always aim at seeking for one of their number a post as sub-prefect, army officer, or Government *employé*. But although this august body is democratically constituted, it is not open to all, since it can only be entered after a novitiate, and in accordance with certain rules ; the novitiate of all public schools, gymnasiums, universities, polytechnic and military institutes, whose diplomas accord a right to compete for the highest posts, thus practically reserving these for the well-to-do classes.

Thus the election of the executive in France, at the outset of the new *régime,* was an act distinctly favourable to the bourgeoisie, in which manner the State demonstrated itself to be the successor of the Church. But logic is an inexorable law of life. The Jacobin Government was no foe to modern civilization ; indeed, its programme favoured progress in opposition to the conservatism of the clergy and of feudalism. But with the growth of civilization the State multiplied its favours, and made of all modern discoveries, from railways to science and hygiene, a pretext for its protective generosity. Thus the French Government developed into a gigantic system of private interests that collected, by means of a thousand channels, prodigious riches which it redistributed to a thousand emissaries. Thus it can annually assign a sum of about a milliard francs for the benefit of its officials, while nearly another milliard francs is put by every year to pay those who make Government loans. Fabulous sums are spent every year on subventions and bounties in aid of mistaken industries and doubtful speculations, in supporting educational and philanthropic schemes. Immense credit is given to contractors for public works, useful or otherwise ; huge fortunes are spent on the army and navy, and for the exercise of large Government monopolies, such as tobacco and matches. Conspicuous sums are spent on the maintenance of expensive colonies, and on paying out a large number of small salaries to satisfy the needs of public mendicity, whose forms are infinite : such as subsidies to race-courses, theatres, exhibitions, scientific and literary publications. In other words, the State has to be lavish with all manner of assistance, to spend freely on public works for the army and navy, not because it benefits them, but so as to provide work for a number of workers, and to *faire marcher les affaires*. It has, above all, to make debts so as to offer a safe though modest investment to the savings of middle-class families. It has to maintain intellectual men and warriors. It has to be the patron of genius hidden in the depths of misery, giving artistic and scientific education at an absurdly low cost.

Moreover, this administration indirectly serves private interests. By means of its custom-houses, it stops at the frontier such foreign goods as would render competition difficult to the national manufacturers. Of this privilege the French Government has made considerable use, more particularly during the last ten years, with the special object of protecting certain industries and branches of agriculture from a depression in price. Modern civilization is admirable, but it has this disadvantage, that wealth is extremely precarious. A permanent and definitive debasement in value was once a slow historical event which followed at the distance of centuries, nowadays the most formidable variations incessantly occur, entailing the destruction of established fortunes and the creation of new ones. But in a society where the spirit of protection is strong, where individual energies are restrained by many bonds, a certain stability of fortune is desired and demanded of the Government, as one of the many forms of its protection. Such, at least in part, is the aim of protectionism in France.

III

When this is admitted we can clearly understand how it is that the Jacobin State is the government of a minority. Its function was to assure to France, by means of a vast protective system, an intellectual liberty in opposition to spiritual tyranny, and a political freedom from the abuses of an absolute monarchy. It therefore freed writers and thinkers from a large portion of those perils that threatened them from a jealous ecclesiastical censorship, it accorded a fair freedom of the press, and scientific education.

But to do this, the work of the Jacobin State had necessarily to be aristocratic. The uneducated majority, occupied only with money-making, did not care about intellectual liberty, which, moreover, appeared impious and dangerous to those who had been most influenced by the restricted education of the Church. These naturally regarded an authoritative scheme of official belief as a salutary system rather than a *régime* of liberty and discussion.

Moreover, the vast protective system exercised by the Jacobin State for the benefit of the middle class was necessarily oligarchical. Such a protection can satisfy a certain number on one condition only : that it takes little in taxation from a large number, and that it confer great favours on a few. Thus it compels the majority to contribute to the well-being of a minority, which latter alone is really interested in the maintenance of the *régime*. There is always an upper-class minority which receives more than it contributes, and another class which receives less than it contributes, that is the majority of workers and the lower bourgeoisie. Now, it is clear that such a state of things can only exist on one condition, *i.e.* that authority be in the power of a minority which avails itself of this vast system of protection, and feels the necessity for intellectual liberty. This singular combination led the Jacobin State into another self-contradiction when it wished to fulfil the second promise made to the French people, that of conferring on it political liberty. According to their formula the majority was to rule, and yet it had to serve a minority which it entrusted with power. In order to escape from this contradiction, the Jacobin State imagined a thousand expedients by whose means it eluded the political formula which gave it birth. Indeed, a great part of the political ability of France has been thus expended during our century.

Every few years, all adult males are called upon to elect members for the Chamber of Deputies. By means of this legislative assembly the majority might express and enforce its will—it might, that is, if practical possibility corresponded to theoretical. But such is not the case, for many reasons, and primarily on account of the party divisions, which are such as to always ensure rule to the minority, under one form or another. The men who take part in French electoral struggles all belong to the category of those who divide public wealth, or at least electoral contests are conducted as though these only were concerned. French party contests are not waged with a view to affirm with precision the desire of the majority, they consist of cliques and *coteries* who dispute the favours of State protection. Between Opportunists and Radicals the only real difference is this: that the Opportunists have a programme for aristocratic protection in favour of the higher bourgeoisie that shall promote the interests of a small class of wealthy financiers, while the Radical programme favours the lower bourgeoisie of shopkeepers, small landowners, and even, to a certain extent, the workers. The former party desires to cut huge slices out of the public cake to satisfy a few ravenous appetites, the latter would divide it into a number of small biscuits to distribute among the crowd. There are rarely found in the Chamber as many as twenty real adversaries who oppose, not the system by which the cake should be divided, but any division at all of a toothsome morsel made of flour stolen from the workers' mill. A few exist among the Socialists, but these are timid and uncertain, entangled in an indissoluble contradiction which they fail to notice, because at one moment they oppose protectionism as unjust and tyrannical, and then incline to test the extreme absurdity of the system by applying it to the working multitudes, thus inventing proletarian Cæsarism.

Thus political contests in France consist in the infernal clamour of a thousand competitors, who crowd around the public banquet, fighting and scrambling to get their share. Those who reach the feast first gorge ravenously, while occasionally flinging a few crumbs to the crowd to keep them quiet. The competitors in parliamentary, senatorial, municipal, or county elections vie with one another in making promises that shall procure them public favour and votes. One man promises his most ardent partisans one of those positions that carry with them neither heavy work or responsibility, of which there are so many in the French bureaucracy. Another pledges Government support to some declining local industry. A third promises to classify the local tobaccos among the most expensive qualities. Yet another promises a school or railway to his electors, while all try to get into favour by rendering such small services as exemptions from fines, decorations, the remission of small penalties, *i.e.* by distributing among the mass those crumbs which remain over from the feasts of Cæsarism.

The majority of the people—that is to say, those who provide the banquet—are unable even to approach it. But, owing to the fact that they are dispersed, disunited, unconscious of their ills, and often ignorant, they can do little against a well-organized and active minority. As a Frenchman on entering the world finds the State ready constituted, so also he finds ready made the various factions who dispute the enjoyment of its protection. No party exists to represent his confused desire to be less exploited by the State. Of what use, then, is the right to vote at elections if, amongst all the candidates who solicit his favour, he cannot find one to express his thoughts and wishes? All those who suffer from this method of government should come to a mutual understanding, unite together to found new parties, and seek for new men to rule them. An understanding and union, however, is difficult between so many people scattered all over France, between whom, moreover, there exists such wide differences of education and social position, differences which the unceasing and cunning conduct of the administration tends to increase.

Besides the task of maintaining order, the Government has another more important duty to fulfil : that of rendering universal suffrage a harmless toy in the people's hands. This weapon it was, by force of circumstances, compelled to give to the populace, as you give a child a toy pistol to quiet him. It uses all manner of devices to attain this object. For this end there exists a distinctly political body, served by prefects and sub-prefects, and aided by the executive. Prefects and sub-prefects are scattered in all French towns, and are most especially charged with the organizing of electoral cabals, to render impossible the growth of any real party of reform, and to maintain and, if possible, increase their disunion. By all methods of corruption they successfully bamboozle the working-men and middle-class associations. They keep a keen eye on the local authorities ; they curry favour with rich proprietors, manufacturers, and well-to-do people in general; they disperse decorations, promise favours, judiciously regulate the pressure of certain fiscal laws. By such means they seek to win over the electors, and to induce the majority to elect, now an Opportunist, now a *rallie*, now a Radical, in accordance with instructions received from Paris. These Government candidates are, of course, men favourable to the traditional politico-administrative system, and prepared to exploit in favour of those who contribute to their victory. The prefects generally meet with success because the chief article of this electoral Machiavellism is very simple and practically infallible : that of blinding a man to the universal interest, which is, of course, indirectly his own, in view of some direct and immediate benefit. Men generally fall into this trap. Hence manufacturers, merchants, and landowners allow themselves to be enticed by a decoration, or some frail promise to favour a policy, which, by gradually augmenting taxation throughout the country, must ultimately lead to their ruin.

To intrigue and corruption, in extreme cases, force is added, the force of a huge army, as useful for internal repression as for foreign wars ; and which has, on more than one occasion, saved the Jacobin State from outbursts of national fury. The Commune forms an instance. This fell a victim, not to the capitalist bourgeoisie, but to administrative Cæsarism. It was crushed down so ferociously, not because it aimed at abolishing private property, but because it favoured a federalist movement which would by centralization have destroyed the nucleus of the Jacobin State.

IV

But nowadays the possession of arms and money does not suffice, a Government must also have a moral basis founded on some popular sentiment. The French Jacobin State has, therefore, sought to impress the people with an almost mystical idea of its own power and greatness, and to persuade them that it is the strongest, most infallible, and invincible of all Governments.

We have already observed that man's greatest source of pleasure consists in the consciousness of his own superiority. Personal pleasures originate in a sense of our own individual worth, collective ones in a belief in the superiority of the society to which we belong. This latter satisfaction is stronger in inferior men. The enjoyment of collective superiority is, in short, a species of recompense to the mediocre crowd, and this explains its universal prevalence. The scholars of one school consider themselves superior to those of another ; the soldiers of one army to those of their rivals ; the members of one class or profession to those of another.

Patriotism, in some cases, arises from a similar sentiment. French patriotism, in fact, consists in the complacent belief that France is, and must be, the greatest, the most invincible European nation, that is destined to rule the rest. This belief, flattering to the universal vanity, may become a real pleasure and generate that sentiment which M. Tarde—who laments its diminution since 1870—defines as : "*Le sentiment delicieux, intime,* presque inconscient à force d'être continu et profond, qui était le fond de l'état d'âme de tous les Français avant 1870 ; la foi absolu en la France, en son hegemonie, en sa mission supérieure et providentielle" (*Figaro*, October 11th, 1898).

Now, this pleasant sentiment of superiority |over other nations resolves itself into devotion and admiration towards the Government that maintains it by its arms and policy. The majorities may be discontented with the Government for its impiety, its oligarchic administration, or its constant self-contradictions, but all parties indiscriminately are grateful to it as the author and custodian of this national moral superiority over other countries. From this point of view we can judge the vastness of the service Napoleon rendered to the Jacobin States, because from that extraordinary epoch of war and victory dates that general passion for military and political greatness which, in France, is such a precious element of administrative stability.

Hence we can easily understand that the Government is interested in diffusing and feeding this passion in every manner, and principally by means of its officials. A well-armed Government, generous, amply provided with money, which shows itself even when commanding half a million officials, inspires the masses with respect and admiration.

The French official class, more especially its better-educated portion, are well enabled to inspire the people with respect for the State. In small towns and country districts the sub-prefects and magistrates, all those officials who possess a certain grade of education and come from afar, sent by the Invisible which rules over all, to represent that unmeasured thing capable of doing so much good and so much harm, appear as small sovereigns, more particularly to the bourgeoisie, who, possessing a little, have more to expect and more to fear from the State. Thus, partly from the genuine humility of the weaker towards the stronger, partly from servility and interestedness, these classes easily accept as aphorisms of Supreme Wisdom the political ideas circulated by the officials. In the same manner much of a priest's authority is not personal, but the result of the accumulation and growth of centuries.

The ideal which the French bureaucracy represents, and which it impresses on the minds of the middle class, is that of military patriotism, according to which French prosperity depends on its military power, its diplomatic superiority, therefore every victory or the conquest of any territory is a happy event conducive to the greatness of the fatherland. The French military and civil authorities can profess the most varied religious and philosophical theories. They may call themselves atheists or believers, materialists or spiritualists, but all of them, under whatsoever political *régime*, under the third republic as under the first and second Napoleonic empire, are bound never publicly to deny this ideal. I do not affirm that they all believe in the justice of these principles as in gospel truth. Some may have grown so inured to them as to regard them with fanatical faith, many accept them passively, for love of peace and quiet, without worrying their brains to analyze. No one, however, dares publicly express his aversion or indulge in too free a criticism. An official who, in writing or in a public speech, maintains that the military honour of France is an absurdity, and the military policy fatal to the country, would be evicted. Therefore the more liberal spirits are forced, by fear of poverty, to keep silence.

Thus the French executive, even to-day, is the custodian of the bellicose traditions of the country, just as the clergy is the defender of its faith. It is assisted by many auxiliary, literary, religious, political, and economical influences, which together build up an ingenious system of mutual intimidation that works admirably.

Public schools are carried on in the same spirit. The Jacobin State organized its educational system in opposition to that of the Church, making of it a tool to cultivate the sentiment of the politico-military greatness of France. These schools are mere gymnasiums where youths are tired out with useless fatigues and stupid mnemonic exercises that only result in procuring the ephemeral glory of " first-class certificates" to a few boys gifted with feeble intellects and good memories. But French schools, by way of recompense, foster military and patriotic enthusiasm. All the chief personages of French military history are paraded before the boys, aggrandized into ideal proportions : Clovis, Charlemagne, Bayard, Louis XIV., Napoleon. The great events of national military history are narrated in glowing and sentimental language. The belief in national and military greatness is fostered in every way. Indeed, these beliefs are perhaps the only ones which have any real hold on the minds of modern French youths.

Religion collaborates with the public schools. From the village pulpit the priest preaches to the peasants concerning the fatherland, the army, the honour of arms, the standards blessed by the Almighty. In the remotest villages of the Alps and Pyrenees, where the schoolmaster possibly would be useless, the priest penetrates, sent thither by the State to represent religion, on condition that he will also put in a good word for the military greatness of France.

The most perfect side of this subtle and varying work of propaganda is to be found in the system of mutual intimidation, thanks to which the most thoughtful men are prevented from rebelling against the tyranny of absurd military prejudices.

The patriotism of the cultured classes in France resembles, to a certain degree, those walls in which the bricks support one another without cement; or, if you prefer, a prison in which every one is in turn the gaoler of his neighbour on the left, and the prisoner of the one on the right. Many Frenchmen are intimately persuaded that much of this high-flown patriotic agitation is mere bluster, nor could it be otherwise, as prepossession has been pushed to the extreme of absurdity. A recent event furnishes an example :—The Madagascar expedition cost the nation £5,000,000, and the lives of 5000 soldiers, raised by conscription and sent there by force. How was it possible that several deputies—and I have known many who admitted it in private conversation —should not regard as insane such waste of life and money for the conquest of an island whose only use would be to institute new expensive bureaucratic sinecures, and which commercially would be exploited by Englishmen and Germans? And yet, in this small matter, as in many more important ones, no one dared to declare openly that the talk about the honour of the French standard in Madagascar was absurd, and that the first duty of a Government is to waste neither men nor money. Thus it always happens, in matters where the traditional ideals of French military glory are concerned, many persons are more or less conscious of the same opinion, but each would be ready to stone for his boldness any one who dared proclaim the truth hidden at the bottom of every one's mind. Were this audacious spirit a journalist, he would find his readers rapidly diminish ; were he a deputy he could never again speak in public ; a university professor would be ruined, an independent literary man would never enter the Academy. French public opinion is ferocious against the crimes of *lèse-patriotisme,* and the Press, which understands this, and speculates on the most ardent passions of the human heart, occasionally goes in for wild outbursts of patriotism, which so excite the public that they positively lynch—metaphorically speaking—all those suspected of little or no patriotism.

Thus it happens that journalists, officials, scientists, and literary men, *volens nolens,* all live in terror of the threatened anger of the public, and are compelled to become the accomplices of this colossal military-territorial delusion which is hurrying France to its ruin.   The revolutionist Rochefort is as great a "jingo" as the imperialist Cassagnac; the socialist municipality of Paris is forced to receive the Czar; Pasteur has to refuse a title of honour from the Emperor of Germany; Ferry becomes the object of universal detestation from the day he is suspected of wishing to reconcile France with Germany.   The sincere fanatics for revenge are few, because all know in their heart of hearts that war with Germany would have disastrous results for European civilization.   And yet, how many years will pass before any of the parties which come into power will publicly renounce this idea, and set Europe at peace?—a universal and fatal error in which all mutually imprison one another, from which all would be only too happy to escape.

V

Thus the cultured classes, if not the whole nation, accept in silence these ideals which correspond so ill to the requirements of the age, and consequently military traditions are transmitted from generation to generation, and fossilized into integral parts of the administration.   We have seen that the majority does not and cannot rule in France; that the

various *coteries* and small minorities, who from time to time
come into power, take no trouble to reform the Government.
The only aim of a ministry is to satisfy the "clients" which
raised it to power. All the rest, the reform of abuses and
so forth, except what is brought about by the force of circumstances, is treated by the various Governments with a
very Mussulman indifference. As a general rule, the more
unjust the constitution of a Government, the greater its need
to emphasize some ideal to play on, some disinterested and
altruistic passion of the human heart. In our day, the Government which, more than any other, depends on an ideal is the
Turkish. Why are its officials and soldiers ready to die
heroically wherever the caprice of a foolish Government
chooses to send them ? Not for any consideration of personal
gain, certainly, for the Government lets them hunger twelve
months a year, ill-treats and oppresses them, but out of
devotion to their religious beliefs. Is anything found to
equal the barbarous but infinite heroism which the Turkish
Government lives in the Swiss *régime?* In comparison with
the Turkish Government, that of Switzerland is a prosaic
company of tradesmen ; its virtues consist in pedantry, in an
orderly and economic spirit, in the subordination of everything to saving. Nor should this surprise any person who
well considers the question. The unjuster a Government,
the more it has to fear from the resistance or aversion of its
subjects. If it can manage to inspire its victims with some
generous passion, and ingeniously connect itself therewith,
then it frequently succeeds in gaining the affection of those
it oppresses. Throughout history an ideal has mostly been
the sentinel of injustice.

Owing to an analogous phenomenon, the satisfaction of this
sentiment of national pride has, in normal times, diminished

in France, and obscured any feeling of aversion or discontent
towards the Government.   Political parties have always
availed themselves of this public passion for military glory
as a cover for their injustices and errors.   Napoleon III.
managed for eighteen years to popularize his government
by continued fortunate military expeditions, for which he
found opportunities and pretexts in every quarter of the globe,
in China, Germany, and Mexico.   Under the present Republic the various parties try to animate the people by visions
of colonial trophies.   When General Duchêne disembarked
at Marseilles, on his return from Madagascar, where he had
waged a greater struggle against malarial fever than against
any troops, the socialist mayor of the town went to meet him,
made a complimentary speech, and thanked him as a bene-
factor of his country.   General Dodds, who conquered the
King of Dahomy, met with an absolutely triumphant reception from the Parisians.   But the strongest proof of the
strength of French bellicose sentiments is found in the attitude
of the socialists who, in their war against militarism, display
none of the violence shown by socialists in other lands.   I
remember attending a meeting of the Association of Rail-
road Workers, men who are nearly all socialists, presided
over by the socialist deputy, Claude Hugues, that was held
to protest against a law, approved of by the Senate, which
prohibited railway *employés* from forming themselves into
syndicates.   The chief complaint was that one of the principal
motives in favour of the law was this: that permitting the
railway men to associate would facilitate strikes, and that these
would offer a favourable opportunity to some hostile nation
to declare war against France.   All the orators expressed
their indignation at the idea that any one could believe them
capable of continuing a strike after the outbreak of war;

that the railway men, as Hugues put it, would not have
failed in the performance of their duty "under the fire of
German cannons." In the project for a general strike, prepared by an association of railway *employés*, was included
a clause which became the object of considerable jocularity
in the conservative press, but which was very characteristic.
It proposed that a member of the strike executive should
place himself in direct communication with the minister
of war, so as to be able to give orders for the immediate
termination of the strike as soon as the necessities of
national defence demanded it.

VI

But European society is changing with the times. Thus,
also, French militarism must of necessity alter its character,
and, above all, modify itself.

Herein lies all the significance of the colonial policy inaugurated in France since 1870, at enormous expense, chiefly
through the influence of Ferry. What a difference from the
English colonial policy !—that is, the colonization of Sancho
Panza: a commercial colonization entered upon prudently
and by degrees, with the object of getting buffeted about as
little as possible. The French policy is that of Don Quixote,
all for military glory, without any thought for vulgar
material interests. The French colonial policy signifies this :
the executive realizes that the age of great military undertakings is now for ever past in Europe. It therefore tries to
perpetuate the glory of its arms in Asia and Africa. The war
of 1870, the downfall of Napoleonism, and the altered condition
of European politics, rendered wars in Europe impossible to
the Jacobin State, which always—but more particularly under

the two Napoleonic Empires—had mixed itself up in all European conflicts, and had even sought after more distant ones in Algiers, the Crimea, Mexico, and China. To-day the military spirit, still so prevalent in France, seeks satisfaction in colonial expeditions, by whose means officers, generals, and all the military unemployed are able to practise the skill which in Europe finds no scope. How can we otherwise account for the absurdity of this policy? France, of all countries, has the least necessity to found colonies. Her population steadily decreases; so that, instead of requiring fresh territories for emigration, it possesses them for immigration. The character of the people, as moulded by the long-standing traditions of French civilization, is suited rather to the exploitation of ready formed civilization, by means of its commerce and luxurious trades, than to the cultivation of fresh lands. A Frenchman is much better adapted to sell champagne, fashion-books, and perfumes to the rich of a refined society, than to burn down the virgin forests of desert continents or construct railways across marshes inhabited by serpents and crocodiles who devour the engineers. New York and St. Petersburg render far more to French commerce than all its enormous colonial empire which took such long years to create.

In short, all the French colonies are the last efforts of an antiquated militarism. They are undertakings of administrative exploitation, which cost men and millions to the nation, and only enrich or give social power to a few officials, speculators and adventurers. French colonies merely serve to augment lucrative bureaucratic posts, to create a movement of fictitious affairs, under the form of financial undertakings (railways, navigation, etc.) subsidized and guaranteed by the State, whose profits are derived, not from the colony but from the

national treasury.   One of the first acts of the French Government, after the conquest of Madagascar, was the despatch of a
numerous body of officials.   The sick and wounded from the
terrible expedition of 1895 still crowded the hospitals, when,
by decree dated December 30th, 1895, the Government constituted at Tananarivo a court of appeal, and appointed
counsellors, although it was not yet known what law ruled
in the country, whether the French or that of the island.
Inspectors of the French schools were appointed before
these schools existed.   Such is the nature of all the profits
made by the French Government out of its colonial policy,
a fruit of the military traditions that have survived from
the monarchy that existed prior to the Revolution, right
through the two Napoleonic Empires, until our own time.

VII

Certainly this curious mixture of democracy and militarism,
of republican institutions and imperialist ideas, is most
original, and is a proof of great national strength, despite of,
I might almost say by reason of, its absurdity, because absurd
institutions are those which maintain themselves with the
greatest energy.

This system has several grave defects, partly proper to it
and partly inherent to all Governments based on protection.
Amongst these, the most important is the indifference of the
majority to public affairs, their sullen hostility towards the
State, in which the better part see only a foe and an oppressor.
Outside France, the ardour of her political contests appear
extraordinarily active, because they are generally very violent ;
but their violence prevents us from perceiving the indifference
of the majority, their lack of enthusiasm for the men who

P

wage them, their disinclination to take any active part.
Social egoism is intense in France, not only among the
ignorant masses, but also among the richer and educated
class, who, in sharp distinction from this class in England,
regard politics as a vulgar and dirty business to be left
strictly to ambitious men and demagogues, or at the very
best as an amusing spectacle by reason of its *bizarrerie* and
extravagance.

This is the inevitable result of the vast protection exercised
by the State over the bourgeoisie, whereby the Government
awards this class the temptation, or places it under the
necessity of living on public employments. A class cannot
both serve and control a Government. The Jacobin State,
by protecting with so many favours the middle class, divides
and weakens the moral strength which this class would
possess were it independent, reducing it to petty family
interests, because every family is seduced into availing itself
of the largest possible share of State favours. Politics, in
short, take the shape of family interests. In this respect
Catholic education has been of service to the Jacobin State,
because this system was elaborated for centuries as the best
means of preparing men to receive Church favours. Thus it
has, with certain modifications, also prepared them to receive
those of the Government. Catholic education aims at the
suppression of personality, at the development of docility,
timidity, and reserve, encouraging selfishness and a dislike of
taking trouble, qualities which are all more suited to a class
of officials who regard the State as father and master, than
to strong and energetic political men. Moreover, Catholicism
gives great power to women in family life. It constitutes the
family on authoritarian and selfish principles, and encourages
the idea that politics are merely a field for the promotion of

private and family interests. This is more particularly the policy of women in Latin countries. These exert great influence in the French middle-class family, perhaps of all the most authoritarianly constituted, so that France is more under petticoat government than any other European land.

There are a great number of intelligent and cultured men in the bureaucracy who are thus unable to take any part in politics or exercise any influence on public opinion. Hence the sentiment of social solidarity is feeble in France, public opinion passive and inert. And this is one of the reasons why political struggles are so fierce, for a man who wishes to influence public opinion knows what a heavy weight he has got to move, and realizes that he must use strong measures. France is rather like a bull before whose eyes we must wave a flaming flag in order to excite him. The hatred of Jews, of Italians, of English or some similar class, the panic of spies or fear of revolution : all these matters tend to keep more refined men from mixing themselves up with politics. It is not every one who cares for this trade of exciting the bull with red rags, as also there are many who do not care for the office of agent of favours, of which a French political career consists. No deputy or minister can long retain the good-will of the public if he does not manage to procure many Government favours for his partisans and *entourage*, a business in which mediocre men frequently make a great success, but in which men of intelligence fail. Thus the political class is of the commonest order, and consists of men with slight culture and of a low moral standard.

This leads to another evil : the bureaucracy are too powerful and not sufficiently plastic. It is composed of ill-paid officials, who as a recompense receive life appointments. Each possesses a certain degree of protective influence, and many of the higher are able to place their own caprices before the public welfare, retain positions to which they are not suited, oppose reforms which for some reason or other they do not approve. The ministers, who are at the head of the bureaucracy, ought to insist on the executive serving France, not France the executive; they ought, in short, to temper and control faction spirit, known in France under the name of *mandarinism*. But the ministers are, for the better part, commonplace men, political intriguers of little importance and limited education—at the best they are elegant writers and orators, not intelligent men of action made to rule. What authority can they have over the administration, composed of fixed officials, who know all its mechanism, and have been for years the centre of influence and favours? The executive is the real master of France. The ministers have no power over it, and have to content themselves with being responsible before the public for all its errors. Above all, the heads of a popular administration, such as the army, are all-powerful; no ministers could ever prevent them from doing as they chose.

Thus, contrary as it is to the general belief, the greatest defect of the French social system lies in conservatism. The European public sees the French Ministry change with bewildering frequency; they hear statistical *dilettantes* repeat that the average duration of a French administration is eight months and sixteen days, that from the 4th of September, 1870, to the end of 1897, thirty-seven ministries followed one another; and they conclude that all continuity and seriousness is lacking in the French Government. But the mutability of the ministry is, on the contrary, a guarantee of the immobility of the routine whereby France is governed. France is the most conservatively governed land in Europe, because the ministries, by remaining in power for such a short period at a stretch, have no chance of altering or modifying the methods and traditions of the bureaucracy. What could the most energetic of ministers do? He arrives and studies, but no sooner does he begin to understand the nature of the executive which he has to direct than he is dismissed. The reforms of public services are generally only possible when the bureaucracy itself wakes up to their necessity. The initiative is generally given by the permanent officials of the ministry, not by the ministers themselves.

A third drawback to the Jacobin State is the alarming destruction of wealth it entails ; its military policy, which is its outcome, costs millions to the nation. Moreover, the executive is anything but thrifty ; on the contrary, it is extravagant and wasteful. The balance sheet of a Jacobin State normally shows a deficit, whose necessary consequence is the continual increase of taxes and the national debts, the slow or rapid impoverishment of the country.

In short, and this is where chance is the greatest evil, the Jacobin State constantly wears itself out in self-contradictions which augment the number of its enemies. It is composed of an official class abounding in clever but ill-guided men, and of a body of politicians of mediocre worth. Before all else, these all have to uphold their power as a minority, in opposition to the majority, and then satisfy as best they can the various parties, insuring intellectual and political liberty to the liberal minority. They have to make the Catholic population forget their impiety, by distributing money favours ; they have to keep the people contented, and satisfy the universal military patriotism, which is the soul of the French Government. We can easily understand how these efforts result in contenting no one.

And so it happens that, under the sway of whatever Government France may be, the true nature of its political system is always Cæsarism—that is, a universally protective, prodigal, and warlike state. The republic may attenuate the Cæsarism of the second empire, it cannot abolish it. It, too, is prodigal of public money to give to the people, in a more refined and civilized form *panem et cirsenses*. It also is ambitious for trophies, not from Europe, but Africa. It also is weakened by the military oligarchy, which devour thousands upon thousands in an administration which is almost irresponsible.

In short, the evil of evils is that the Jacobin State appears too liberal to the Catholics, too authoritarian to the Liberals. The first consider it impious that the crucifix should be removed from the schools, nuns from the hospitals, and that the publication of books which deride human and divine authority should be countenanced. The others consider as tyrannical a state where free principles are professed rather than practised, where the highest ministerial officials enjoy almost uncontrolled authority, and where citizens have scarcely any means of defending themselves against their injustice. This latent discord assumes every day more and more the shape of antagonism between the Government and executive. Men from Jesuit schools, who have received Catholic education, predominate in the executive. In the political world, on the contrary, liberal ideas prevail. In the French parliament, radical liberalism is represented by a larger number of socialists and radicals than anywhere else in Europe. Thus France has already witnessed radical ministries, that have filled conservatives with terror, who likened them to a vanguard of the revolution that was coming into power. But what could they do, when their instrument of rule was a narrow-minded and bigoted executive ? Even had these ministers been bolder reformers than they were, they would have been none the less impotent at the head of so slow and conservative an executive.

But the greatest contradiction of all can be observed in the policy of the State towards the Church. The Jacobin State is founded on a system of protection, and, as we have observed, no education is so well suited as that of the Church to prepare men for a *régime* of patronage. The lay education which the Government attempted to organize was very imperfect in comparison : the result of a few years' labour is weak beside the work of ages. Thus the Jacobin State is tempted to avail itself of the Church as an excellent implement for disciplining the masses, but it had never been able to do anything very definite in this direction for fear of rousing the Church's dormant ambition for absolute power. Thus the spiritual policy of the Jacobin State has always wavered during this century, and still wavers. When it feels itself threatened by the insubordinate disposition of the people, it attempts making advances to the Church, sacrificing part of that intellectual liberty which it is its historical function to insure to France. When this policy rouses too much discontent in the intellectual classes, it abandons the Church and returns to more liberal methods.

VIII

This continuous state of vacillation and contradiction, so characteristic of the educated classes in France, finds a unique expression in those three popular Parisian journalists : Henry Rochefort, Paul Cassagnac, and Edward Drumout. Here are three men and three papers which would be quite incomprehensible anywhere but in France, and which represent marvellously the state of feeling that accompanies so singular and curious a form of government as the Jacobin.

Who are they ? The titles of their journals are equally *bizarre*. The name of Cassagnac's paper is *L'Autorité*, dry and concise as a shield borne by a brawny arm ; that of Rochefort's is *L'Intransigeant*, which is proud and emphatic as a challenge ; Drumout's organ bears the name *La Libre Parole*, which title is unprecise and transcendental, like to a mystical book. The one wishes to express his contempt of the crowd ; the other his hatred of the tyrannies of the powers that be ; the third his insufferance of any lie respected by universal abjectness.

In reality all three represent the same thing : a spirit of desperate malignity towards everything. It would seem that each of them aims at a special target: Cassagnac at the republic, Rochefort at the bourgeoisie, Drumout at the Jews. But this looks like an artifice to direct public attention to the tricks of the shooter, who really aims far beyond his little target. Angry discontent at everything, insolent contempt for all that was, furious hatred towards all that is, gloomy pessimism for the future, combined with vague prophesies of extraordinary events ; such are the airs which these singers of political woes, these Jeremiahs of French society at the end of the nineteenth century, never tire of singing. Regularly every morning they write that France is on the verge of perdition, that her arsenals are empty, her frontiers exposed to the enemy, her powerful ones at discord and more ambitious for personal gain than for public glory, her soldiers desperately resolute to do their duty, but without confidence, France was never so humiliated and badly served as she is to-day. What other ambition have her foreign ministers than to be the servitors of the German Emperor ? France is the most wretched country on earth ; her industries are ruined, agriculture is no better off, her wealth is stagnant : in a few more years' time she will be reduced to sleep on straw. And what about their verdicts on the best-known and most popular politicians ? They are all low comedians, rogues and idiots destitute of ideas, of dignity or energy, their only care is to stuff their pockets ; and when the reader, exasperated by this angry criticism, asks, " But what can be the end of so desperate a country ? " the three *confrères* answer him with vague but fearful premonitions ; they speak of imminent convulsions, they hint at universal slaughters, at the renewal of bloodshed and disorder, of supreme judgments and supreme justice.

Such is the tone in which the three most popular Parisian journalists, these three *canailles* of the pen, these pavement Cassandras, treat social and political questions both great and small. The temperament of the three writers are certainly diverse : Cassagnac is stormy, Drumout mystical, Rochefort ironical. But their daily task is the same : a task of furious universal onslaught, to which we find nothing similar in history excepting the mission of the Hebrew prophets. These three Parisian journalists have conceived the idea, like the Hebrew prophets, of making themselves little *colporteurs* and retail salesmen of discontent and pessimism among the people, like so many greengrocers and fishmongers in the market ; to find the merchant in his office during a pause in business while he seeks a moment's repose ; to stop the worker on the way to his shop, and the scholar on the road to school ; to seat himself besides the business man eating a hurried lunch at an eating-house ; to go and exchange a few words with the lazy official slowly looking over the work at his office. By means of their papers, which circulate everywhere, they speak to every one, to rich and poor, women and men, the educated and the ignorant; and in the minds of all they try to insinuate the same discontent, or, perhaps more correctly, to express well what these already feel confusedly.

Insult and defamation are the two weapons necessary to papers such as these. The axiom on which is based the philosophy of these three men is, that every one who opposes them are rogues of the lowest grade. Honest but mistaken belief is a thing which, according to them, does not exist. Thus they speak of all their enemies in a lofty tone of contempt, and the form with which they express this corresponds to the sentiment: it is violent and furious, composed of a choice collection of extreme adjectives and substantives. To express the fact that a man is anti-pathetic, one of these writers will say that he is disgusting and revolting; to say that another is not intelligent, he calls him a d—d fool. A third is labelled a thief, brigand, violator. This simply signifies that, in the writer's opinion, the probity of this person is not entirely free from doubt. It follows that as the most virulent adjectives are used in mild cases, there is no means of sufficiently increasing the penalty when grave faults are to be treated. As in those societies where the lightest offences are punished with death, no stronger punishment can be found for grave crimes, and the notions of crime and punishment grow confused, so these executioners of the pen so massacre their enemies, guilty of small transgressions, that they are unable to graduate the chastisement to meet the case of worse scoundrels.

Insult and defamation are twin sisters. Not only are these writers prodigal of insults, but they recount horrible and totally false tales about their enemies, which they affirm with the utmost impudence, as though they possessed authentic documents in proof. The laws against defamation of character remain paralyzed in face of such audacity, because timid and weak-kneed laws always recede before fearless crime.

But surely the French conscience must be in a bad way to be able to take any pleasure, even a purely literary one, instead of feeling moral nausea, in reading these invectives and lies, invented every day to satisfy blind party hatred! The world, as represented by these maniacs, is like those Chinese pictures, devoid of perspective or proportion, where all the figures are squashed out flat, near objects are smaller than distant ones, the lodgers taller than the roofless houses they inhabit, the horses larger than the trees round which they graze. What would become of the senses and reason of a man who for years saw nothing but Chinese figures of this order? He would lose all count of the reality of things, of their proportion and solidity. Thus it happens also to those who accustom themselves to consider the moral world without perspective or proportion, as represented by these enraged denouncers, to whom the smallest venial offence is equal to the greatest mortal sin. In the end they lose all sense of moral reality and its gradations, and grow to look upon the world as a horde of horrible scoundrels, created to be observed by the only four honest pairs of eyes that exist : the journalists' and his own. But precisely because with this bitter pessimisim they satisfy a social need, the public permits them to say all that they choose, even the most repulsive thing. They allow Rochefort, in the midst of Catholic France, to call the Pope "ce vieux roublard de Pecci ; " they allow him to associate the name of Mary with a filthy word. What matters it to the public? He loves his journalist none the less because he wounds his feelings so

roughly ; he likes him because he expresses well the cold
bitterness which lies in the human heart suffering from the
stings of unrevenged hatreds.   These terrible literary *frondes*
represent one aspect of the revolutionary spirit, that deep-
rooted unrest which knows no definite direction, that species
of nervous tremor which from time to time seizes a multitude
weary of long oppression and not comforted by the hope of
any near relief, whence are born mystical revolutions such
as Christianity, outbursts of war-like ardour such as the
Napoleonic conquests, revolutions which swamp cities in
blood like the French Revolution, a psychological epidemic
like Boulangism, or a violent, and I might almost say Neronic,
journalism like the Parisian.   A serious disease for a people
is that revolutionary spirit which vaguely dreams of change
and knows not of what order it should be, a disease which
can only be cured by the spirit of continuous progress ; but
this spirit is never found under a despotic Government, and
the Jacobin State, despite its appearances, is despotic.

IX

The conclusions to be drawn from what precedes are
these.   Notwithstanding its military character, a Government like the French, whose executive is so conservative, slow,
and ill-controlled, degenerates into a permanent condition
of military weakness.   The power of an army nowadays
depends on its organization, which should be constantly
improved in accordance with the mutability of our age.
French ministers are not sufficiently plastic to fulfil this
work.   It is by no means rash to suppose that many of the
milliards spent on the army since 1870 have been wasted ;
this is easily comprehensible to any one who knows what

these uncontrolled administrations are worth. The French executive was capable of organizing a good army under Napoleon I. because the organization of armies was then a rudimentary affair, and, slow as it was, it was then the most rapid and perfect administration in Europe. Now it has been improved on, and armies require to be more delicately made and with less clumsy tools.

THE MILITARY OUTLOOK
IN ITALY

CHAPTER VIII

THE MILITARY OUTLOOK IN ITALY

I

THE second Napoleonic empire was a splendid blazing sun ; the kingdom of Italy, which was formed out of the revolutions and wars of 1859-60, was its moon, small, pretty, and shining with reflected light.

The ancient oak of absolutism, and the spiritual theocracy of the Catholic Church, blasted by the Napoleonic victories, had reflourished in Italy after 1815. The old *régime* was restored there much more effectually than in France ; monarchism was re-established ; the Church regained possession of a large portion of her wealth, by means of which, in league with the State, she once more extended her protection over society. With the consent and deferential supervision of the State, she then undertook the education of the middle and upper classes, in whom she hoped to inspire a healthy respect for secular and ecclesiastical authority ; whilst to the working classes no instruction was imparted, as it was deemed too dangerous a charity.

The Government endeavoured to check, by every means in their power, the development of trade and industry, and to impede the formation of a class of independent, cultured, and wealthy tradesmen, which would most probably have been a hotbed of liberal ideas. In short, the object aimed at was

Q

to keep the middle classes in subjection by forcing them to rely solely on State or Church employment. Italian society was composed of an aristocracy of large landed proprietors, bigoted, ignorant, and charitable ; of a middle class studying only the Latin and Italian languages, intolerant of the revolutionary culture of France and England, living on Government posts and ecclesiastical benefices ; of an ignorant, narrow-minded class of merchants, whose only occupation, beyond their antiquated commerce, was to cheer the king when he walked abroad, and to fulfil scrupulously their religious duties, not forgetting to give liberally to Church charities ; and of a working class composed of artisans and peasants, for the most part ignorant, boorish, lazy, and pugnacious, who lived partly by their own work, and partly on charity doled out by State and convents.

Fortunately, the revolution of 1848 was an earthquake which so shook and battered the walls of this citadel of tyranny and ignorance, that it could not stand much longer. In Piedmont a liberal party was formed, calling itself the Moderate party, headed by a great man, Camilla Cavoir. Availing themselves of the help of diplomacy, this party succeeded in overthrowing the mainstay of reaction in Italy and Austria, and in conquering the peninsula by force of arms, and in substituting an united state for the many ancient ones it found existing.

The Moderates who, under the leadership of Cavoir, commenced from Turin, and, on his death, completed the military conquest of Italy, were the Jacobins of Italy. The title of Moderates, which they assumed, must not delude us. They represented a cultured minority, a handful of " intellectuals," who hated the mean and petty *régime* of political and spiritual tyranny prevailing in Italy. They admired the flourishing civilization which France and England enjoyed, thanks to their more liberal institutions ; and desired to confer on the Italians political and intellectual liberty, and all those benefits of modern civilization, trade, railways, the telegraph, which had been opposed by the former Governments. They were able to confound and strengthen this desire with another great political dream which then fascinated all cultured minds, and which had been roused to life in Italy by the Napoleonic conquests : I allude to the patriotic fever, the desire for a united national Government free from foreign intervention. Patriotic ambition, combined with a love of freedom and admiration for the industrial civilization of the nineteenth century, formed the programme of the men who made modern Italy.

The Italian Jacobins, however, had to face the same difficulty as their French brethren. The grandeur of modern civilization, the necessity for liberal reforms, was only realized by a small minority. Members of the nobility courageously and devotedly took part in the Italian revolution, but we cannot say that the nobility, as a whole, ever sided for the new order of things. For the most part, their education had been too narrow to permit of their being anything but devoted to the ancient *régime*. The bourgeoisie mostly lived under the protection of State and Church, in Government posts, or in the ranks of the clergy ; so that, even discounting the ignorance and narrow bigotry prevailing in most families, we could not expect them to revolt against a system by which they lived. The working classes, ignorant and boorish, only wished to eat well and amuse themselves, and cared nothing for parliamentary rule and liberty of thought and Press, for they did not read, and their only thought was for horse-racing, the game of Pallors, and the Lotto.

The good fortune of the small Jacobin minority consisted in the fact that in 1848, owing to circumstances and intrigues which it would take too long to enumerate, it was able to seize the reins of power in Piedmont, and make that province, which had adopted parliamentary institutions, the basis of operations for a military conquest.

The new Piedmontese Government was strengthened by those intellectual Italians who were forced to emigrate from their country. It procured the assistance of France and of all those *déclassés*, discontented men, rebels, heroes, and maniacs who abound in a country so fertile in great men, criminals, and fanatics as Italy. But the conquest once achieved, the Jacobin State found itself in the same straits as in the French Revolution—that is to say, they had to *enforce* by violent means a *régime* of liberty on a country that was, as a whole, indifferent or adverse ; to establish the minority rule in the name of popular sovereignty ; to substitute their own protective system for that of the Church.

In short, a Jacobin State similar to the French, and initiated in a great measure from it, was established in Italy in 1859-60. It gave freedom to the intellectual minority weary of Church tyranny ; it organized secular education ; it instituted civil marriage ; it suppressed the convents, and in many ways diminished the Church's privileges, and despoiled it of its wealth. But the middle class had for centuries been accustomed to live under Church and State protection, and thus the Jacobin Government was forced, for the same reasons which led to similar results in France, to become its protector, or it would never have found favour in a society whose interests it injured by reforms, whose conscience it wounded by its impiety. The same reasons, in the same example, further led to the foundation of a vast civil and military bureaucratic class. It was thus possible to give salaries and livelihoods to a large number of persons, drawn chiefly from the bourgeoisie. Thus a nucleus of men interested in the maintenance of the new *régime* was formed, and as this administration became the centre of universal protection, it rapidly collected round itself a crowd of jobbers and mendicants whose affairs the Italian Government administers to this day in the interests of a small oligarchy. This protection, in some respects, took the shape of an effort to introduce the new Anglo-French type of civilization, to which the previous Governments had always been hostile, and which the country would certainly not have adopted of its own accord, so strong was the spirit of conservatism, timidity, and ignorance bequeathed by the old *régime*. Everything had to be done at the instigation of the Government. It opened new roads and forced the municipalities to do likewise ; it constructed public works of various descriptions, established schools, telegraphic communication, and railroads ; it founded banks, and improved the various public services, over which it expended fabulous sums and contracted heavy debts. All these novelties being imitated from France, the parliament finally grew to resemble the French parliament, and became an instrument in the hands of an oligarchy. This enabled them to turn to their own advantage all the institutions of the nascent state. Thus the Italian parliament appears to be modelled on the English, but it is in reality similar to the French, more especially in two essential characteristics which we should seek for in vain in England : the interference of the Government and executive in elections, and the disintegration and mobility of parliamentary parties.

In other words, the Jacobin State in Italy consists of permanent functionaries, democratically recruited from all

classes, but more particularly from the middle, and of a
parliamentary oligarchy which was very restricted until 1882,
because, till then, the rights of suffrage was accorded to very
few. In the first years of the new rule the electors of
deputies numbered only 300,000, of whom little more than
a third exercised their prerogative ; so that 100,000 persons
were the masters of the State. Since 1882 electoral rights
were conceded to all those who had received elementary
education, but the number of electors was always small,
because many neglected to vote. Thus in 1897, the citizens
who took the trouble to inscribe their names in the voters'
registrar only numbered 2,120,900, and of these in the
general election of 1897 only 1,199,175 voted, *i.e.* about
3 per cent. of the population.

II

Now, amongst the other institutions which it was attempted
to introduce into Italy, along with the rest of Napoleonic
Cæsarism, there was militarism, with which we have principally to deal. It was planned to give to Italy a great army
and a formidable navy, without any thought of the expense.
Two factors played a part in this policy : one ideal, the other
material. The ideal was the renewal of the political and
military greatness of Italy ; the material, the need felt by the
Government for the possession of a strong force to quell the
resistance to the new *régime* which, more especially in Southern
Italy, was much more serious than it has been represented
hitherto in the histories written by the victors, the need to
excite the sympathy of the population in the new *régime* by
attractive illusions of glory, and to find a social position for
a large number of persons.

The creation of a strong army and navy led the new Government to spread throughout Italian society those sentiments and prejudices which lie at the bottom of French militarism. It was necessary to rouse the educated classes to an enthusiasm for military glory and territorial expansion, to organize that system of mutual intimidation which works so well in France. It was a delicate moral undertaking which the ruling classes had set themselves, and at which they have worked with energy ever since 1860.

But this work was rendered difficult by an inherent contradiction which greatly reduced its moral efficacy. The traditions of the Italian revolution are full of a fine spirit of justice, a broad humanitarianism, which manifested itself practically in the plebiscites, and in that theory of respect for nationality according to which it is wrong to coerce a people into subjection to foreign rule. This sentiment is one of the most beautiful inheritances that has come down to the Italians from the revolution, and it is all the more valuable for being deep-rooted and universal and belonging to no party in particular.

Now, a militarism like the French cannot prosper if it does not popularize the contrary principle : that victory is always glorious whatever be the motive for the combat, that one nation must bully and coerce other peoples. The Napoleonic were able to establish the traditions on which French militarism depends, because they represented anything but the brutal spirit of conquest. The wars of Italian independence could not have this effect, because they were waged—those against Austria, at least—in the name of international justice. The principles of conquest, and those of justice between nations, are diametrically opposed ; but the Italian Government long wavered between the two. It dared not altogether relinquish the principle that gave it birth, but it sought at the same time to insinuate the passion for conquest in the Italian mind. This contradiction was a source of military weakness to Italy, which had the misfortune to be born, not with an original sin, but an original virtue. An indestructible spirit of international justice, widely diffused, more especially amongst the educated classes, which renders impossible the popularity of those bellicose-patriotic sentiments so prevalent in the French bourgeoisie.

The Abyssinian War is a singular proof of Italian public feeling on this point. It was the work of a few high-placed military functionaries and foreign ministers, in collusion with a parliamentary faction that recognized Crispi as its leader. At Court, and in the ministries among bureaucrats, a "project" for vast colonial conquests found favour, not because it represented any national interests, but with a view to military prestige, and to forward dubious speculations that should give work to unoccupied officials and financiers in search of lucrative investments. Parliament, which was more directly in touch with the people, has always been anti-Africa, but with that docility which characterises its dealings with the Government, wherever private interests are not concerned, it did not interfere. The people, who are always attracted by military theatricality, applauded the first expedition, believing it would prove innocuous and successful. But by degrees the matter assumed a tragic aspect. This, however, was ignored or unknown except by a few whose foresight was vain. Suddenly the moment arrived when the whole nation should have assisted the Government in its war against Abyssinia. But at that moment the country felt that it lacked strength for several reasons, amongst others, because the undertaking roused scruples in the minds of many, the result of those liberal traditions in the name of which United Italy had been created.

The fate of the campaign was not even known, owing to the rigour with which the Government enforced silence on its adversaries. Hence a continual hesitation perplexed the minds of the public. This invasion of a foreign country, whether barbarous or not, was repugnant to a large majority ; but the disgust of the peace faction would possibly have been less evident if matters had gone well. It naturally grew stronger after the crushing defeat, and contributed towards compelling the Government to abandon all ideas of re-conquest.

Another reason why the Italian Jacobin Government did not succeed in popularizing the passion for military glory among the upper classes, was the poverty of military traditions in Italy.

The military history of France, more especially in our century, is of grand proportions, and furnishes copious material for the formation of a military reputation. The French do not merely feed their military fervour with the great records of national history ; each family has its own recollections : grandfathers and great-grandfathers who fought under Napoleon I., fathers, uncles, and relations who took part in the Italian wars of 1859, in the Mexican campaign, in the defences of 1870, a whole immense archive of family traditions, which are bequeathed from father to son, and which reanimates in young men the military passion of their fathers. In Italy, on the contrary, the history of the *risorgunento* is relatively poor in heroic deeds, because the revolution was made as circumstances permitted, *i.e.* much more by diplomatic manœuvres than by cannonades. The year 1859 was not an epoch of great conquests and wars such as those which disturbed the early years of the century. Such would have convulsed European society too profoundly, and the Powers would not permit Italy to turn the world upside down. The only truly great and terrible war would have been that of 1859, if it had had its full evolution ending with the conquest of Vienna. But that was cut short at its best point. In the other wars, those of 1860 and 1861 not excepted, the force of arms was always combined with diplomatic manœuvres and the underground work of corruption. But diplomatic ability, combined with patience and good luck, is capable of founding a State, not of establishing a warlike reputation. This can only arise from great victorious wars generating in the people a passion for military glory, and such wars were no longer possible in the years that saw the establishment of Italian unity.

III

But all these were secondary causes, which do not entirely explain the military weakness of contemporary Italy. The tragic history of the African campaign has demonstrated the fact that Italy lacks the strength to resist a long and painful aggressive war. Look at France. Twenty-seven years ago, both reason and humanity counselled peace after Sedan. And yet, if the peace had then been concluded, the military pride of the people would have received a severe shock, while the desperate resistance which followed the first decisive repulses, contributed to save the military sentiments of the public from that dejection which follows on defeat. Now, this resistance was possible because a minority of madmen had the courage to enforce it, at the cost of terrible cruelty to the country which was in need of peace, urging on by martial trials and death sentences the forcibly recruited armies. Indeed, the army, during this inhuman cruel effort, was finally seized with a species of collective homicidal mania, that lasted several months, whose most terrible manifestation was the suppression of the Commune. Those were terrible days of bloodshed, during which every person lived in such a state of sanguinary excitement that no more was thought of shooting a man than we should think of dealing him a blow. If the Italian Government had possessed the cruel energy which the French displayed in similar emergencies, it would, after Abba Carima, have forcibly repressed the demonstrations in Rome and Milan ; it would have threatened the most turbulent provinces with siege ; it would have despatched a great army to Africa, and severely applied all the penalties of the penal code to any soldier who did not properly control his reluctance ; it would have had no scruples about ruining the country in order to raise the necessary funds. In short, it would have tried to quell the feelings of the nation by brute force. Instead, the Government hastened to reassure the country by concluding peace, and the nation renounced without a pang all hopes of revenge. Nothing is so detested and unpopular in Italy as the subject of Africa. The thought of another war horrifies the people to such an extent that the little *coteries* of soldiers and politicians who, in their hearts, sigh after another campaign, dare not manifest their ideas, however feebly, despite the fact that Italy is also one of those countries where the desires of the majority are less considered than those of the ruling oligarchy.

The real cause of the weakness of Italian militarism must be sought in the weakness of its Jacobin Government. This Jacobin State did not find in Italy the same favourable conditions as in France. Hence what were tolerable evils in

France, in Italy became terrible crises which weaken the country and render its future uncertain and perilous. No ordinarily sane politician believes himself to be omnipotent, and yet nearly all act as though this were their opinion. No policy or institution can be created out of nothing. Like chemical compound, or works of art, they must be drawn from certain materials or necessary elements, without which all creative force is futile. The majority of political errors arise from the fact that men do not realize that, without certain human intellectual and moral elements, it is as impossible to create certain institutions or carry out certain policies, as it is impossible to make a lamp burn without oil. This is the case of latter-day Italy. A small group of politicians dream of military glory without observing that, not only the social elements necessary to build up a vigorous militarism are lacking, but that the Government has scarcely sufficient strength left to drag on its existence. They have always kept their eyes fixed on French example, and imitated these, but without noticing that the conditions of Italy were very different from those of France.

IV

The superior wealth of France is one of the many reasons why militarism and the Jacobin Government are more prosperous there than in Italy. We have seen that the Jacobin State is essentially wasteful; that it inevitably squanders a large part of its wealth in useless expenditure, in subsidies, bounties, protections, arms, and wars; that it is compelled continually to increase taxes. We can *à priori* affirm that a rich country like France is better able to support the extravagance of its Government than a poorer one. France

consists of a vast plain protected by two mountain-chains, which
are to her like water *reservoires*, from whose summits the ice
constantly melts to irrigate the fertile land. She is warmed
by a sun which shines on her from a safe distance, without
being fierce enough to scorch her, or so pallid as to freeze.
She is covered with ancient and beautiful towns, densely
populated by a conservative people deeply imbued with the
mystical oriental spirit of Catholicism, hard and ferocious at
bottom, but clever, industrious, and energetic. She looks out
on the Atlantic and the Mediterranean, is situated in the
centre of Europe so as to be almost its heart. By land and
sea her frontiers touch those of nearly every other European
country—Italy, Switzerland, Germany, Belgium, England,
and Spain. What a magnificent position whence to carry
on all manner of commerce and industries, and to exercise
a powerful influence over European society! Further, her
traditions of civilization are more deep-rooted and ancient
than in any other European country with the exception of
Greece and Italy. Consequently, France was able to direct
the democratic and Jacobin movement which has played such
an important part in the social and political history of the
century, during the whole of which she has, politically and
intellectually, been at the head of Europe—Prussia, England,
and Russia not excepted—whilst, at the same time, enriching
herself.

Italy, on the other hand, is a much less fertile land.
She is covered with rugged mountains which men have only
succeeded in inhabiting at the cost of immense labour. The
increase of population necessitated the cutting down of all
the mountain forests. But the forests once destroyed, the
mountain torrents poured down into the valleys, flooding
and ruining. In those parts of the country which do not

suffer from this scourge, such as Southern Italy and Sicily, there is a lack of water, the rivers are few and poor, the sun does not warm and fertilize, but scorches. Drought is the terrible foe of agriculture. Few countries, in short, are as badly off for water as Italy. The only part of the country well adapted to agriculture is the valley of the Po. Nor is the position of Italy in Europe so favourable as that of France. It is more isolated, and was still more so during the first half of the century, before the opening of the Suez Canal, and when relations with the Orient had not the importance they now have. Italy looks out on that species of internal court-yard of civilization, the Mediterranean ; from no side does she survey the immense Atlantic, now traversed by the high-roads of the human race. To sum up in a few words, the value of Italy is now calculated at 55 milliard francs, or a quarter of the sum at which France is estimated.

For this reason Italy would not have been able to tolerate, with French facility, the same degree of waste such as a Jacobin State entails, had this waste been of equal intensity and proportion. But such was not the case. This Jacobin Government was constituted in a much more dangerous way in Italy, and disastrous for its economic future. In France it was established at the end of last century, before the great discoveries and inventions of modern civilization had been made, when civilization was less costly and more simple. Thus the State was able to introduce and develop modern civilization under its protection, by degrees, as industrial progress advanced. In Italy, on the contrary, the ancient Governments had kept the country in a state of barbarism, so that when the new Government came into power it had to make up for lost time, and to introduce rapidly that civiliza-tion which in France had slowly penetrated in the course of half a century. But these sudden changes, introduced by a new State, in the midst of an indifferent or hostile country, demanded immense capital, which was procured partly by loans, partly by increase of taxation. To give an idea of the enormous sums which the new civilization cost to Italy, it suffices to say that the expenditure of the Italian Governments, anterior to 1860, amounted to little more than 500 million francs, and that after thirty-six years' continual increase it reached, in 1896, the sum of 1,830,753,509 francs. From the 525 million francs which public expenditure reached previous to 1860, in 1863 it had reached 900 millions; in 1871 it had already reached one milliard and 250 millions, which increased to nearly one milliard and 518 millions of francs in 1881, to rise to one milliard and 936 millions in 1888. Since then, the expenditure vacillates between 1700 and 1800 millions. These increases naturally represent in part the interest of the loans borrowed, which were gigantic, not counting the period from 1860–70, which was an epoch of war necessary to the unification of Italy. The public debt, which in 1871 stood at 9 milliard francs, had increased in 1897 to something more than 13 milliards—a debt of 4000 million francs contracted during twenty-six years of peace! If we add to this increasing expenditure and debt of the State those of the communes, which have also notably augmented, we can gather some idea of the waste of money which followed in Italy on the foundation of the Jacobin State.

V

Such immense expenditure would have been bad for the country even had it been made wisely, with the sole object of rapidly civilizing Italy. But the Jacobin Government was

little capable of performing this task judiciously and economically. It was composed, as we have seen, of a bureaucracy
imitated from the French and of a parliamentary oligarchy ;
but the bureaucracy, recruited in haste from diverse elements,
was still less suited than the French to fulfil its task with
economy and perfection. The parliament was at first led by
a small number of educated, honest, and wise men, who had
grown up under the influence of Cavour, and who knew how
to temper the faults and errors of a revolutionary Government.
But this *élite* disappeared with time, and the cultured classes
were unable to find others to replace it. An idea has survived
in the Italian middle class—a heritage from the former protective Governments—that the only decent position that can
be held by the son of a not wealthy family is some Government post, and that the Government is something sublime
and superior to ordinary men, which it is madness to oppose
or criticize. The Oriental idea of the sanctity of authority,
inherited by the Church from the Roman Empire, has survived through the middle ages to our own times. The
middle class passively accepted the new Government as it had
accepted its predecessors. Any policy which favoured the
increase of expenditure, employment, and public works was
popular. It was popular with the workers, who thought it
would be good for work ; with the middle class, for whom
new posts were thus created ; with the higher classes, who, in
the extensive State loans, saw a good investment for their
money. These classes were timid, unaccustomed to business,
and disinclined to run any risk, like all well-to-do people who
live under a protective system ; they therefore found it convenient to make State loans. Thus, after 1882, when the right
of suffrage was extended, it sufficed for an ambitious man to
promise his electors that he would make the Government

spend a lot of money to their advantage in order to get returned. Thus the Italian parliament, more particularly after 1878, became filled with ambitious men of mediocre intelligence, and too often rogues, who were powerful because they knew how to procure, not the well-being of the public, but the transitory well-being of their *coterie* and friends.

In this manner, public opinion in Italy can exercise no control over expenditure. It is a well-known fact that military expenditure is unproductive, and leads to the destruction of capital, because the money invested in a fortress or a barrack is consumed for ever, and has not the power of reproduction like that invested in a prosperous business. Therefore, it is evident that a poor country should avoid such expenditure, unless it seeks its own ruin. And yet, by playing on the ignorance and pusillanimity of the parliamentary oligarchy, the heads of the Italian army easily managed to persuade the Government to augment, beyond the bounds of all reason, the military expenses of the State, and to spend, in twenty-six years (from 1871–97), 8 milliard and 223 million francs on the army and navy, an enormous waste of capital to a country whose total wealth is reckoned at 55 milliards!

Now, this was not all. Money was spent equally lavishly and foolishly on public works, railroads more especially, by whose construction many contractors enriched themselves, through resorting to all manner of fraudulent tricks. It suffices to cite, as an example, that certain railways which the contractors had agreed to build for 202 million francs, in consequence of various intrigues in the end cost 352 millions to the State.

The nation, however, paid little attention to this waste, living happily in the midst of the abundance which so much money spent by the State diffused, without reflecting that

R

such prosperity must naturally be of a transitory character, and that the Government could not long continue such liberality. The better part of the public wealth was spent by the State on these undertakings, and very little remained for the development of national commerce and industry. The result was that while schools, roads, and railways increased, production flagged ;· and this led to heavier taxation. Besides State loans, a large proportion of Italian capital, after 1860, was spent in the cultivation of the monastic lands, which the monks had kept most negligently, in the purchase and untimbering of mountain forests, and the cultivation of unwooded land. Agricultural investments were regarded as safer than hazardous industrial undertakings, in a land where the conservative spirit is strong, and in which, since three centuries, agriculture was found the basis of all riches. But, unfortunately, these agricultural investments proved on trial to be even more dangerous, because fifteen years later agricultural products began to diminish in value, and more especially cereals, owing to the cultivation of new continents and countries.

VI

Increase in population must be added to the former evils. In 1881 the Italian population numbered less than 29 millions; in 1891 it had increased to 31 and a half millions. In France the decrease of population is much deplored, and its cause is earnestly inquired into. Few seem to perceive that the cause lies in the universal State protection applied by the French State to society. Where the middle class, instead of depending for its livelihood on some useful productive pursuit, lives principally on the favours of a public body, stability of population is an advantage, because there the population does not augment, so neither do those who demand its favours and protection, and consequently the lucky minority who benefit by it are better off. The Church fully realizes this, and it therefore made celibacy a necessary condition to its priests and monks. Prudent Malthusian practises take the place of celibacy with those favoured by the State. Moreover, as the Jacobin Government is by its nature a dissipater and destroyer of wealth, sterility by all classes is advantageous to the society it governs, for the country is forced to make up by private economy for the extravagance of the administration. In France and Italy domestic economy is much greater than in England ; more especially in France, where, amongst other economies, economy in children is strictly observed. France borrows many of the workers, necessary to the growing development of civilization, from neighbouring countries, Italy more especially ; and thus other lands have to bear the expenses of rearing these labourers, whom France receives ready to render service. Consequently, there exist in France only a very small number of unemployed.

In any case, the most important point is that the middle class does not augment in France, therefore the State is not constantly forced to satisfy increasing demands for employment and favours. In Italy, with the constitutions of the kingdom, on the contrary, there sprung into being an extensive bureaucracy ; but this class was no more economical in its prolific energies than with the public funds. Almost every one of these middle-class families generated numerous sons, whom their fathers set to study, so that they might fill official posts, whilst many families of the lower bourgeoisie aimed at similar positions for their children. This fecundity resulted in the consumption of the great part of the savings of middle-class families, which are spent in educational expenses, and by diminishing their reserves it ended in impoverishing them, and in the same ratio the chances of finding employment for their sons diminished. For twenty-five years the Italian Government has been continually multiplying official posts ; it has created regiments, schools, divisions, manufactured railways ; the communes have found new jobs for their officials, and augmented the number of public services ; but with the increase of bureaucratic expenses on the one hand, and the waste of public funds on the other, the finances of both State and municipalities came to an end, and they were forced to receive no more functionaries.

When the fountains of Government abundance began to dry up, when, through lack of funds and the impossibility of negotiating fresh loans, the State was forced to check the extension of the bureaucracy, and to put a stop to public works, then, and then only, did the Italians realize what it meant to have allowed themselves so carelessly to be made one of the most heavily taxed nations in the world. The average of State expenses (apart from those that are purely communal) stood at 1821 million francs from 1890 to 1895, whilst the French was 3665 millions, the English 2266 millions, the Belgian 320 millions. Now, as the value of Italy is calculated at 55 milliard francs, while that of France is reckoned at 225, that of England 270, and that of Belgium at 34 milliards, the Italians find themselves in the condition that the French would if they had to pay 7449 milliards in taxes, the English if they paid 8939 milliards, and Belgium if its taxation amounted to 8124 milliards. It is easy to conceive what a terrible drag on industry such gigantic taxation must be. The nation's capacity for consumption is necessarily much reduced by these fearful taxes, which every year withdraw an immense amount of wealth from useful employment to pay huge military expenses. And consumption naturally limits production, since what object is there in producing what cannot be consumed? When the number of the bureaucracy was complete, and the diminution of public works had thrown innumerable workers and middle-class youths out of employment, it proved difficult to them to obtain occupation in private industries, because the enormous taxation had checked their development.

To this must be added a final scourge: protectionism. Availing themselves of the ignorance of the Italian public, who understand economic problems still less than the French, a small number of interested men in 1887 deluded the Parliament, by means of all manner of intrigues, to vote for a new customs tariff, which replaced the free-trade system then prevalent in Italy by an exaggerated *régime* of protectionism. The old fable of protecting national industries was employed to persuade opponents that this project was a means of enriching the country. But its real effects were the inevitable ones of protection, the impoverishment of the masses, which grew worse in Italy than elsewhere, for this class had been so very poor to start with. Protection, moreover, by impeding or rendering impracticable the exportation of agricultural produce, reduced the value of exportable goods (wine, oil, fruit, cereals), and thus it artificially rendered the investment of large capital in land still less profitable. Protection, in short, though it may have benefited a few industries, increased the demand, and raised the price of most manufactures, just as the earnings of the middle class diminished ; so that though it made millionaires of a few fortunate men, and conceded a few brief years of well-being to the working population of certain industrial districts, it rendered the conditions of the middle class and the multitude still more miserable.

VII

The increase in taxation to which the increase in the wealth of the country did not correspond, careless destruction of capital, protection, augmentation of population, impoverishment of agriculture, brought about the crisis which was fatal in a country where one of the three factors of production, men, continually increase ; the second, land, remains stationary ; and the third, money, diminishes, being either destroyed or squandered. Work, in consequence, is miserably paid. Country labourers work, more especially in the rice districts, for wages under a franc a day. Small proprietors, it is calculated, rarely earn so much as £40 a year. In the little towns, where hands are plentiful, there are numbers of men and women who willingly work at the weaving industry fourteen hours a day, for from 1 to 2 francs per diem. In large towns and in trades which demand a higher grade of instruction, a wage of 3.50 francs a day is considered quite princely. Very few workers earn as much as 5 francs a day, and the luckiest are those who succeed in obtaining employment in the Government arsenals and in the great railway offices, where higher salaries are given, and where men cannot be dismissed when work is lacking.

Yet worse is the condition of the middle class. The liberal professions are ill-paid on account of the keen competition ; intellectual ones are not paid at all. Crowds of doctors and

barristers squabble over patients and clients ; lawyers employ
all manner of tricks and ruses to multiply disputes, being more
fortunate in this respect than doctors, who cannot make men
ill by artificial means, in order to be able to cure them afterwards. Thus, with the exception of a few lucky men who
succeed in monopolizing the rare rich clients, the majority
who attend the class of bourgeoisie and workers, that are
growing poorer year by year, have to content themselves with
even poorer remuneration. In large towns excellent young
doctors are to be found who accept 50 centimes for a visit,
and the most capable, those who consider themselves highly
privileged, never ask more than 2.50 or 3 francs. The
richest newspapers rarely pay more than 25 or 30 francs for
an article, and then it must be by some well-known man,
otherwise it is paid 20, 15, 10, or even 5 francs. For 100
francs any publisher can find a person to translate a huge
octavo volume on political economy or medicine from some
foreign language. Young ladies can receive instruction in
the pianoforte for 50 centimes a lesson. The best paid
schoolmasters receive 2000 francs, but the number of these
are few ; they very rarely are paid more than 750 or 800
francs. In a city like Turin there is a certain set of young
teachers who give lessons every day for 100 francs a year !
University professors rarely earn more than 2000 francs.
They are divided into various classes, of which the best paid
receive 5000 francs a year, but the others receive salaries
varying between a minimum of 1200 to a maximum of 3500
francs. A lieutenant in the Italian army receives 5 francs
a day, a captain less than 10. The higher officials are also
relatively poorly paid. The highest salary a judge can receive
is 3500 francs. The president of the Court of Cassation, who
is the highest magistrate in the land, receives 15,000 francs,

a State councillor 9000 francs.   The general director of a
ministry, who is the highest permanent functionary after the
president and vice-president, receives 12,000 francs.

VIII

The ultimate result of this state of things is that in Italy
the Jacobin Government has reached such a degree of weakness that it scarcely manages to drag on.   In France the
State is weakened by many vices and contradictions, but the
middle class, the better educated portion more especially, has
a reserve of moral energy.   One portion of the French
population is really enthusiastic for the ideal of the military
and political supremacy of their nation, another for the great
liberal and democratic principles of the Revolution.   Let an
unfortunate war, like that of 1870, come to pass, or a dark
and tragic history of injustice and horror commence with
the condemnation of an innocent man, and a large number
of energetic and generous persons are found to stir up the
public conscience.   The military formula of the national
honour and the national flag, the formula of the Revolution,
Liberty, Equality, and Fraternity, are still, to a certain
extent, living things to educated France, and the Government
derives thence considerable strength.   Trouble begins, however, when the military and revolutionary formulas are at
variance.   Here also the Jacobin State can depend, with a
fair degree of certainty, on its bureaucracy, which served
the Empire as faithfully as it served the Monarchy and the
Republic, but which believes firmly in the religion of the
army and the French Revolution.

But this state of the French mind is not due to any quality
innate in the people, but in a great measure to the social

conditions of France, more especially to the superior remuneration of labour, more particularly in the middle class. We
have already stated that an essential social condition on
which the morality of a community depends is the remuneration of labour. Where man's labour is badly paid, where the
educated classes—the backbone of modern society—are compelled to work hard for a wretched pittance, ideal energy
slackens ; men abandon themselves to pessimistic indifference,
and seek consolation in exaggerated mysticism. And thus it
happens that the educated class in Italy, disgusted at the
wretched remuneration they receive for their work, weary of
the hard labour they are forced to endure in order to exist,
irritated at their own squalid existence, give themselves up to
a universal *laissez faire,* lack the energy to trouble themselves
about anything outside of the sufferings and bitterness of their
daily life, and grow indifferent to national interests. The
honour of the flag! The absurdities which have taken place
in France on account of this phrase would never have been
possible in Italy. After the battle of Adna the military
party was compelled to abandon any idea of revenge, for
otherwise it ran the risk of creating a revolution. Even to-
day the fate of the monarchy depends to a certain extent on
the future aspect of the African policy. The country wishes
for peace, and cares little about great international questions.
It does not trouble itself in the least about the problem of the
East, or the equilibrium of the Mediterranean. It has no
ambition to share in the division of China. In no country,
perhaps, is there so little interest displayed in international
problems.

In short, the educated classes have sunk deeper than ever
into that condition of political inertia which was always natural
to the Italian bourgeoisie, and which is the sad inheritance

from past Governments. So long as the Government possessed money to spend, this class took some slight interest in the State. Now that they have nothing to hope from it, they abandon it to its own devices. We have already seen that only a small proportion (three per cent. of the population) take part in the elections, and we must add that these consist chiefly of men in humble positions, and that abstention from voting is much more general in large rich cities, such as Milan, than in country districts. The fact is, that the elections are carried on almost entirely by small *coteries* of ambitious men, who naturally recruit their partisans principally from among the ignorant workers, whom they bribe to go to the ballot, while educated men abstain from voting out of indifference or disgust. This abstention is rendered still more general by the Catholics, who have always preached indifference to State politics in the hope of rendering matters intolerably difficult. The Catholic party is very strong, and is led by the High Church prelates, who are clever and ambitious, men who hope to witness the return of the good old days when society could not get on without them. Have they any precise political ideas or programme? None, beyond that of exploiting the Jacobin Government in so far as it can be of use to them, and of creating difficulties for it by preaching abstention from the ballot. Thus the followers of the Catholic party are not above accepting Government posts and investing their savings in Government funds. Indeed, the richest section of the party, which consists of nobles and great land-owners, has succeeded in obtaining from the hated Government protection for corn just when its price was going down in the American markets. But the Catholics have never agreed to recognize the Government they exploit.

Difficulties are thus ever on the increase, because the

indifference of the middle class is still the least danger which threatens the Jacobin State in Italy. A large proportion of the middle class, and even of the bureaucracy, is, in fact, growing hostile to the Government. The Government can depend on the bureaucracy in France ; in Italy it cannot. Here many officials, dissatisfied with their careers, which are blighted by the poverty of the State, burdened with families and in debt, frequently disgusted by the injustice to which they are subjected, and the intrigues necessary for promotion, hate the Government they serve. In the ranks of the bureaucracy there are many who profess republican-socialist ideas. In political elections in large towns it has been observed that socialist candidates run a better chance of getting elected in the districts inhabited by Government officials and the educated classes generally. Let us add to this, disaffection of another order, but equally grave, against the parliamentary oligarchy. That portion of the middle class which has received a university education and represents the cultured Italy of to-day, by reason of its poverty and the hard work to which it is condemned in order to live if it follows a liberal profession, if it enters the bureaucracy is excluded from taking any part in politics. Thus parliament grows ever fuller of rich noodles who look upon politics as a species of sport, and of ambitious intriguers, who see in it only a means of satisfying their vanity and private interests. What greater dilemma could one conceive for a country than for its enlightened men to be condemned to inertia whilst perceiving the evil and its cause and remedy ; and for education, which should be a fountain of courage and faith for State reforms, to be only another ground for discouragement, and to afford merely the vain knowledge of an apparently incurable evil ?

In the midst of this universal indifference with regard to

politics, one party only prospers, and that is the socialist. The only seriously organized party which knows how to keep ambitious men and intriguers at bay is the socialist, which is led by intelligent and educated men. It organizes the workers and collects the votes of the discontented members of the middle class, meeting everywhere with a success which, not without cause, alarms the Government. The elector frequently has to choose between two candidates : the one a socialist, the other an ignorant and dishonest rogue. How is he to act ? Many belonging to the upper classes abstain ; others, in disgust and despair, vote for the socialist. We can easily understand how all this favours the socialist and perplexes the Government. But the socialist party, in its turn, although it is strong, owing to the weakness of its rivals, is undermined by an indissoluble contradiction. Is it, or is it not, a revolutionary party ? Equally good arguments could be found to prove either of the two hypothesis, because the true nature of the party is very ambiguous. It knows that the sympathy it inspires in the cultured classes is due to the fact that it is considered solely as a party of reform, which desires to ameliorate the existing Government, not as a party which desires at an early date to upset property and society. It therefore makes a great point of insisting on its evolutionary character. But another branch of the party conceives socialism in a far more revolutionary light, which affrights the Government, just as the evolutionary faction assuage the intellectual minority who intrigue against the Government.

IX

Is it difficult now to understand the reason of the bankruptcy of Italian militarism ? The Jacobin State, which is like the scaffolding of militarism, is too weak in Italy. This Government rests on three pillars : military prestige which arises from fortunate wars ; money ; and the material strength of the army. In France, the State still possesses much money, although less, perhaps, than at one period ; a military prestige which, though somewhat antiquated, is still considerable ; and a strong army. Italy no longer possesses either military prestige or money ; the army alone remains.

Surrounded by the indifference of that portion of society which it chiefly benefits, pursued by the discontent of another class which it oppresses, not master of its own bureaucracy, poor in funds, opposed by some as impious and an enemy of the Pope, by others as being corrupt, wasteful, having exhausted all the resources of taxation, with a population so miserably impecunious that a rise in the price of bread, such as that which took place in 1898, reduced large numbers to the verge of starvation and drove them to rebellion—the Jacobin Government is too much in need of the army to maintain internal order to undertake great foreign wars. In the social crisis which convulses Italy, militarism is altering in character and object. It has become a State weapon for internal defence. The Jacobin Government, by its constitution and origin, is obliged to concede to the country a certain degree of intellectual liberty ; it cannot rule despotically like the Russian. In order to suppress and efface the tradition of liberty which it itself introduced into the Italian State, it would need to be very strong. On the other hand, if it were thus strong it would have no more need than the French to suppress the liberties of press, speech, and meeting. At the same time it has to contrive so that this *régime* of freedom should not prove too favourable to its enemies. In this state of things we perceive the contradictory character of the Italian Government. It has established a *régime* of liberty based on periodical epochs of military dictatorship. The Italian army has become the tool of these intermittent dictatorships, which grow more and more necessary to protect the State against those periodical crises to which it is falling a victim. The first great experiment of this order was made in the spring of 1898, when, owing to the famine riots, half of Italy was declared in a state of siege, the constitution suspended, military law declared, and the officers charged to decimate the ranks of the opposition (the socialists and clerical more especially) by a series of arbitrary trials whose absurdity and extravagance it would be difficult to imagine. Criminals, vagabonds, honest workmen, loyal and courageous writers, priests, monks, even merchants, political men, and deputies—more than 5000 men in all—were, in the course of two months, brought before the military tribunals, tried, and condemned in hot haste, without any preliminary examination, frequently condemned for offences not written in the penal code to punishments not assigned there. Then by slow degrees things resumed their natural course, and the *régime* of semi-liberty which Italy enjoys by degrees returned. The unjust sentences of the courts-martial are gradually cancelled by royal pardons and amnesties, for which the excuses are found in regal birthdays, and, once all the men are liberated, national life will return to its pristine calm until the next convulsion.

Until several important reforms will have been made, the

Italian Government will be compelled periodically to rouse itself from its habitual apathy to these attacks of dictatorial cruelty, during which it will endeavour to frighten its enemies, red and black, socialist and clerical, threatening them with the sword which twenty-five years ago it forged, according to its own saying, in order to spill foreign blood. For this reason we need not fear that the peace of Europe will be disturbed by Italy. Nevertheless, any initiative for partial disarmament, whether it come from the Pope, the Czar, or any other powerful personage, will always meet with a cold or hostile reception, whether open or covert, from the Italian Government. Although it has no longer any desire to wage war, neither does it wish to discontent the military class, of whom it stands in need periodically to strike and weaken its enemies in order to prolong its own infirm existence, and to postpone, as long as it may, the reforms necessary to its cure.

MILITARISM IN ENGLAND AND
GERMANY

CHAPTER IX

MILITARISM IN ENGLAND AND GERMANY

I

FRANCE is a bellicose country, Germany a military : herein lies the essential difference between the two hostile and rival nations.

If we disregard the number of soldiers each nation keeps under arms, and consider only the popularity of the ideas and sentiments of military glory that prevail among the educated classes of the respective countries, the Germans are immediately found to be less warlike than the French. The barrack of Germany, the country in which military traditions are oldest and strongest, is Prussia ; but though the whole of Prussian society looks as though it had been moulded in a barrack, the bellicose spirit in the upper and middle classes is, and was always, feeble. From Frederick the Great to Bismarck, Prussia only fought in the wars against Napoleon. Not much for a truly bellicose nation which desired to reap military trophies. From 1815 to 1863 Prussia stood aside, contenting herself with a humble position that was somewhat humiliating at times, as, for instance, under William and Frederick IV., when it tolerated the public interference of Tzar Nicholas I. with its home politics. How, then, would it be possible to affirm that a people, which allowed its Government so to

debase national dignity, possessed any great passion for
military glory?

Bismarck's new policy became necessary—and herein lies
one of his principal merits—in order to reanimate by some
dignified sentiment the debased soul, first of the Prussians, and
afterwards of the Germans.   But Bismarck was a cause of alarm
to all—to the Prussian nobility, and in a yet greater degree
to the people, so frightened were these timid folk at his bold
and aggressive rule.   Thus he was forced to lead them all by
force—court and parliament, nobility and people—to the war
of 1866, the only war absolutely necessary to the social
progress of Germany, *the* great political creation of Bismarck.
But this, too, was not a war of conquest.   Its real object was
to strengthen the union of the various German States, and
to exclude Austria from the German Confederation—that
country without original character, without nationality, without any political reputation beyond intrigues, makeshifts, and
diplomatic tricks.   Had the German States always been compelled to tolerate the interference of this mean and petty
government, they would never have been able to manage their
affairs with that liberty which is indispensable to any real
progress.   And yet the German people were actively hostile to
this war, which was so necessary in order to cut the Gordian
knot of diplomatic and political problems, so feeble were their
warlike tendencies.

A still more remarkable indication of public feeling consists
in the fact that the Germans never allowed themselves to be
inebriated by their victories in 1870.   The unexpected greatness of the triumph did not suffice to extinguish the old love
of peace and tranquillity.   At first it seemed to rouse a passion
for war in the people; but this rapidly dispersed in smoke,
despite Bismarck's efforts to fan this commencement of fire.

No unprejudiced person travelling in Germany can fail to be surprised at the feeble enthusiasm which survives for the two victories of 1870. Even the French are astounded. Indeed, one of their most famous writers told me, that what struck him more than anything else in Berlin was, that he saw there a much smaller number of pictures, engravings, and illustrations of the war than were to be found in the Parisian shops. The twenty-fifth anniversary of the war passed amidst general indifference : the people scarcely raised their heads a moment from their work to watch the processions of soldiers passing in the streets. What did these processions recall to their minds other than an historical recollection ? In fact, the armour with which Bismarck invested her weighs heavily on the shoulders of Germany, who cannot rid herself of it as she would desire, because modern militarism is an armour so curiously constructed that a people can easily don it, but once on, it is with difficulty cast off.

In no country is the treatment of soldiers by their officers so continually controlled by the press as in Germany. The denunciations of brutalities committed in barracks are frequent and virulent. The sovereigns of various German States have been compelled, owing to these press protests, to charge the heads of the army to keep their officers under proper control. In no other great European country has funds for military purposes been so difficult to obtain. While in France, ever since 1870, the Government has obtained milliards of francs from the parliament for the asking, merely stating that it was necessary for the national defence, Germany has always provided money for military purposes with a reluctance which grows with the increase of her wealth. Bismarck succeeded several times after 1870 in persuading the country that more money was needed for military uses, but at the cost of endless disputes with the *Reichstag*, and by alarming the public with terrible tales of the approaching wars of reconquest. In no other country is such an energetic crusade made by the press, which represents the upper classes, against duels. So strong was this crusade that the Emperor William was compelled to publish an edict regulating and controlling the practice among officers. Propaganda against duelling is a sign of aversion to militarism ; so distinctive a sign, indeed, that the present aspect of public opinion in Germany very much resembles that in England during the first half of this century.

But however true it may be that public feeling is not bellicose in Germany, and that anti-military tendencies are strong, it is none the less a fact that the constitution of Germany has a more military character than that of almost any other European society. Soldiers occupy the most important positions in the official world. The military class is a class apart. Officers lead a separate existence ; they have their own habits, laws, jurisdiction, and almost a *weltanschaung* all their own ; they take more part in civil government than in other countries. Thus, while in France you can find a bourgeois minister of war, in Germany, on the contrary, civil ministries are to be found directed by generals, notwithstanding the fact that officers on active service have not the right of suffrage. Bismarck was originally a doctor of law, who had only fulfilled the ordinary period of military service, and yet, when it was wished to consecrate his high position in the State, he had to be made a general ; and in a general's uniform he was wont to make his appearance in the Reichstag. The second chancellor was also a general. All the citizens belonging to the *landwehr*, or reserve list, have to appear in uniform at official ceremonies. At the inauguration of the new

Reichstag palace the president actually appeared in the uniform of a *landwehr* major. The German emperor always appears surrounded by swarms of generals at official ceremonies, and sometimes he has even criticized the conduct of the Reichstag at a military assembly.

II

In England, on the other hand, militarism is reduced to a minimum.

Let it be understood, however, that militarism being reduced to a minimum does not signify the lack of an army or inconsiderable military expenses. The English land forces are not very numerous (they number little more than 200,000 men), but to make up, they are the most expensive in Europe, costing the nation an annual sum of from £18,000,000 to £20,000,000. The navy costs from £14,000,000 to £16,000,000. The total military expenditure thus stands annually at from £32,000,000 to £36,000,000.

Neither is there a lack of admiration for military display, which is proper to all countries possessing a strong military reputation. From certain points of view this feeling is stronger in England than in France, because the army has preserved, in a sense, a more aristocratic constitution. The grade of officers has remained much what it was in France before the Revolution, *i.e.* a privilege of the rich. Before 1870 commissions were bought and sold.

Under Gladstone's first ministry the purchase system was abolished, but this has not greatly altered matters. Regimental life is still so extravagant and showy, that an officer's mere pay does not suffice to maintain his position. The mess, which ought to be an economical system, has become a most luxurious affair, in which officers vie with each other in extravagance.

To be an officer, more especially in certain regiments, is a diploma of elegance, a distinction which attracts the sons of rich and noble families. Among the people there is the same silly ambition to wear a showy uniform as in continental countries. Hence the uniforms of the English army are the absurdest and most eccentric in the world. Lord Wolseley has said that the British soldier needs to wear a grotesque uniform in order to rouse admiration in the breasts of members of both sexes. On the enlistment posters displayed at every street corner in London, the fact that the cooking is good and the uniform attractive is never left unmentioned.

If the middle classes do not entertain the same vulgar admiration for the uniform as does the populace, even if they do not regard the career of an officer as a particularly desirable one, they are not the less Jingo on this account. The victories of the British army, even over some little African monarch, lend prestige to the Government in power, for the public mind is distinctly bourgeois. In no country have so many monuments been raised to generals, or so many histories of wars been written, as in England ; few other countries are so proud of their military history or their naval power. Bellicose outbreaks of public feeling are not rare. There was one in 1878 during the Russo-Turkish war, and another one is now in full swing.

III

And yet, of all European countries, England is the one where militarism is reduced to a minimum, because the military class does not possess a code of morality of its own, nor any special laws or manner of life. An officer is merely a Government official, like an employé of the Minister of Finance, or public-school inspector. He is in no manner distinguishable from them ; he observes the same laws and customs. Only his office is different, because, instead of looking after accounts or inspecting schools, he is expected to lead soldiers under fire with firmness and courage.

In the officers, who represent of course the better educated portion of the army, this civilian tendency is marked. While in continental Europe it is considered a special duty for a soldier never to refuse a duel, in England it is regarded as disgraceful for him to fight a duel as for any other well-conducted person. The old barrack code no longer holds good, with its strict rules concerning the personal relations of one officer to another. These are taking the form of the ordinary relations between gentlemen, who do not command one another, but politely request the performance of certain services. The mess does not live enclosed in a barrack ; it opens its doors and windows to the world ; it gives balls and entertainments, organizes parties and pleasure trips. Officers of all ranks preside in turn. Within its precincts there are no longer superiors and inferiors, but only men of the world, comrades disciplined by the common sentiment of professional duty. The English officer scarcely possesses a special uniform ; he has dropped his livery. While Italian, French, and German officers have a special uniform which they have to wear always when moving in the midst of their fellow-citizens, the English officer only wears his on duty. Each day when his barrack duty is over, he returns home, puts on civilian dress, and in civilian dress goes into society. Uniform is for him not a class uniform, but a professional one, like a judge's gown and a clergyman's surplice—a costume which is donned from time to time to fulfil a duty, not to represent a caste. This fact alone proves that the army in England is a profession not a caste.

The same thing on a lesser scale is to be observed among the soldiers—a more boorish and ignorant class. The English soldier is not recruited by conscription, but is a volunteer who enlists for a given period, lasting rarely less than ten years, and who receive a minimum pay of a shilling a day. He adopts soldiering as a trade to earn a livelihood. And yet this military and caste spirit is not so strong in the English as in other European temporary soldiers. Their feelings, their relations to superiors, are much like those of ordinary workers. English barracks have lost much of that odious character, a cut between a monastery and a prison. They more and more resemble the traditional *cottage*, under whose roof English families live and work in all parts of the globe. It consists of small pavilions, surrounded by little gardens, and cheered by the green of vegetation, and by all manner of games, such as cricket, football, and lawn-tennis.

The canteens are not the brutal taverns they are in continental countries, but species of clubs whose profits are divided among the soldiers; and where these are not only furnished with food and drink, but with books, papers, games, and even small theatrical entertainments. The soldier, too, wishes to take his share of the comfort of bourgeois life of those luxuries which industrial progress places within reach of the workers. The life he aims at is not that of European armies, but of the British workman. As his conditions improve, so do his pretensions—the better he wishes to eat, to dress, to be lodged. When he is discontented he combines with his comrades, and they go on strike like other workers; and discipline does not threaten such strikes with the terrible punishments that would be meted out in continental countries. Thus, also, the relations between soldiers and officers are not the harsh ones of slave to master which they are in other armies. They are the relations between men and men ; where superiority of education is recognized by reasonable subordinates ; where it is enforced on riotous ones by means of chastisement both barbarous and familiar—the cat-o'-nine-tails.

English militarism is bourgeois, and observes the bourgeois moral code ; it is a profession like any other. Nor does this special characteristic appear to have rendered it inferior to other armies, in any case as far as the valour of the soldiers is concerned, for during this whole century—in Asia, in Africa, and in Europe, at the siege of Sebastopol as in the campaign against King Cetewayo—these regiments, made up of all the ne'er-do-wells, all the scrapegraces and vagabonds of the United Kingdom, have displayed unflinching calm and courage. Although the English army has often been badly led by incapable generals, it has always displayed great courage in its common ranks, who rarely give way to vulgar terror, the result of their excellent professional education, which teaches them a necessity of their trade, never to be afraid, just as a postman learns to walk quickly. This education meets with the better success because as the soldiers all enlist voluntarily they mostly consist of men who feel some natural aptitude for the life. An army recruited from volunteers has a greater chance of consisting of men to whom courage is easy ; so that the English army, if it is largely composed of soldiers whose requirements, even in time of war, strike their European brothers-in-arms as absurdly luxurious, is nevertheless composed of soldiers who are not inclined to run away, a fact which is not without importance.

IV

Thus soldiers form a caste in Germany, whose power is more composed and controlled by public opinion than in France. In England they no longer form a caste, but a special branch of the bureaucracy that is entirely in the service of the civil authorities : a class that does not give orders but receives them, which follows the policy of the civil Government but does not direct it.

To what can we attribute this condition of things, so different from what we have observed in France and Italy? To one sole cause : in England, to the existence of an independent, well-to-do, and educated middle class, which directs the Government and executive by means of parliament and numerous organs of public opinion, and formulates and modifies the existing moral code ; in Germany, to the daily growth of this class, whose every progress is a progress in bourgeois morality, and a fresh step towards the decadence of militarism. In both countries this class is composed of those who live comfortably by industries, commerce, and intellectual professions independently of governmental aid : such as the directors of factories and businesses, rich merchants, manufacturers, and business men, professors, journalists, etc. Protestantism has practically abolished Church protection in Germany and England since the sixteenth century. It has destroyed monasticism, an oriental institution which has very largely contributed to enervate the bourgeoisie in Latin countries. Since this date this class has had to depend principally on its own resources in England and Germany. These countries now receive their reward for any sufferings this may have caused in past times, because we find in them to-day those conditions which, according to the keen observation of Gaetano Mosca, are most necessary to the exercise of a free government. He writes : " No condition is better suited to the relative perfection of the political organization of a society, than the existence of a numerous class economically independent of those who are in power—a class sufficiently well-to-do to be able to devote part of its leisure to improving its mind and to take an interest in public concerns, an almost aristocratic sentiment I might call it, which alone leads men to serve their country for the mere satisfaction of their *amour-propre*. In all countries in the vanguard of freedom, such a class is to be found."[1] This class, owing to its being distinctly bourgeois, although it may be willing to make use of a military class in case of need, naturally conceives life very differently to professional soldiers, and therefore, as its power augments, it invariably comes into conflict with the military caste, and seeks to weaken it as in Germany. When in the end the bourgeoisie become masters of the State, they transform the military class into a profession dependent on the Government as in England. The decline of militarism is everywhere connected with the rise of this bourgeois class, which introduces a mercantile spirit of calculation into every branch of life, and which, though it may be accessible to bellicose enthusiasm, is too intensely utilitarian ever, in the most heated moments, to lose sight of its monetary interests. Hence, in those countries where this class is in power, war loses any romantic character of poetical glory, and becomes merely a matter of £ s. d. But from the moment that a people looks upon war as a mere matter of business, it rapidly becomes pacific, so far as other European nations are

---

[1] G. Mosca, "Elementi di Scienza Politica," p. 153 (1896).

concerned, because the risk of such an undertaking would be too great in proportion to its advantages. The policy of the country consequently becomes prudent and cautious. These nations, then, even if they preserve or augment their armies, regard them merely as a defensive weapon as does Germany, or make use of them for distant wars in barbarous countries as does England. After the fall of Napoleon, England has only taken part in one European war, the Crimean ; since when it has grown more and more cautious, and more disposed to resort to diplomacy than to arms.

V

In a certain portion of the German people these conditions take the shape of an anti-military feeling, which is much stronger than in England, because both the Prussian and the Imperial Government have an aristocratic constitution. The German State is neither lay nor democratic ; it is ruled by two equal forces, legislative power and a civil and military bureaucracy. The ministers are chosen by the king-emperor from any class he pleases ; and they remain in office until it suits the sovereign to dismiss them. A parliamentary vote does not suffice to depose them. As the ministers are at the head of the bureaucracy, this depends on them, and therefore on the sovereign. Consequently the monarchy act and work in accordance with laws made by the assemblies elected by the people, but is not under their control. In other words, whereas in France the bureaucracy is theoretically controlled by the ministers elected by parliament, and emanates from the people's will, in Germany it professes to emanate from God by the will of the sovereign, the king of Prussia and German emperor, who is at the head of the Lutheran Church. Thus unconverted Jews are excluded from many posts in this bureaucracy, which professes to be strictly Christian. The army is naturally its most important department.

Now, in a society thus organized, if anti-militarism were not very strong in the educated bourgeois class, the power of the army and bureaucracy would rapidly degenerate into a tyranny. France may adore her soldier, and be happy to be ill-treated by him, like certain hysterical women who are fond of brutal lovers who beat them. The French army depends theoretically on the minister of war, who is dependent on parliament, and if this power is smaller in practice than it is in theory, the fault lies, not with the constitution, but with the men. England is similarly situated. But in Germany, on the other hand, whatever abuses the army might commit, the Reichstag would be impotent to reform it, and it would remain with the army to decide to alter itself. Civil society would have no power to enforce the rights of reason and morality against the usurpation of the military class.

Therefore a latent spirit of hostility, in the educated class towards militarism and war, is necessary in Germany, to control the strong desire of the army to supersede civil power. If a war, or foolish prejudices like those of the French people, were to augment the moral power of the army, the constitutional *régime* would easily degenerate into a military tyranny. Peace, therefore, is an essential condition to liberty in Germany. If Germany wished to oppress other nations by force of arms, it would itself be punished by falling a victim to a military despotism. And as the desire for freedom is strong in Germany, thanks to the strength and number of the independent bourgeoisie, military fanaticism is not so rampant there as in France. Therefore, paradoxical as the assertion may appear, Germany is not a bellicose nation, because the constitution of its Government is very military.

VI

But it will be objected, this large, well-to-do, and educated middle class exists also in France : why does it not therefore slowly undermine militarism as in England ? Because in France it is slave, not master, of the Jacobin State, and it is to the interest of the Government to propagate warlike sentiments. The independent bourgeoisie is less strong in France than in England and Germany, because Cæsarism ties it in a great part to the Government, to its traditions and principles ; and those few who are not thus tied can do little. Thus inertia favours these traditions, and prolongs, to the detriment of France and Europe, that militarism which is a mere anachronism to-day, the shadow of something which once had life and being. The traditions survive, but grow feebler from day to day, whether it be that public opinion is modifying in France, or that the spiritual and social conditions of the rest of Europe indirectly influence his.

But in France, at least, the middle class, though the slave of the Government—which it obeys instead of guiding—lives under materially and morally good conditions ; and while a few may grow unjustly rich, the majority are not reduced to such a wretched and squalid condition as to render odious to them the Government under which they live. Thus the bourgeoisie preserves sufficient enthusiasm for those military ideals which still play such an important part in French politics ; and though it be *frondeuse* and discontented, it is neither sceptical nor so embittered by its conditions as to grow revolutionary and anti-patriotic.

Italy, on the other hand, lacks the independent bourgeoisie which prospers in England and Germany ; the middle class is tied down to the Government as in France. Thus it lacks all influence to modify the political traditions that govern the country. Although these traditions are recent, shallow, and unpopular, nevertheless they drag on through lack of any contrary influence to destroy them. Supported as they are by the Court and a few groups of interested men, who avail themselves of universal sloth and stupidity, they drag on more through general inertia than any essential virtue of their own. But the middle class is declining in Italy, slowly ruined by the increase of population, and by the reckless waste committed during the last thirty years by the rising and thoughtless Italian Cæsarism, by the Government's policy. The middle class being reduced to such a miserable condition, corrupted by having to beg their bread of those in power, degraded and exhausted by the hard work they are forced to endure and the poor remuneration they receive, by the emptiness of an existence rich only in mendaciqus appearances, this class degenerates into a state of bitter scepticism. It grows to hate the Government, or, worse still, grows indifferent towards it. A middle class in such a dangerous moral state, passing through so terrible a period of passion and unrest, cannot be the creator of a militarism that has any chance of success, nor indeed, anything else of a serious kind, so that Italian militarism is nothing but an expensive lie, which can bring only shame and injury to the country.

Such, in broad outline, the picture of European militarism, from the English, a mere profession, to the Italian, a mere appearance.

T

PAX CHRISTIANA

CHAPTER X

PAX CHRISTIANA

I

WE have studied the military constitution of some of the principal European States, and seen how it corresponds to certain requirements and characteristics of the societies themselves. But though these armies have an internal social function, they have also an external one—they are organized to serve against each other. The whole military organization of Europe necessarily presupposes one or more reasons of rivalry between the Governments, on account of which they are every now and then led mutually to attack or defend themselves.

Economic rivalry is considered by many as the chief cause of conflict, that mania for wealth which torments all European nations, on whose account all seek to conquer new colonies and open fresh markets. It is commonly believed that this rivalry must ultimately lead to a terrible conflict, whose dimensions and consequences it is difficult to conceive. Are these fears legitimate and reasonable, or are they merely a survival of ancient ideas no longer corresponding to the necessities of the age?

Doubtless, one of the most general features of history is, as we have observed, the desire of a small number of men to accumulate wealth. We have seen that wars in ancient times were nearly all directly or indirectly caused by the efforts of these minorities, who ruled society, to enrich themselves, in an age when capital had small reproductive power. Is it to be supposed that human greed will lead to the same results amongst the nations of to-day? Or is it not more probable, on the contrary, that by slow and uncertain stages a *novas ordo* of human things is beginning for the civilized world? It is as difficult to a man to realize the full importance of events in whose midst he lives, as for a traveller to realize the motion of his conveyance. Things often appear mere trifles to contemporaries which, by their descendants, will be judged as events of prime importance ; for great historical events are like the façades of monumental cathedrals, that can only be understood in their entirety when seen from a distance. Most people think that we are living in an age like any other, which will merge into the course of time, just as the hours which have preceded it, and those which will follow. As a matter of fact we are living perhaps in an age that is witnessing the greatest social and moral revolution history has ever chronicled. Those who regard the introduction of machinery as the chief characteristic of our century, show that they have only looked at things from a superficial point of view, and understood nothing but the external features of the great moral revolution, which is the real work, whether enduring or temporary, of our time, thanks to which the ruling classes have at last realized that it is their duty to take their share in the work of civilization.

In the past, nearly the whole responsibility of the work whereon the life of society depended, was left to the ignorant peasant and humble artisan, compelled by force to provide the leisure of their ignorant and stupid masters with pleasures. Nowadays, on the contrary, the ruling class collaborates with the masses in working, and although it is frequently overpaid, and often squanders the people's strength in creating unreal wealth, nevertheless it notably enchances the universal activity. England, Germany, America, and, in a minor degree, France and Italy—all civilized nations, in short—are no longer governed by oligarchies of idle sybarites, but by social groups who direct, more or less efficiently, the work of society.

Owing to this change, it was possible that between societies which for thirty centuries had not ceased for an instant to persecute one another with wars, a sudden desire for peace should grow up : a desire which many have derided because they were unable to understand it owing to its novelty and the rapidity of its growth. But it arose principally from the fact that since the ruling class ceased to acquire wealth by brigandage, seizing it forcibly from other nations or classes, war lost its essential function, and commenced to grow repugnant.

II

We must not imagine, however, that greed has lost its hold on the human heart. The legend of the Argonauts, who set off for the conquest of the golden fleece, not that of Prometheus, who ventured, for the good of mankind, to rob fire from a capricious and malignant god, still symbolizes the doings of modern men. The passion for accumulating treasure is still the strongest of the motives that sway the minorities who govern European society ; and though it no longer resorts to such violent means in order to satisfy itself, it is still as strong in the heart of a highly Christian English banker as in a Roman proconsul or an ancient Pagan chief. But these minorities are no longer composed of warriors and statesmen, but of financiers, merchants, and industrials. As we have already seen, the supreme characteristic of modern civilization is the indefinite variety of productive investments for capital, due to the extent of our scientific knowledge and the universality of laborious habits. In opposition to ancient civilizations, which were, above all, artistic, unlaborious, frugal, and poor, modern civilization is learned, laborious, rich, and has many requirements ; universal industry and a continual increase in demand are its salient characteristics. Hence nowadays the ruling classes, instead of devoting their time to war and the State, occupy themselves in putting accumulated capital to good use, directing work, perfecting and multiplying instruments and machinery, not from any noble sentiments of social duty, but for the same reasons that the aristocracies of the past went to war so frequently—for the accumulation of great and superfluous wealth. This was the chief cause of the creation of modern commerce and industry.

On this account there is a certain spirit of conquest innate in modern trade by reason of which it resembles a species of tempered war. Many economists affirm that industry exists in order to prepare the necessities of life, and that the object of commerce is to organize the exchange of these goods between men, families, classes, and nations, so that by dividing their work they can satisfy all their requirements. An impartial observer can discover in modern business another reason beyond either of these : an elaborate machinery which in part serves the purpose indicated by the economist, in part serves to enable certain classes and nations to rule over other classes and other nations—in short, taking the place and function filled by armies in the past.

III

Modern civilization is founded entirely on the development of work and consumption, for the increase of supply always entails a relative increase in demand. Certain economists make a great error in believing that the only object of industry is to satisfy the needs of man. It serves, above all, to create and diffuse these needs, so as to be able subsequently to satisfy them. In order that it may enrich and support so many people, it is a necessary condition that it should not remain the humble slave of human requirements. An infinite number of objects are every year invented, and made in thousands upon thousands of factories, by rich capitalists in the hopes of gain, by means of powerful and expensive machines, and an immense number of workers whose desires for an easy life every day increase, under the direction of brain-workers, who also demand ample recompense. These goods are then sold by merchants more anxious to make profits out of them than even the very manufacturers, who travel to the most distant countries in search of the strangest and most various products of the globe. Now, how could so many desires and greeds be satisfied, if the price of goods sunk too low? In order to prevent this it is necessary that production should never surpass a certain measure of abundance, or that consumption should so augment as to constantly exceed it. For various reasons, which it would take us too long to develop, every effort to bridle production has failed of late: hence the necessity to increase demand.

To succeed in this bold and difficult undertaking, it has been necessary to modern commerce and industry to attempt a new and very hazardous conquest in the world—that of inducing other people to adopt a more expensive and complicated mode of life. It is not necessary to enlarge on this subject in order to demonstrate the fact that during this century innumerable things have been invented to satisfy fresh requirements, and introduced into distant countries. The fact is well known, as it is also well known that the ever-increasing cost of living, which is, curiously enough, combined with the lowering of the price of single objects, is caused by the prolificacy of industry and trade. Now, these new needs were felt because in a certain sense they had been latent in the minds of men ; but it is also certain that they would have continued in this latent state had it not been for a few greedy and ingenious men, who found the means of developing these inclinations. Thus modern commerce, by means of numerous agents, has succeeded in spreading the temptation of these new methods of life throughout the whole of our planet. Everywhere it has despatched apostles, not to preach a new gospel, but to persuade men of all colours, tongues, and customs to consume their ever-increasing fresh productions. No difficulty has ever succeeded in baffling these slow and patient conquerors—neither the inertia of men in matters which entail the alteration of old customs, the diffidence, ancient traditions, and diversity of customs of the races unused to our civilization, the invincible prejudices of primitive religions and Governments, nor the barbarism of wild unknown regions, abounding in traps and perils, wild beasts, and still wilder men. By plodding persistence, by all manner of deceit to delude the ignorant, by corrupting the great ones of the earth, and, in some desperate cases, by forcing their way by arms, filling the desert roads, abysses, and little cemeteries of far-away lands with corpses, these obstinate invaders from the great industrial centres have succeeded in vanquishing the world, as though they had all united together for one supreme object, and worked unanimously as one body from the centre of Africa to India, from Siberia to California, from Sicily to Australia.

IV

In this manner, what we may call the mechanical-industrial civilization of the nineteenth century has diffused itself throughout Europe, from Italy to Russia, and also throughout America. Partially, also, it has penetrated other continents. But it would be too simple to imagine that this spread of civilization was merely like an exchange of produce between various nations for their mutual benefit. Its result has been the division of the civilized nations of Europe into two classes— the *creditor* nations, who are those which contributed towards this new order of civilization ; and the debtors, which are those who have merely profited by it. Let us recall to mind the simple primitive scene narrated in the " Odyssey."

The Phœnician merchants landed on the Greek shores, took from their ships the merchandise of their country, and exhibited it ; then from the neighbouring villages came troops of women and girls to gaze at them, and through these samples of a more refined industry, the desire for more luxurious things took birth in the minds of the barbarians. Our latter-day great manufacturers and merchants have repeated the undertaking of the Phœnician merchant a thousand times during the course of this century. They have penetrated everywhere, amidst civilized, barbarous, and savage nations ; they have exhibited on the seashore, in the village squares and city streets, samples of an infinite number of things manufactured in their country by millions of human hands, and by machines working rapidly as lightning. A few savage races have expelled and slaughtered them ; but generally, even in the remotest mountain villages, the merchant has met with a ready welcome from the simple folk. Men and women have surrounded him, curious to inspect the new goods introduced by the stranger ; and one having given the example, another and another followed suit, until all bought a specimen, thinking that they thus satisfied an innocent desire. But the merchant's treasure-bag was inexhaustible. Every day he produced thence some new object, and the temptation to indulge in them grew ever stronger ; so that the better part having spent all their ready cash, dug up the little hoards hidden away by the old people ; all their savings gone, they gradually got into debt with the village usurer and the merchant himself. And the merchant, in the mean time, grew richer and richer.

This little fable sums up very characteristically one of the least known episodes of modern history. It accounts, in a certain manner, for the mysterious growth of fortunes which our century has witnessed. Leaving the smaller nations out of account, among which there are many creditor nations, such as Belgium and Switzerland, which, although in a flourishing condition, pay little attention to politics, among the great nations of Europe, France, Germany, and England count as creditors, Italy, Spain, Russia, and Austria as debtors.

V

Now, the superior or inferior condition of modern nations all depends on this matter of *debtor* and *creditor*. The creditor nations are to-day in the same condition that countries ruling by force of arms found themselves in ancient civilization; the debtors represent the conquered tributary populations.

The creditor nations are the centre of world-wide capitalism, *i.e.* capital is so abundant as to be superabundant for internal requirements, and consequently can be used for productive investments in other lands, for Government loans, industrial, banking, and commercial speculations. By means of this capital these nations have become a world empire. We cannot gauge the real extent of the English and French empires by those territories marked yellow and red on geographical charts, but by the gigantic investments English bankers have made all the world over, in United States industries, as in those of Moscow, in the diamond mines of the Cape, as in the hydraulic works in the Italian Alps; in the loans made by France, the great usurer of this century, to all the Governments of the globe, in the international commerce of money of which she is the centre. The power and empire of Germany are not extended by the coreografic journeys made by the emperor to Palestine, got up in the costume of a Crusader, but by those patient business men who, in Russia and Italy, in the two Americas, and the extreme Orient, manage to find new productive investments for capital. This is an empire without geographical dimensions, invisible and intangible, above all political divisions of nations, but one which assures well-being to the creditor countries.

Wherein did the greatest privilege of the ruling nations of antiquity consist? It was the tribute they enforced by arms from the conquered nations. To-day the ruling nations still extort tribute which takes this form, that they are able to import a larger quantity of goods than they export. Any one who examines the English, French, and German statistics of exportation and importation, immediately perceives that these nations import much more than they export. In some years, for instance, England has imported as much as a milliard of francs more than she exported, and France 800 millions. This signifies that these nations obtain an enormous amount of goods from other countries without giving anything in exchange; that from those countries which are in their debt they take every year a quantity of useful and beautiful things as payment of interest without contributing anything in exchange; they carry away what they choose, whilst the wretched debtor nations pay back as interest on the sums they borrowed all their most valuable possessions. English and German millionaires drink the best Italian and Spanish wines; they purchase the historical palaces of Venice, the villas and lakes of the Alban hills; they keep a keen eye on the masterpieces of ancient Italian art, which, but for governmental prohibition, they would carry away from Italy in larger numbers and more effectively than did Napoleon. British workmen batten on the best oranges of Spain and Sicily. The first effect of the abolition of feudalism in Russia was that the peasants had to leave off eating wheaten bread and to content themselves with bread made of rye, because all their corn was exported to nourish German and English workmen. As in the ancient world all countries sent their goods to Rome, the universal ruler, in homage to the final victress of so long a contest of interminable wars, so to-day half the world sends the best produce of its agriculture, its art and industry, to London.

This vast lucrativeness of capital employed productively in foreign countries, is a cause of well-being to the creditor nations, who are well off from the workmen to the upper class, the middle class, the backbone of modern civilization, being the most prosperous of all. Capital abounds; the desire to invest it profitably is universal; hence work is also plentiful, the standard of life tends to improve in all classes, individual energies have ample scope, and the whole of society becomes a vast field of scientific, industrial, social, political, artistic, and literary experiments. Those who are desirous of enriching themselves can do so without being noxious to society whilst promoting its interests, while intellectual men have much fuller scope for doing their best. Prosperity being so widespread, the workers are satisfied, and the Government has an easy task.

In the debtor nations, on the contrary, the conditions of the middle class and workers are hard; capital being scarce there is little work, salaries and profits are small; little is consumed, the vast exportation renders life dearer to the middle and working classes—indeed, to the whole of society life grows more and more difficult. All aspire to a broader, more dignified, and intellectual life, but they are daily reduced to a meaner and more squalid existence. The very rich are comparatively poor and ungenerous. There is little scope for energy, originality has small chance of displaying itself; wherefore those countries which used to be the seat of an ancient and vast civilization, and which to-day abound in intelligent and clever men, find themselves in a most unfortunate condition to compete in the field of intellect with the newer creditor nations, to whom belongs in a great measure the honour of directing the intellectual movement of our times. Nations which are economically in a tributary position are imitative intellectually.

What country has contributed so much to the history of civilization as Italy? And yet for the last forty years she appears to have lost all originality. With the exception of a few men who have managed to preserve their individuality at all costs, and who have generally been persecuted by the envy of their country, nearly the whole intellectual movement of Italy is borrowed from abroad; her literature is in a great measure imitated from the French, her experimental science from Germany, her social and political ideas from France and England. The latter country has also exercised considerable influence on those general theories which have contributed towards the development of Italian thought: Spencerism and Darwinism. Such a pass has been reached that in the country of Raphael and Michael Angelo artists take the paintings of English Pre-Raphaelists as their model. Debtor countries, in short, are in such bad internal conditions that they find it relatively difficult to develop their intellectual energies.

But the greatest evil is that in the debtor countries also greedy plutocracies are formed anxious to draw profit out of the direction of some social work. However, in these countries the scarceness of capital renders the few people who possess it very cautious; they are unwilling to risk more than a small sum at a time, and that only with the certainty of good profits. Thus industry finds it difficult to compete with richer nations, and it seeks to augment its profits by protectionism. Whilst the world-wide industries of creditor nations prosper, little provincial traders struggle on in the conquered nations, protected and assisted in all manner of ways by the Government. A small minority manages to live and prosper, and does its best to imitate the life led in powerful countries, thanks to the eternal historical law by which the conquered always seek to imitate the conquerors.

Thus a ruling class is growing up in these countries which attempts to augment the social value of their work by the help of Cæsarism in its many various forms, including protectionism.

In other words, while all creditor nations — with the
exception of France, which is an eccentric exception to
everything—display a decided tendency towards free trade,
in debtor countries the great industrials and landowners
seek to augment their profits, by artificially raising the prices
of goods by customs-house tariffs, thus paying a higher price
than could rightly be demanded by the producers, whilst
obtaining State favours in the shape of subsidies and other
artifices common to the not very scruplous finance of European
nations. Thus we find the Spanish industrials up to last
year drawing large profits from being able to export to
the colonies under a lower tariff than other countries. The
idleness of the Sicilian landowners is insured by the Government by means of taxes which raised the price of bread.
Then again we see that the great Russian merchants by
introducing a vast system of customs tariffs, became the
masters of Russian consumers. In the same way the Italian
cotton and wool manufacturers, by the customs revolution of
ten years ago, procured themselves a few years of great
prosperity.

By such means in those weaker countries which were
not sufficiently favoured by fortune to become centres of
capitalism, the greedy and ambitious succeeded in accumulating large fortunes by impoverishing their fellow-
countrymen, by exploiting their brothers who speak the
same tongue, and this not by violent, but by insidious means,
in the name of industrial patriotism—a catchword capable of
seducing many minds, and which represents the economic
sophisms of protectionism as salutary truths. Protectionism
aggravates the already hard condition of tributary nations,
and becomes at the same time a partial means of enriching
the creditors, who always invest large capital in the protected

U

industries. Thus Russian protectionism has enriched English capitalists, Italian protectionism has enriched Germans ; the first founded many industries in Moscow, St. Petersburg, and Lodz, the latter have done the same in Lombardy.

VI

But these world-wide empires of capitalism are based not on territorial extension, but on the abundance of capital and the capacity of men to use it productively. Therefore, as has already been demonstrated, societies founded on free principles run a better chance of success than those where the middle class depend on governmental protection. The only exception to this rule is France. All the remainder, Austria and Spain, Russia and Italy, are debtor subject nations. This explains at the same time the relative decadence of Catholic countries as compared to Protestant ones ; as Catholicism is still the most potent protective system.

Moreover, as this empire does not depend on territorial extension, military power is not essential to its stability. Little countries, like Belgium and Switzerland, may be creditors and rulers ; huge empires, like Russia, debtors and tributaries. Militarism may in some cases be an auxiliary of the capitalist empire, but only on one condition, *i.e.* that it does not entail such an immense expenditure on arms and wars as to impede or arrest the accumulation of capital. Italy is a terrible example of how a nation can be reduced by debt to a tributary and inferior condition, from having squandered too much of its wealth on arms. Moreover, a creditor Government finds itself to-day *carteris puribus*, and capable of becoming stronger than other States, also from a military point of view, because armament expenses are continuous and recurrent. Who is not aware that, nowadays, arms and all the apparatus of war have to be renewed nearly every ten years, thanks to the mad fury for military inventions which afflicts Europe? This continuous change renders militarism too expensive a matter for debtor nations, who find themselves constantly embarrassed at each fresh renovation of the army and navy to find the necessary funds.

VII

A world-wide commercialism in a creditor country or a large system of commercial and industrial Cæsarism producing large profits for a fortunate plutocracy in a debtor country, are then the greatest, pleasantest, and least immoral means for satisfying the greed of the governing minority, which in the past sought to satisfy itself by means of war. This is so true that in those countries which possess a world-wide commerce, or where a vast national financial Cæsarism exists, the State grows ever less bellicose, by mere force of circumstances, even if it be unaware of the fact, and go on increasing its military armaments.

I will give two examples—England and Russia. England is the seat of the vastest and most powerful world-wide capitalism existing, and may, in some respects, be considered the first military power in the world ; for it possesses the largest fleet, and the European army most exercised by continual wars. But, notwithstanding, her policy grows ever more prudent and conciliating. Her diplomatists never make demands which are likely to require enforcing by wars ; in the East and in the Far East they have always preferred to manage matters in a friendly spirit, and to give in rather than to display her naval superiority in one or more wars.

English diplomatists always prefer slow solutions and transitions; if in the Fashoda question they acted with unaccustomed energy, it cannot be said that in other questions which have arisen with France, Germany, and Russia, they have not displayed great consideration. The Fashoda question had become one affecting the national pride more than interest, and served to interrupt by energetic action a system of conciliation, which seemed in its turn likely to become perilous. Moreover, an English ministry has recently declared that British imperialism strives above all things to avoid conflict and expense. By so doing the United Kingdom provides both for its own well-being and that of European civilization, for wars occasioned by thirst of power would arrest its magnificent development. History will be grateful to England for not having abused her naval power, for having recognized the right of other nations to their place under the sun, for realizing that the prosperity of others does not entail her loss, and that war, whatever its result, would damage her power. The English Empire stretches beyond its territorial confines; it extends wherever English capital is invested, and becomes one of the motives of civilization. Thus a war resulting in the annexation of new and vast territories, but also implying a huge destruction of capital, would diminish the grandeur and power of the Empire, for every million of capital consumed represents a square million of ideal empire lost. Thus England is, and daily becomes, more pacific, because no class of society is interested in war, no one wishes to avail himself of it to satisfy his creed, which can be better appeased by other means. War with civilized countries is repugnant to her, she accumulates huge armaments merely for self-defence, which remain idle, and were only used in petty colonial wars, whose one object is to open and maintain roads across savage continents for the use of her merchants, at a comparatively trifling cost.

Russia is another example. No European Government presents so military an aspect. Russian society appears to an outsider to be ruled by a military despotism. Yet the very heads of this system, the Czars themselves, rank to-day amongst the upholders of peace ; a Russian policy during the last twenty years has become ever more pacific in its relations with other European nations. If the external form of Russian society, the military absolutism, remains unchanged, the internal is rapidly modifying. The old Russian aristocracy, composed of land and serf owners, which diminuted by force of arms till the abolition of serfdom, is decaying, ruined by usury and idleness, and the social reforms which for the last thirty years, ever since the second half of the reign of Alexander II., have hastened the introduction into Russia of the mechanical industrial civilization of the West ; and the place which it is leaving vacant, as it disappears into the shades of the past, is filled by a very powerful financial oligarchy composed of merchant princes and manufacturers, to whom the Government abandons, with the most shameless protectivism and Cæsarism, the whole of the immense empire. For the past twenty years Russia has been seized with the industrial fever, with the unlimited ambition to accumulate huge fortunes by means of industries, protected by tariffs, subventions, and encouraging rewards prodigated with princely generosity.

Thus the military pride of ancient Russia is disappearing, that pride which dreamed of new conquests, and hoped to expand the Sclavonic empire, contemplating the conquest of Constantinople and India, and the establishment of a political and military dictatorship over Europe ; and it is replaced by the desire to develop all over Russia an immense system of traffic and industry. Hence the gigantic projects for public works, first among which ranks the trans-Siberian railway, which will open up to adventurous Russian capitalists an empire vaster and richer than that which Alexander the Great conquered for himself with his sword—Macedonian legend ; hence the laws to protect industry and commerce which engross more and more the cares of the State to the detriment of war. But as this new spirit grows the ancient military spirit declines ; so that the Russia of to-day, instead of being governed by generals, is at the mercy of a band of ambitious financiers, who dream of an age of gold for Russia. The wealth they dream of would fall to the share of a few capitalists, however, not to the people ; for the terrific expense entailed by this gigantic Cæsarism is, and will be, paid above all by the peasants, the citizens, and the middle classes, who contribute the greater part of the money necessary for the construction of railways, for paying the liberal rewards assigned to the encouragment of absurd and mistaken industries, and for supplying the deficit entailed by a banking system which enriches a few unscrupulous speculators whilst despoiling the masses.

The first concrete proposal for disarmament has emanated from Russia, and this fact, though it has taken the world by surprise, appears, on deeper study, less astonishing than one would think for. Russia is a debtor State, poor in capital, which has accomplished the progresses of the past thirty years by borrowing money from France, Germany, and England. The growth of wealth is slow there, accumulated capital scarce, whilst the need thereof is great, for civilizing huge countries, opening up new roads, building railways, and meeting the annual deficit incurred by a wasteful administration. Hence Russia is one of the countries which finds most difficulty in meeting the ever-growing burden of military expenditure, a difficulty proportionate to the immensity of the empire, and to the gigantic capital necessary for civilizing it ; and thus it is interested in maintaining peace even more than is its rival creditor.

VIII

All that we have said about creditor and debtor countries applies to Europe, but not to America. Another proof of the privileges enjoyed by the new continents is that there a society may be economically a debtor and yet enjoy those material and moral conditions which in Europe belong to creditor countries. Such is the case with the United States, which is a debtor country, inasmuch as English capital is largely employed there, and whose exports exceed its imports. But, owing to the reasons which we studied in our first chapter, fruitful investments for capital are very numerous ; and hence the governing classes are intensely pacific. The recent Cuban war must not lead us to think that America is entering on a new epoch of military conquest, unless, indeed, its governors go mad. If such were the case, the prosperity and strength of American society would rapidly decline ; because all the capital which would be expended in conquering territory in Asia and Africa would be withdrawn from useful employment in the mother-country, from which we must expect the ever-growing greatness of American civilization. This decay would be all the more rapid, as recent events have proved that if Americans know how to conduct wars successfully, they are unable to manage it cheaply.

IX

But, it may be objected, although already these social conditions have flourished nearly all over Europe, our century can chronical an infinite number of wars from its commencement until 1870. Firstly, the Napoleonic wars ; then, after a long interval of peace, the various wars from 1848–49 : the Crimean war ; the war between Austria, France, and Germany of 1866 ; the war between Germany and France of 1870. A long list indeed, even if we omit the minor wars, for a century which is considered destined to witness the disappearance of war from the history of Europe! But the greater part of these wars had a political, not economic motive, and were necessary in order to modify a condition of things which rendered life impossible to many European nations. This work having been completed by the war of 1870, the era of peace commenced afresh. It has endured now for twenty-nine years, and to all appearances it means to endure a long time yet.

There were two principal causes for war during our century : the policy of Austria prior to 1866, and the turbulent Napoleonic spirit. That curious spirit of intrigue, interference, and conservative fanaticism which characterized the Austrian policy from 1815 to 1866, rendered that country a potent cause for disturbance to Europe—a base and intriguing diplomacy which was energetic and sterile at the same time ; a brave but stupid military class ; an honest, diligent, but retrogressive and bigoted executive ; a small oligarchy which the French Revolution had maddened with terror. Such were the elements which together went to build up this curious military empire, which since 1815 attempted to

solve by force the problem, not of perpetual motion, but of
the eternal immobility of European society. The prejudices
and stupid obstinacy of this Government retarded the progress
and development of three countries: Italy, where Austria
tried to compel even those provinces which were not under
its domain to submit to the barbarous rule which tormented
her; Prussia and the German States, in whose confederation
Austria represented the spirit of negation and disorder; and
Hungary, which was subjected to the tyrannical rule of the
Austrian army and executive.

On the other hand, no sooner had Napoleonism reopened
the tomb of St. Helena and Napoleon III. mounted the
throne of France, than the turbulent elements of French
politics, which had appeared dormant since 1815, began to
reassert themselves. The French Government immediately
armed and took to the road in search of adventure, a little
like a mediæval knight, and not altogether unlike a brigand.
Now we find it defending the weak, here again associating
itself with the masterful. Whether side by side with Turkey
or fighting against Austria; whether in defence of the Pope
or in opposition to the growing power of Prussia; whether
against China or in aid of the poor Italian provinces suffering under the tyranny of barbarous Governments; wherever,
in short, an occasion presented itself for fighting and glory,
Napoleonic France stained the earth with blood. What was
its object? To what motive can we attribute her actions?
Little matters it whether, in a few of these various adventures,
the Napoleonic Government served a useful social or political
purpose;—for instance, as in the Italian war. It was not with
this object that it so often resorted to arms, but in order to
obtain the approbation of France by satisfying a vain passion
for military glory. It could thus also constitute a vigorous

and well-disciplined class of professional soldiers, who would be a solid weapon to the Government to keep its subjects in order. Was it necessary periodically to disturb the peace of Europe in order to attain this end? Little mattered it so long as the traditions of Napoleonic glory were well re-established with the new empire.

Even bad things contain an element of good. Napoleonism and the Austrian empire, both intrinsic evils, served the useful purpose in respect to one another of each weakening the other by wars, until Prussia and the German States gave them both the *coup de grace*. Since 1866, Austria has wisely resigned herself to passivity. Of the unmeasured ambition that used to characterize her, she only preserves a short programme of negations, whose principal object is to prevent Russia becoming too powerful in the Balkan peninsula and the Orient, and from preventing Hungary, which is independent in reality, from becoming so also in name. The French Republic, on its part, has not entirely broken with the military traditions of the nation. This would have been impossible, but its policy of European warlike adventures has, in the course of time, been modified and softened into one of colonial expeditions to Asia and Africa. We might almost say that it is gradually lulling it to sleep in the public conscience. France, the warrior all in arms, like the legendary Valkirie, is gradually sinking into an enchanted sleep on the mountain of things that have been, beside the stake of Time, which reduces everything to a heap of ashes; and here she must sleep until some hero shall arrive to rouse her from her slumbers. And she will sleep for a long time yet, you may be sure. The race of such heroes is extinguished in Europe; if it is rash to say for ever, for a very long time to come at least. With Austria converted to a more reasonable policy, and Napoleonism dead, Europe was able to establish an equilibrium which, if not perfect, is at least tolerable—one which has resisted many perils and disturbance during the past twenty-seven years, and which will grow better in the course of time. Germany merits no small credit in having contributed towards this new phase of European politics, a merit which she has done her best to efface by the annexations of 1871—a useless annexation which concluded madly a useful work. The war of 1870 was the rudest blow given during the century to European militarism, because it destroyed for ever the Napoleonic spirit ; but that fatal land-grabbing which concluded it must have appeared as a triumph of militarism, giving back to this spirit a little of that sign of which Germany was rapidly stripping it by means of those fierce blows known as Gravelotte and Sedan. Many imagine that the war of 1870 gave a fresh lease of life to militarism in Europe. In reality it killed it by destroying Napoleonism. But the annexations which were its contradictory conclusion, the increase of armament which were a transitory consequence, led many minds totally astray with regard to this historical event. History, however, will judge differently, because, though Europe may never have been so heavily armed as it has been since 1870, desire and opportunity to make use of these weapons have never been so reduced. Now, arms are the body of militarism, while the desire to resort to them is its soul. Lastly, the Spanish-American War arose, also, from a purely political cause. The United States demanded of Spain to alter its policy in the government of Cuba. A political incompatibility existed between the United States and Spain analogous to that which existed between Germany and Austria, and Austria and Italy, and therefore war became inevitable in the end. But this political incompatibility is everywhere diminishing in the civilized world, while colonial and commercial jealousies are everywhere on the increase—troubles which, as we have demonstrated, can in no way be solved by war.

X

Thus the duty of every well-meaning man to-day is to diffuse knowledge of the fact that war no longer serves the purpose it once served in the struggle for civilization. The aspect of society in whose midst we live is continually changing; but we persist in seeing it as it *was*, not as it *is*, owing to that inertia and misoneism which are fundamental laws of the human mind. Were I to ask a man: "In what century do you suppose that you are living?" he would probably think that I wished to deride him. And yet, although we all live bodily at the end of the nineteenth century, a great number of us are still living mentally in past ages : we see the world as it used to be, not as it actually is. As, every night, millions of eyes lift themselves to heaven to contemplate the radiancy of those stars which, though they have been dead for years, still shine so brilliantly, thus for years and centuries men see around themselves things which once were, but which are no more. Facts follow one another at a rapid pace, more especially in our times, while human thought limps after them with halting steps. In this problem of war, as in every other problem, that incredulity which is due to the debasement of ideas to facts must also be overcome, the conscience of man must be awakened to the greatness of the historical moment in which we live, to the rapid progress going on around us, to the process of transformation of which we are in part the subject, and in part—whether consciously or not—the tool. Now, none of the diplomatic conflicts which actually divide the nations of Europe are of a kind which could not be settled without resort to arms. Indeed, modern civilization is so organized that the most powerful countries are those which most benefit by peace; because not war, but the accumulation and right use of capital, is what gives a nation supremacy nowadays. Yet many people still believe that problems of social and political supremacy can only be settled by the sword—a common error which is one of the obstacles to a rapid and reasonable solution to many international problems.

It is our duty to free the eyes of the multitude from this veil of error which blinds them, by proclaiming the truth that war in Europe is to-day nothing but the ghost of dead injustices, which, like the bogies of fiction, return from time to time, but only to alarm. During those thirty centuries from which dates our historical knowledge, war has been more a social system than a cruel pastime of kings—the first most violent and brutal means adopted by ruling minorities to acquire wealth. At last, after so many centuries of iniquity, the absurdity of the social system of war has been demonstrated by the decay of all the triumphs which war, in its mysterious caprices, conferred on men and people. A new form of civilization has arisen in which men can appease their greedy instincts by the productive investment of capital —a wise, laborious, extravagant, and magnificent civilization, which produces and consumes a prodigious quantity of material. Thus, for eighty years, since the fall of Napoleon— the man who had tried to reanimate the spirit of warfare in modern society—the civilized nations of Europe have renounced the exercise, to each other's hurt, of that systematic brigandage named warfare, and from that moment war was a dead thing.

A few campaigns have been fought since then which arose from political problems which prejudices inherited from past ages rendered it impossible to settle by other means; but war, in its true and proper sense, was dead. So long as our present civilization shall continue, so long as men and their needs shall augment, so long as in new lands and old countries the productive investment of capital can be multiplied, war between civilized nations for economic motives will be impossible; and those more pacific countries which have become the centres of world-wide capitalism will be the most powerful. Only some access of insanity, contagiously communicated from one European Government to another, could rekindle war over questions of colonial dominion; and hence arises the necessity of intellectual propaganda with the object of bringing about a clearer and more profound understanding of the truth among the governing classes.

Thus propaganda against war is intimately connected with any movement for social progress and any agitation which has this object in view. War in the past was the daughter of ignorance and vice and the mother of injustice. Were it to assume its former sway in modern society, it would generate sloth, ignorance, and injustice in an aggravated form. War is, in itself, a pure injustice, and this alone ought to suffice to induce men to do all in their power to abolish it; for injustice is the origin of all evil, of the physical evils of disease, pestilence, and premature death, of the moral ones of madness, crime, and all the suffering which is the invisible but inseparable companion of mankind on earth. How many men have not asked themselves, in face of so much atrocious suffering which appears inexplicable because unmerited: "What is the cause of so much pain in life?" A terrible and august reason there is, be sure of it. The baby who dies in its cradle, the youth who is killed by consumption, the man who goes mad in the flower of his years, the son who inherits his father's disease, the degenerate who becomes a criminal, the neurotic who passes his existence tormented and tormenting, the unfortunate who succumbs to a broken heart on account of one of those thousand injuries which men blindly exchange in the thick of the struggle for wealth and honour,— all of these are the expiatory victims of the innumerable injustices which every society tolerates in its midst, and for which we are responsible, one and all, by reason of an iron law of solidarity which admits of no immunity nor privilege. The sin may not always have been committed by the man who expiates it. But what matters this? The process by which justice is dealt does not directly affect individuals, but the whole of society. Only in a society totally free from injustice would man be absolutely liberated from evil. That society would no longer be afflicted with invalids, criminals, lunatics, paupers, vicious or unhappy men. The seed once destroyed, the bitter fruit could no longer ripen.

For this reason society unconsciously always tends towards a greater degree of justice, because injustice leads to suffering, and man ever tries to avoid pain. The history of mankind is merely the history of these efforts : slow efforts, of which a single one frequently fills a whole epoch in history ; incoherent efforts, which, in one age or one people, often differ from those of a former age and another nation ; intermittent efforts, where long pauses often alternate with periods of feverish energy ; vain efforts, not unfrequently, because, seduced by an apparent or transitory happiness, man has found pain instead. But the great work is equally well accomplished because it is necessary ; because man, considering in the light of experience one after another all the many mendacious and apparent forms of happiness, naturally approaches to a better comprehension of the nature of true happiness ; and in face of this inevitable final success, all the most shameless triumphs of injustice are but mere episodes of which the very recollection will be lost when the term of expiation shall be fulfilled. Certainly these expiations of injustice, that stupefy the human comprehension by reason of their greatness, are often very slow in comparison to the brevity of a single life. But, after all, what is man in the universal mystery of existence ? Let us, then, take hope when we consider the past, and rejoice in the thought of the great events and doings in whose midst it is our lot to live. At the present moment the Christian world has before it, if its wisdom is not less than its fortune, a long respite of peace. How many great and good things might it not accomplish ! Oligarchies, whose only object was to enrich themselves, filled past ages with their violent iniquities, from that which reigned in ancient Rome to that which sprang up last century around Napoleon. To-day nothing remains of them but dust, and from their ashes they shall arise no more. If men are wise, the age of *Pax Christiana* can now be inaugurated, of longer duration and more glorious than the *Pax Augusta ;* and this should herald a fresh chapter in the history of the white man's civilization—an unheroic chapter if you will, but, let us earnestly hope, a less lugubrious and less bloody chapter, and one less replete with atrocities than those which have preceded it.

FINIS

WARD, LOCK AND CO., LTD., LONDON, NEW YORK, AND MELBOURNE.